P9-CLQ-568

Carnegie Commission on Higher Education
Sponsored Research Studies

THE MULTICAMPUS UNIVERSITY:
A STUDY OF ACADEMIC GOVERNANCE
Eugene C. Lee and Frank M. Bowen

INSTITUTIONS IN TRANSITION:
A PROFILE OF CHANGE IN HIGHER
EDUCATION
(INCORPORATING THE 1970 STATISTICAL
REPORT)
Harold L. Hodgkinson

EFFICIENCY IN LIBERAL EDUCATION:
A STUDY OF COMPARATIVE INSTRUCTIONAL
COSTS FOR DIFFERENT WAYS OF ORGANIZ-
ING TEACHING-LEARNING IN A LIBERAL ARTS
COLLEGE
Howard R. Bowen and Gordon K. Douglass

CREDIT FOR COLLEGE:
PUBLIC POLICY FOR STUDENT LOANS
Robert W. Hartman

MODELS AND MAVERICKS:
A PROFILE OF PRIVATE LIBERAL ARTS
COLLEGES
Morris T. Keeton

BETWEEN TWO WORLDS:
A PROFILE OF NEGRO HIGHER EDUCATION
Frank Bowles and Frank A. DeCosta

BREAKING THE ACCESS BARRIERS:
A PROFILE OF TWO-YEAR COLLEGES
Leland L. Medsker and Dale Tillery

ANY PERSON, ANY STUDY:
AN ESSAY ON HIGHER EDUCATION IN THE
UNITED STATES
Eric Ashby

THE NEW DEPRESSION IN HIGHER
EDUCATION:
A STUDY OF FINANCIAL CONDITIONS AT 41
COLLEGES AND UNIVERSITIES
Earl F. Cheit

FINANCING MEDICAL EDUCATION:
AN ANALYSIS OF ALTERNATIVE POLICIES
AND MECHANISMS
Rashi Fein and Gerald I. Weber

HIGHER EDUCATION IN NINE COUNTRIES:
A COMPARATIVE STUDY OF COLLEGES AND
UNIVERSITIES ABROAD
*Barbara B. Burn, Philip G. Altbach, Clark Kerr,
and James A. Perkins*

BRIDGES TO UNDERSTANDING:
INTERNATIONAL PROGRAMS OF AMERICAN
COLLEGES AND UNIVERSITIES
Irwin T. Sanders and Jennifer C. Ward

GRADUATE AND PROFESSIONAL EDUCATION,
1980:
A SURVEY OF INSTITUTIONAL PLANS
Lewis B. Mayhew

THE AMERICAN COLLEGE AND AMERICAN
CULTURE:
SOCIALIZATION AS A FUNCTION OF HIGHER
EDUCATION
Oscar Handlin and Mary F. Handlin

RECENT ALUMNI AND HIGHER EDUCATION:
A SURVEY OF COLLEGE GRADUATES
Joe L. Spaeth and Andrew M. Greeley

CHANGE IN EDUCATIONAL POLICY:
SELF-STUDIES IN SELECTED COLLEGES AND
UNIVERSITIES
Dwight R. Ladd

STATE OFFICIALS AND HIGHER EDUCATION:
A SURVEY OF THE OPINIONS AND
EXPECTATIONS OF POLICY MAKERS IN NINE
STATES
Heinz Eulau and Harold Quinley

ACADEMIC DEGREE STRUCTURES:
INNOVATIVE APPROACHES
PRINCIPLES OF REFORM IN DEGREE
STRUCTURES IN THE UNITED STATES
Stephen H. Spurr

COLLEGES OF THE FORGOTTEN AMERICANS:
A PROFILE OF STATE COLLEGES AND
REGIONAL UNIVERSITIES
E. Alden Dunham

FROM BACKWATER TO MAINSTREAM:
A PROFILE OF CATHOLIC HIGHER
EDUCATION
Andrew M. Greeley

THE ECONOMICS OF THE MAJOR PRIVATE
UNIVERSITIES
William G. Bowen
*(Out of print, but available from University
Microfilms.)*

THE FINANCE OF HIGHER EDUCATION
Howard R. Bowen
*(Out of print, but available from University
Microfilms.)*

ALTERNATIVE METHODS OF FEDERAL
FUNDING FOR HIGHER EDUCATION
Ron Wolk
*(Out of print, but available from University
Microfilms.)*

INVENTORY OF CURRENT RESEARCH ON
HIGHER EDUCATION 1968
Dale M. Heckman and Warren Bryan Martin
*(Out of print, but available from University
Microfilms.)*

*The following technical reports are available from the Carnegie Commission on Higher Education, 2150
Shattuck Avenue, Berkeley, California 94704.*

RESOURCE USE IN HIGHER EDUCATION:
TRENDS IN OUTPUT AND INPUTS, 1930–1967
June O'Neill

TRENDS AND PROJECTIONS OF PHYSICIANS
IN THE UNITED STATES 1967–2002
Mark S. Blumberg

MAY 1970:
THE CAMPUS AFTERMATH OF CAMBODIA
AND KENT STATE
Richard E. Peterson and John A. Bilorusky

MENTAL ABILITY AND HIGHER EDUCATIONAL
ATTAINMENT IN THE 20TH CENTURY
Paul Taubman and Terence Wales

AMERICAN COLLEGE AND UNIVERSITY
ENROLLMENT TRENDS IN 1971
Richard E. Peterson

PAPERS ON EFFICIENCY IN THE
MANAGEMENT OF HIGHER EDUCATION
*Alexander M. Mood, Colin Bell,
Lawrence Bogard, Helen Brownlee,
and Joseph McCloskey*

AN INVENTORY OF ACADEMIC INNOVATION
AND REFORM
Ann Heiss

ESTIMATING THE RETURNS TO EDUCATION:
A DISAGGREGATED APPROACH
Richard S. Eckaus

SOURCES OF FUNDS TO COLLEGES AND
UNIVERSITIES
June O'Neill

NEW DEPRESSION IN HIGHER
EDUCATION—TWO YEARS LATER
Earl F. Cheit

PROFESSORS, UNIONS, AND AMERICAN
HIGHER EDUCATION
*Everett Carll Ladd, Jr. and Seymour Martin
Lipset*

*The following reprints are available from the Carnegie Commission on Higher Education, 1947 Center
Street, Berkeley, California 94704.*

ACCELERATED PROGRAMS OF MEDICAL EDUCATION, *by Mark S. Blumberg, reprinted from*
JOURNAL OF MEDICAL EDUCATION, *vol. 46, no. 8, August 1971.**

SCIENTIFIC MANPOWER FOR 1970–1985, by Allan M. Cartter, reprinted from SCIENCE, vol. 172, no. 3979, pp. 132–140, April 9, 1971.

A NEW METHOD OF MEASURING STATES' HIGHER EDUCATION BURDEN, by Neil Timm, reprinted from THE JOURNAL OF HIGHER EDUCATION, vol. 42, no. 1, pp. 27–33, January 1971.*

REGENT WATCHING, by Earl F. Cheit, reprinted from AGB REPORTS, vol. 13, no. 6, pp. 4–13, March 1971.

COLLEGE GENERATIONS—FROM THE 1930s TO THE 1960s by Seymour M. Lipset and Everett C. Ladd, Jr., reprinted from THE PUBLIC INTEREST, no. 25, Summer 1971.

AMERICAN SOCIAL SCIENTISTS AND THE GROWTH OF CAMPUS POLITICAL ACTIVISM IN THE 1960s, by Everett C. Ladd, Jr., and Seymour M. Lipset, reprinted from SOCIAL SCIENCES INFORMATION, vol. 10, no. 2, April 1971.

THE POLITICS OF AMERICAN POLITICAL SCIENTISTS, by Everett C. Ladd, Jr., and Seymour M. Lipset, reprinted from PS, vol. 4, no. 2, Spring 1971.*

THE DIVIDED PROFESSORIATE, by Seymour M. Lipset and Everett C. Ladd, Jr., reprinted from CHANGE, vol. 3, no. 3, pp. 54–60, May 1971.*

JEWISH ACADEMICS IN THE UNITED STATES: THEIR ACHIEVEMENTS, CULTURE AND POLITICS, by Seymour M. Lipset and Everett C. Ladd, Jr., reprinted from AMERICAN JEWISH YEAR BOOK, 1971.

THE UNHOLY ALLIANCE AGAINST THE CAMPUS, by Kenneth Keniston and Michael Lerner, reprinted from NEW YORK TIMES MAGAZINE, November 8, 1970 .

PRECARIOUS PROFESSORS: NEW PATTERNS OF REPRESENTATION, by Joseph W. Garbarino, reprinted from INDUSTRIAL RELATIONS, vol. 10, no. 1, February 1971.*

. . . AND WHAT PROFESSORS THINK: ABOUT STUDENT PROTEST AND MANNERS, MORALS, POLITICS, AND CHAOS ON THE CAMPUS, by Seymour Martin Lipset and Everett C. Ladd, Jr., reprinted from PSYCHOLOGY TODAY, November 1970.*

DEMAND AND SUPPLY IN U.S. HIGHER EDUCATION: A PROGRESS REPORT, by Roy Radner and Leonard S. Miller, reprinted from AMERICAN ECONOMIC REVIEW, May 1970.*

RESOURCES FOR HIGHER EDUCATION: AN ECONOMIST'S VIEW, by Theodore W. Schultz, reprinted from JOURNAL OF POLITICAL ECONOMY, vol. 76, no. 3, University of Chicago, May/June 1968.*

INDUSTRIAL RELATIONS AND UNIVERSITY RELATIONS, by Clark Kerr, reprinted from PROCEEDINGS OF THE 21ST ANNUAL WINTER MEETING OF THE INDUSTRIAL RELATIONS RESEARCH ASSOCIATION, pp. 15–25.*

NEW CHALLENGES TO THE COLLEGE AND UNIVERSITY, by Clark Kerr, reprinted from Kermit Gordon (ed.), AGENDA FOR THE NATION, The Brookings Institution, Washington, D.C., 1968.*

PRESIDENTIAL DISCONTENT, by Clark Kerr, reprinted from David C. Nichols (ed.), PERSPECTIVES ON CAMPUS TENSIONS: PAPERS PREPARED FOR THE SPECIAL COMMITTEE ON CAMPUS TENSIONS, American Council on Education, Washington, D.C., September 1970.*

STUDENT PROTEST—AN INSTITUTIONAL AND NATIONAL PROFILE, by Harold Hodgkinson, reprinted from THE RECORD, vol. 71, no. 4, May 1970.*

WHAT'S BUGGING THE STUDENTS?, by Kenneth Keniston, reprinted from EDUCATIONAL RECORD, American Council on Education, Washington, D.C., Spring 1970.*

THE POLITICS OF ACADEMIA, by Seymour Martin Lipset, reprinted from David C. Nichols (ed.), PERSPECTIVES ON CAMPUS TENSIONS: PAPERS PREPARED FOR THE SPECIAL COMMITTEE ON CAMPUS TENSIONS, American Council on Education, Washington, D.C., September 1970.*

INTERNATIONAL PROGRAMS OF U.S. COLLEGES AND UNIVERSITIES: PRIORITIES FOR THE SEVENTIES, by James A. Perkins, reprinted by permission of the International Council for Educational Development, Occasional Paper no. 1, July 1971.

FACULTY UNIONISM: FROM THEORY TO PRACTICE, by Joseph W. Garbarino, reprinted from INDUSTRIAL RELATIONS, vol. 11, no. 1, pp. 1–17, February 1972.

MORE FOR LESS: HIGHER EDUCATION'S NEW PRIORITY, by Virginia B. Smith, reprinted from UNIVERSAL HIGHER EDUCATION: COSTS AND BENEFITS, American Council on Education, Washington, D.C., 1971.

ACADEMIA AND POLITICS IN AMERICA, by Seymour M. Lipset, reprinted from Thomas J. Nossiter (ed.), IMAGINATION AND PRECISION IN THE SOCIAL SCIENCES, pp. 211–289, Faber and Faber, London, 1972.

POLITICS OF ACADEMIC NATURAL SCIENTISTS AND ENGINEERS, by Everett C. Ladd, Jr., and Seymour M. Lipset, reprinted from SCIENCE, vol. 176, no. 4039, pp. 1091–1100, June 9, 1972.

THE INTELLECTUAL AS CRITIC AND REBEL: WITH SPECIAL REFERENCE TO THE UNITED STATES AND THE SOVIET UNION, by Seymour M. Lipset and Richard B. Dobson, reprinted from DAEDALUS, vol. 101, no. 3, pp. 137–198, Summer 1972.

COMING OF MIDDLE AGE IN HIGHER EDUCATION, by Earl F. Cheit, address delivered to American Association of State Colleges and Universities and National Association of State Universities and Land-Grant Colleges, Nov. 13, 1972.

THE NATURE AND ORIGINS OF THE CARNEGIE COMMISSION ON HIGHER EDUCATION, by Alan Pifer, reprinted by permission of The Carnegie Commission for the Advancement of Teaching, speech delivered Oct. 16, 1972.

THE DISTRIBUTION OF ACADEMIC TENURE IN AMERICAN HIGHER EDUCATION, *by Martin Trow*, *reprinted from* THE TENURE DEBATE, *Bardwell Smith (ed.), Jossey-Bass, San Francisco, 1972.*

THE POLITICS OF AMERICAN SOCIOLOGISTS, *by Seymour M. Lipset, and Everett C. Ladd, Jr.*, *reprinted from* THE AMERICAN JOURNAL OF SOCIOLOGY, *vol. 78, no. 1, July 1972.*

*The Commission's stock of this reprint has been exhausted.

The Academic System
in American Society

The Academic System in American Society

by Alain Touraine

Professor,
Ecole Pratique des Hautes Etudes, Paris

Third of a Series of Essays Sponsored by
The Carnegie Commission on Higher Education

MCGRAW-HILL BOOK COMPANY

New York   St. Louis   San Francisco   Düsseldorf
London   Sydney   Toronto   Mexico   Panama
Johannesburg   Kuala Lumpur   Montreal
New Delhi   Rio de Janeiro   Singapore

*The Carnegie Commission on Higher Education,
2150 Shattuck Avenue, Berkeley, California 94704,
has sponsored preparation of this essay as a
part of a continuing effort to obtain and present
significant information for public discussion.
The views expressed are those of the author.*

THE ACADEMIC SYSTEM IN AMERICAN SOCIETY

Copyright © 1974 by The Carnegie Foundation for
the Advancement of Teaching. All rights reserved.
Printed in the United States of America.

Library of Congress Cataloging in Publication Data
Touraine, Alain.
The academic system in American society.

"Third of a series of essays sponsored by the
Carnegie Commission on Higher Education."
Bibliography: p.
1. Education, Higher—United States—History.
2. Student movements—United States.   3.   Comparative
education.   I.   Carnegie Commission on Higher Education.
II. Title.

LA226.T68   378.73   73-3322
ISBN 0-07-010054-3

1 2 3 4 5 6 7 8 9 MAMM 7 9 8 7 6 5 4

Contents

Foreword

The Carnegie Commission on Higher Education has asked several persons from abroad who are thoroughly familiar with the United States to look at higher education here from their individual perspectives. The first volume to result was *Any Person, Any Study* by Sir Eric Ashby, formerly Vice-Chancellor of Cambridge University; and the second was *American Higher Education* by Joseph Ben-David of the Hebrew University of Jerusalem. This essay by Alain Touraine, professor at the Ecole des Hautes Etudes in Paris, is the third.

Professor Touraine approaches American higher education quite differently than either Eric Ashby or Joseph Ben-David. Among his basic themes are these:

- The university is intimately tied into society; and American society is being forced to reexamine its values and how it translates these values into action. The university is much affected by this process of reexamination.

- The production of knowledge is now more central to society, and the university is the main focal point of that production. Thus the university is a more important institution in society than in earlier times, and there is more of a contest over who should control it.

- Intellectuals, including those within the university, are now a more important class within society, but they also include many critics of society. This results in a new form of social struggle over the rate and the directions of change.

For these and other reasons, the university finds itself in a new period of tension unlike anything that has occurred before. This period of tension is not a fleeting event of the 1960s but constitutes a new stage of history. This view of higher education within the broad sweep of history and within a context of its manifold interrelations with society is set forth with great precision.

Professor Touraine is most understanding of the torment of the university within this new historical and societal context. He sees its future as greatly affected by its ability:

- To perform effectively the intellectual tasks of research and persuasion as a new type of society is being produced
- To incorporate the students, and other constituent elements, into the processes of the university in such a way that the university itself may be preserved as an effective intellectual community
- To manage its internal conflicts and its tensions with the surrounding society with sufficient success so that it may be a continuing source of great intellectual strength

The contemporary university thus faces a great series of crises within the swirling contradictions and conflicts and historic struggles of an industrial society undergoing basic changes. The university also faces great challenges to preserve its intellectual integrity while becoming more effective in producing the society of the future even as it reproduces the society of today.

This volume is full of points of view unaccustomed to many American academics more involved with day-to-day developments, and more committed to mental outlooks that expect problems to be worked out one at a time in the course of events. Professor Touraine challenges such approaches with his integrated analysis of the total situation, and with his conviction that specific tactical solutions should be informed by a broad strategy related to time and place and social purpose.

Clark Kerr
Chairman
Carnegie Commission on
Higher Education

April 1973

Acknowledgments

As part of an extensive program of studies on the American academic system, the chairman of the Carnegie Commission, Dr. Clark Kerr, wished that some foreign observers could express their views on the American scene. I want to express my gratitude for this opportunity to transform my own reactions and impressions into analysis. I hope I did not behave as either a bad anthropologist, unable to perceive the social and cultural mechanism of the tribe under study, or as a nice friend, too willing to accept the self-image of the American academic.

I was helped in my work by many colleagues who provided me with documents and ideas. I thank especially Sir Eric Ashby, Alexander Astin (who very generously assisted me in my use of American Council on Education publications), Daniel Bell, Joseph Ben-David, Nathaniel Birnbaum, Noam Chomsky, Alain Drouard, René Dubos, John Dunlop, William Freiberg, Dietrich Goldschmidt, Stephen Graubard, Stephen Hoffman, Alex Inkeles, Ivan Illich, Clark Kerr, Paul F. Lazarsfeld, Seymour Martin Lipset, Martin Malia, Herbert Marcuse, Gerry Marx, S. M. Miller, Edgar Morin, Serge Moscovici, Mishio Nagai, Talcott Parsons, James Perkins, David Riesman, Alice Rivlin, Walter A. Rosenblith, Melvin See-man, Neil Smelser, Ralph Turner, Martin Trow, Kurt Wolff, Laurence Wylie.

My colleague at the Ecole Pratique des Hautes Etudes, Clemens Heller (through the library of the Maison des Sciences de l'Homme), and Christiane Guigues helped me to collect books and documents. Colette Didier was once more exceptionally skillful in typing the handwritten manuscript. Yvette Duflo gave me the very efficient help of the secretary office of the Centre d'Etude des Mouvements Sociaux.

Mmes. Coryell, Couper, and Johnstone agreed to translate very rapidly the French text of this essay.

Mr. Verne A. Stadtman, associate director and editor of the Carnegie Commission, helped me with his knowledge of the University of California. Mr. Sidney J. P. Hollister, assistant editor for the Commission, should be considered as co-author of the American edition of this essay. He not only revised the translation very carefully but also often helped me to rephrase or make more precise my own formulations. I would like to be sure that this book deserved such a wonderfully skilled editor.

1. Introduction

Less than a century ago, American intellectuals came to Europe, and especially to Germany, partly in search of their roots and culture, but mainly to locate the main centers of intellectual and scientific activity. Today, students and research workers from Europe, Latin America, and much of Asia go to the United States to become acquainted either with modern scientific trends and the most favorable conditions for research, or with an exceptionally active and varied intellectual and artistic world. The carefully preserved image of a new world more concerned with money making than with culture, more dynamic than educated, needs no further commentary.

The number of young people entering college or university is higher in the United States than anywhere else; in California, for the first time in history, more than half the age group between 18 and 21 go to college. Europeans have long maintained that the educational standard of students entering American colleges was much lower than at the end of their gymnasiums or lycées. This is less and less the case. Considerable progress has been made in American high schools, although this varies according to social category. Furthermore, the greatly improved access to secondary education has led to the disappearance, even in Europe, of the apparent advantages of a system of education that was the prerogative of a very limited social elite. Although certain university towns in Germany, and particularly in England, have kept their reputation, today it is certainly in the United States that we find the highest number of university centers with a history. Whereas, in France most university buildings are less than 20 years old, and therefore are places that have scarcely any past, in the United States dozens of academic institutions can boast of more than a century of scientific discovery, of innovations in teaching methods, and of the role they played in the country's history. Vast campuses, the finest and most convenient libraries in the world, laboratories and research centers from which the world expects the most long-awaited discoveries and whose scientists win most Nobel Prizes in science, constitute one of the most striking aspects of American power.

I can still remember my first introduction to the American academic world at Harvard more than 20 years ago. A few minutes after presenting myself at the entrance to the Widener Library, I found myself among the stacks, surrounded by books, free to take what I wanted from the shelves. If I quote this distant recollection, it is to show how difficult it is for a foreigner to attempt to analyze higher education in the United States; he hesitates to go beyond these first impressions. He is more likely to think of ways of obtaining comparable working conditions in his own country, and, if he is an academic, he will envy both the working facilities and the skill in organization that allow these American colleges to be fully creative. Of course, one can learn from Joseph Ben-David's commentary on the mistakes made by the Americans who went to study in Germany (Ben-David & Zloczower, 1962, pp. 47–48). They went to the best universities and the best departments or institutes; they did not notice the disadvantages of a system which, when they discovered it, perhaps had lost the dynamism responsible for its position as the unchallenged model for the whole Western world. Similarly, foreign academics are more familiar with Harvard, Chicago, Berkeley, or Columbia than with the average state university, the majority of the Catholic colleges, or the black colleges in the South. They are also more sensitive to the beauty of many of the campuses than most American teachers or students. My account stands the risk of distortion and of incurring not only the displeasure of the Americans themselves, who feel keenly the difficulties and conflicts in which they are involved, but also of my fellow countrymen, who are more or less aware that what is a success in one country cannot simply be transplanted to another. Before I begin, I must therefore say a little more about my own impressions and the reasons that have prompted me to run the risk of submitting a number of opinions on American universities to American readers.

In my opinion (I personally have lived at Harvard, the University of California at Los Angeles, Columbia, and Chicago), the experience of the twentieth-century European visiting an American university and that of the American who went to study in a German university are not alike. The latter set out to learn something about universities, not about a society; he was more interested in Göttingen and Heidelberg than in the former states that made up the German Empire. Today, the Europeans who come to study in the United States are primarily interested in American society as it is reflected in its colleges and universities. For many of us to whom this society appears, at least in part, as the model of our own future society, admiration for the American university is partly a general identification with the scientific, economic, and cultural progress of the United States.

I must say that my personal feelings were very different. My admiration for the production and organization of American universities was offset for many years by an attitude of opposition, even of hostility, toward American society. I was accustomed to the attitudes of the French intelligentsia. For general, we may say, political reasons (the time when my first visit took place was the McCarthy era), I was keenly aware of what for me was the cowardliness or extreme timidity of the academics. They were more concerned with preserving their own peace of mind—referred to exaggeratedly as "academic freedom"—than with actively opposing the threats to freedom posed by the conformism, self-righteousness, and complacent ideological outpourings of a society blind to its problems and to its role of domination. For many years, therefore, I was very interested in American intellectual life and read as many, if not more, American than French publications. At the same time, I constantly opposed the ideas that came to France from America— even in my own field, which is sociology—and fought the influence of American interests and ideologies. It was only after 1964, and particularly after 1968, when the American academic world, losing nothing of its creativity, regained its critical faculties in words and acts, that I began to feel that American teachers and students were capable of opposing the established government and of questioning their own role. I felt then that I could rid myself of my ambivalent feelings about American universities and could examine the problem with greater clarity. I could certainly not have written this study before the beginnings of the crisis that shook the academic world and, more fundamentally, American society as a whole. I would have felt that I was consistently unjust and that I was betraying the admiration I had, and always will have, for the achievements of American higher education. On the other hand, I would also have felt that I had betrayed the profound reasons behind my reserve or hostility toward a political system in which I considered the universities ideologically integrated. I no longer feel a stranger in American universities now that they are facing problems that are partly like those that I have known in my own country. What is more, they have escaped from the tiresome rhetoric and its preoccupation with human values, noble sentiments, high-sounding principles, and self-satisfaction and are now questioning their role in society.

This is the essential point. In European countries, with their archaic academic organization and inadequate working facilities, where the capacity for decision making and change seems to be paralyzed, it is easy to confuse the issues: the struggle against material disorganization, the criticism of the decision-making system, and the opposition to the role of science and education within the power structure. Such confusion is less likely in the United States. Even if one is irritated by certain material difficulties, even if one denounces the authoritarianism or the lack of vision of certain presidents, or the indifference of professors who are too absorbed in their research to fulfill their role of educators, it is obvious that the reason for the academic crisis is not simply a breakdown in the functioning of the universities. The uprisings that have undermined the academic world have attacked, primarily, the political system in the United States and the relationship between the university and the government. At the same time, this criticism was directed at a certain type of liberalism, the illusion preserved by many teachers that they are pure scientists serving universalist values — the promoters of liberty, equality, and fraternity.

What is specific in American higher education, at least in comparison with other Western countries, is that it constitutes its own social and cultural world, with its own norms and values and its own particular language. At the same time, it is an integral part of society, supplying very varied and rapidly changing demands in general education, vocational training, and scientific discovery. Latin American universities — at least most of them — are also a part of the social body, but they have less professional autonomy and less ability to innovate. European universities usually have this internal autonomy, but at the expense, it seems, of a sound liaison with society. This applies to the demands of those entering the universities as well as to the demands of those who hire university graduates. In other countries attempts to reform the university system are sporadic, but in the United States reform is almost a permanent process. New demands are usually taken into consideration and the universities are able to respond to them by reflecting on their role and on their aims. There is, in my opinion, no other country where the debate within the university and outside the university is more constant; where academics, or at least their leaders, express more frequently their conception of teaching and research; where public and private authorities take initiatives that change the universities or the colleges materially or intellectually. People from other countries may be amused or express their indignation when they see the most scientific and the most practical studies side by side on the same campuses; American observers have always made similar criticisms of the chaotic situation in higher education. But the increasing diversity is paralleled by an equally strong tendency toward integration and by the attempt to formulate a general conception of education. This constant dialogue, which makes the academic system so flexible and so capable of renewing itself, has a particular consequence that we must keep in mind in our analysis of university education—the existence in the United States of a debate on the problem of the university. That debate, mainly the work of academics themselves, is so forcefully expressed and so widely diffused that the academic system itself appears to be the application of a certain conception of the human mind, of culture, and of education.

It is indeed natural that the colleges and those who frequent them should vie with one another in declaring that the educational system should be in harmony with the values of society. Does the United States not wish to be considered a society of material and social progress based on personal initiative and human solidarity? Is not education, on the condition that it is available to all and is based on open examination and on the molding of responsible citizens, the instrument, par excellence, of this type of progress? The dream of the *Aufklärung* and the Encyclopedists would come true. The values of society are firmly institutionalized, as is demonstrated by the highly developed legal system in the United States; they are also, during childhood, inculcated in the minds of the citizens—by the family, by the schools, and also, for many, by the churches. Hence the importance of the debate on education in the United States—a debate that is all the more impassioned because what is at stake is not a question of handing down to a new generation the codified heritage of the past, but rather the ability of sharing in the progress of a society totally oriented toward achievement and toward individual and collective progress. Knowledge, and all that it means in the way of vigor and freedom, is one of the central aims of a society geared to progress. The internal demands of the academic world are thus in perfect and natural agreement with the demands of society. This belief in the complementarity of personal development and collective solidarity runs through twentieth-century American academic history—from the Progressive Era, and especially during the long period of the ascendancy of John Dewey's teachings, and finally to the recent emphasis on the non-direct techniques of Carl Rogers. It comes close to the ideas on education Emile Durkheim expressed at the beginning of this century in another social context, ideas that could not be put into practice in Europe.

This self-image of education is an important element in the educational system. Within it, many teachers, or those responsible for educational policy, defined their aims and attempted to build and constantly transform academic institutions. But the very forcefulness of the self-image and the reality of its effect are major obstacles to understanding the real relationship between education and society. The crises and failures of the universities in Germany, Japan, or France leave us with some misgivings as to all current views on education in these societies. The quality of the debate is poor and, furthermore, it is not argued by the academics and the political elites simultaneously. In the United States, on the contrary, the university seems to be either the embodiment of a conception of the university idea or the invention of a whole society that is inspired by a certain conception of man and life in society and is bent on educating its youth according to its ideals of progress, of justice, and of freedom. But is the conception of a society serving values and principles, governed by ideas, and, above all, totally dependent on a social and cultural consensus, truly satisfactory? It is easy to understand that a recently constituted society, gradually conquering vast territories and formed to a large extent by people of different ethnic origins, should lay particular emphasis on factors conducive to its integration. Such a society would naturally place the utmost importance on moral values and would strive to instill these values in the minds of its citizens, for the social order would not yet have the basis of traditional hierarchies or frameworks.

In European societies the university is at the same time subjected to the established order and more committed to its role as a critic and emancipator. In the United States it is linked more directly with instrumentality, progress, and the integration of a new society. In France the universities produce the executive personnel of public and private administration; they also produce the opposition elite — an elite that once fought clericalism and now fights capitalism. In the United States, the universities are at the same time more independent yet less free, more progressive yet more dependent, and in general are more concerned with progress and integration. It is therefore more difficult to go beyond the debate on education in the United States and to question the value of the links between the university and society. In Europe it is easy to show how schools and universities, far from promoting democratization, transmit, if not reinforce, social inequality. That equality in education, even when it is practically free up to the advanced level, is clearly a myth is demonstrated by the inequalities clearly outlined by the separation between levels and types of teaching and by the role 'of the elite institutions, so carefully guarded by various methods of selection.

Such a problem would at first seem unthinkable in America, where many people go to colleges and universities. Superior and less superior departments coexist in the same institution, and universities are often discussed, aptly or inaptly, as if they were service stations. The founder of an excellent university announced that he wanted it to be a place where anyone could learn anything. Yet, social selection is just as real and efficient in the United States as elsewhere, as studies over the past few years have indicated. It has even been shown that the huge quantitative progress made in past decades has probably not made it any easier for young people of different social backgrounds to enter the social elite. In fact, inequality has increased for certain categories. But recognition of these facts comes up against the forcefulness of the debate on education, and it is probably not by chance that the studies on unequal opportunities in education have developed particularly since 1964, when this debate was challenged. On a broader level, it was difficult to make the American academic system admit that it did not equally serve all sections of society and that to equate a society with its values is either naïve or an act of propaganda. For the debate on education did not mention the political system, except to say that it was representative. The war in Vietnam, however, reflected an image of America that completely contradicted the idealistic speeches and lofty sentiments so lavishly distributed. At the same time, the black movement violently expressed the lack of a consensus and claimed for more than a tenth of the population a status of exploited outsiders in their own society. The United States had to be confronted with both of these before the universalism of a liberal university was questioned and criticized.

It is therefore not the debate on education that I will analyze here, but rather the changing reality of the relationship between the academic world and society, as it is revealed in its class relations, its value orientations, and its political system. More precisely, I would like to show how the academic world has gradually become an element of the world of production and social domination, and how this progressive integration into the political system has caused the breakdown of the academic self-image, leading many teachers and students to refuse integration into the prevailing practices and ideologies. To do this I will have to trace the development of higher education over the past century, that is to say, since the founding of the modern colleges and universities in the United States.

In effect, during the first period, which extends roughly up to the First World War, the academic system was scarcely integrated. Observers vied with each other in describing it as the synthesis of the English college, the German university, and a purely American conception of service, or, if you prefer, of Yale, Johns Hopkins, and the land-grant colleges. But there was little integration, just as American society, open and preoccupied with internal expansion, was scarcely integrated. The intellectually and materially unifying role of the state was slight. The colleges and universities combined the various roles proposed to them to a low degree, thus giving great importance to the president, the only link between the students, the teaching profession, and the community. At most, one could say that the main role of the colleges was to form a national elite.

In the ensuing period, roughly from 1920 to the launching of the first sputnik in 1957, integration progressed as the academic system developed and became organized. The consolidation of a national elite (that is, the establishment) became the central principle of academic policy, although the other aims, such as developing knowledge and adapting a large proportion of young people to social and cultural change, were not entirely subordinated to it. It was when the federal financing of research became a key element in the functioning of the universities, and especially of the head of the "snakelike procession," to use David Riesman's phrase, that the production role of higher education became dominant and the system became most clearly ranked. In Europe, often, the unity of the academic system seems to be linked to the system's dominant role as the agent of reproduction of the social order. But this implies that this order be highly codified and controlled. In the United States, on the contrary, the academic system was only loosely organized when the colleges assumed the role of reproducers of the social order; it was even less so in the period before World War I when the theme of progress seemed to be its main aim. On the other hand, after the Second World War, and even more so after acceleration in changes brought about by the military and political rivalry with the Soviet Union, the academic world really became a system geared to the needs of the large organizations and to the formation of a hierarchy of various types of participants in a society both technobureaucratic and capitalist. The United States is no longer uniquely a national society, but a national state and the most powerful center of world domination. The increasing interdependence of economic domination, political and military power, and academic production now gives to the universities an exceptional strength and importance while, at the same time, provoking internal clashes and revolts that would be incomprehensible if the academic system did not play this key role.

Consequently, the development of an academic system as an element of the social order is the object of my study. I will describe it in considerable detail, at the same time tracing the evolution of the forces and opposition that, in varied forms, always fought integration within the system before actually challenging it.

It is a history enriched by the fact that it takes place in a society in which constraints, repression, and violence are often very directly manifested, but in which freedom of speech and discussion, recourse to legal and political solutions, and a willingness to reform have never ceased to be real and effective.

2. National Integration

Education, and particularly higher education, has three main functions, or more accurately, belongs to three levels of a society's functioning.

In this general introduction to a study of the relations between the academic system and the American society, my purpose is not to list the various activities of colleges and universities or to pay close attention to the aims and organizational forms of various types of institutions; my intention rather is to examine the society itself and the role higher education plays in it.

I make a distinction between three levels of analysis, for the study of a society must (1) start with a consideration of its cultural and social orientations and class relationships; that is, of the social forces engaged in a struggle for the control of these cultural orientations and of the social organization; (2) next, examine the decision-making mechanisms, or institutions, through which these orientations and these class relationships are converted into social change; and finally (3), reach down to the level of organizations — such as companies, cities, or schools — that are the seat both of technical activity and of ideologies striving to integrate the social system.

Research, general education, vocational training, and socialization of the youth are facets of academic life that can be examined at each of these levels, and cannot therefore be examined successively.

Various types of institutions, however, could have been studied separately, for it is obvious that Harvard and a junior college, a liberal arts college of less than 1,000 students, and a large state university have neither the same functions nor the same problems. This approach was rejected because I found it necessary to acknowledge the unity of the academic system over and above the variety of institutions. This unity is not an observed fact, since the organization of higher education is not subject to centralized direction. It is a working hypothesis that results directly from the outlook referred to above. Indeed, no complete separation can exist between the self-creation of a society, the management of its changes, and the reproduction of its organization. The variety of institutions shows the complex relationships among these functions as well as the diversity and the conflicts among social categories whose future members participate—or do not participate —in higher education. The main object of this book is to describe the nature of an academic system's unity—which changes with the times—and, therefore, the place of that system in its society.

The first level of analysis   In the first place, academic activity contributes to the creation of a culture. The most essential aspect of this activity is the construction of systems of knowledge. These systems are frequently created outside the universities, but no university can ignore the scientific research and debates that lead to their creation. Here I will follow the brilliant analyses of Michel Foucault (1966) and Serge Moscovici (1968), limiting myself to modern times. The "classical" period, from Galileo to Descartes and Newton, invented a "nature"—that is, a cultural conceptualization of the material world—that can be described as mechanistic, with a way of thinking that applied to grammar, biology, and economics, as well as to physics. In the nineteenth century, this nature was replaced by another, characterized by evolution and the historical approach, which dominated the thought of the historians and positivists and of Marx and Spencer. This world view—which is not so much a system of ideas as a system of intellectual categories whose meaning and implications are not necessarily conscious— can be said to have been replaced in our century by systemic analysis. This analysis, which first prevailed in physics, went on to renovate biology, linguistics, and economics.

To study a university we must start by asking ourselves whether it is intellectually creative: that is, whether it participates in the creation of new knowledge. Another basic cultural role supplements the creation of knowledge. While developing a type of knowledge, a society pictures its own creativeness and designs a "cultural model," an image of creativeness that directs its action upon itself.[1] In industrialized societies, where the action of society on itself is powerful, this creativeness is grasped "practically," and it is science itself that constitutes the cultural model of society. The further we go from these societies, the more the cultural models are dissociated from practice. Creativeness can be grasped as that of a creator God, or that of the state as organizer of exchange, or that of the market and the firm. Each of these cultural models is linked to a model of knowledge.[2]

Whatever the specific organizational forms of a university, it must first fit into a cultural model. Therefore, we cannot adequately speak of the development and history of German, American, or English universities as if the continuity of the institution implied the continuity of social roles. Professors readily believe that the development of the universities is determined by the improvement of their working conditions and by their own professionalization. They are not entirely mistaken, but science is not merely a professional activity. It is first of all a cultural model, and its development is linked today to a society's ability to withhold from the consumer market part of its production capacity, in order to

[1] *Cultural model*　A society is not a network of interdependent variables. That would define a "closed system."

Living organisms are able to maintain their equilibrium. Some animals and certainly human beings are able to adjust to change by learning. The human society goes further. It has a symbolic capacity through which it creates what I call historicity: a model of knowledge is the first aspect of it; the second is accumulation—that is, the capacity to withdraw part of the resources from the economic process to invest it. The last is the consciousness of this capacity to act upon itself, in other words, an image of the creativeness. Science is, in our society, a special case: model of knowledge, it is the cultural model too.

The main idea here is to analyze society not as a system of roles or functions but as the transformation of the social and cultural orientations linked with a type of historicity into a concrete practice in a definite historical setting. One of the consequences of this approach is to give a central importance to class relationships and class conflicts. Because the ruling class is not the upper stratum but the group who "manages" the historicity, the capacity of the society to act upon itself carries as a direct consequence the dichotomizations of the actors into opposite social classes.

[2] *Model of knowledge*　Society builds a set of categories through which it analyzes man and nature. A merchant society developed from Galileo to Newton a mechanistic view of the world: God, like the king, was a watch maker. On the contrary, the capitalistic society introduces a historical approach: biology, economics, linguistics, all main aspects of the sciences, are conceived in terms of evolution. A model of knowledge is not a set of ideas but of concepts and categories.

devote it to a particular type of investment. The development of science in our society depends therefore on conditions similar to those that made possible in other societies the construction of churches, palaces, or the great works of nineteenth-century industrial capitalism. The most important of these conditions is the existence of a central decision-making authority, a centralized power able to channel resources toward culturally valued types of investment. Without such an authority, scientific progress could develop in any society, but the importance of science as a cultural model would be considerably diminished. If we look at the nineteenth century, we see that science at that time was still developing largely outside the university. Neither Darwin nor Marx nor Pasteur belonged to any university. On the other hand, academic organization assumed great importance wherever there existed a centralized will to develop a new cultural model — historicism, for example, whose concrete political expression was the national state. Hence the importance of the achievements of the French Revolution and Napoleon, and even more of the University of Berlin — an answer to the Prussian defeat at Jena — and the development throughout the century of a German national conscience. As we shall see, colleges and universities played the same role in the United States, but in the nineteenth century this role was a limited one precisely because of this country's low degree of national integration and the weak role of the national state. However, in a different society and a different culture, when the cultural model had assumed the form of science and growth, rather than of "progress" in the nineteenth-century meaning of the term, and when the university had become the physical site of the development of a model of knowledge, the United States, then a strong national state, established a remarkably dynamic academic system — seat of the creation of the new cultural model. The professional autonomy of the scientists is therefore closely linked to the centralization of political power. The United States is one of the countries where this autonomy, though most constantly demanded, developed most slowly, finally reaching, at the present time, one of the highest degrees ever attained.

These remarks cannot be separated from those concerning the relation between the university and class domination. The cultural model of any society is not the ideology of a ruling class; it is an essential element of the cultural field in which class conflicts arise. Through these conflicts, the classes struggle to appropriate the cultural model as well as the means of production. But the university, like any agent in the development of a model of knowledge and a cultural model, is primarily linked to the ruling class.

When I use the term *ruling class* I do not mean upper strata, as if the academic system were influenced by the social and cultural characteristics of a certain social category. Such an influence is generally very limited and indirect. But education in general, and higher education in particular, are part of a system of social control through which a society is shaped into forms of social and cultural organization. These forms support and reinforce the power of the group that decides and controls the investment and production process, defending the "needs" of property, capital, or corporations against the needs of those who are subject to their decisions. But I am not identifying ruling class with power elite, because it cannot be accepted as a general statement that economic and political power are always in the same hands.

Training of the social elite, propagation of its ideology, activities linked to the demands of the ruling class—these are some expressions of this bond, for knowledge is not neutral insofar as it makes use of social resources. If the Soviet universities resist the development of the social sciences, it is because the technocratic power born of a popular revolution feels threatened by an investigation of its policy, which does not necessarily correspond to its ideology. If in the United States more money has been devoted to advertising than to the study of many social problems, it is because advertising brings more profits to the ruling class. We shall see below that this bond is not the only one that subjects the academic system to class domination. Here I am dealing only with the direct, material, and ideological action exerted by the ruling class in order to orient the knowledge and training efforts, and therefore the productive work, of the academic system. This action is always circumscribed by the autonomy of both the model of knowledge and the cultural model. But it is ever present, for this cultural model has no existence outside the conflictual field of the social classes. The relationship between the dependency and the autonomy of academic production takes various forms. A rising ruling class relies on new knowledge and cultural models to combat the old ruling class. On the other hand, political power is more or less closely linked to the ruling class. As I have just pointed out, when a national state plays an important role, it reinforces the university's role as creator of a cultural model; but this also results in stronger domination of the university by the ruling class.

There is a parallel between the university's cultural creativeness and its social dependence. It would therefore be illusory to think that the universities could be centers of both opposition and creation, except at a time of crisis for the social power, when an outdated ruling class no longer corresponded to the new productive forces. The universities then become instruments of political change. It is also illusory to think that the universities prosper in a situation of "independence" and that universal respect for what James Conant calls the "citadel of learning" is favorable to the progress of disinterested intellectual production.

European universities are well acquainted with this illusory freedom, which in their case has meant nothing but routine and corporate bureaucracy. Academic development is never independent of its political commitment, either on the side of the powers-that-be or that of the forces of social change.

The more "practical" a society's cultural model, the more the ruling class tries to control it directly. The universities' social autonomy is therefore increasingly threatened, or, as a corollary to this statement, the universities increasingly become theaters for social struggles.

Between the nineteenth century and the twentieth, the change is striking. But there is a significant difference between universities controlled by a "voluntarist" state and those which, to use a nineteenth-century expression, are more closely linked to the "civil society" than to the state. Many Latin American universities find themselves today in a social and cultural environment similar to that of the national movements of nineteenth-century Europe and so are experiencing the kind of political activity that is completely linked to national development. Famous examples in the first half of the twentieth century are the Argentinian universities at the time of Hipolito Irigoyen's assumption of power, the National University of Montevideo under Battle y Ordoñez, the National University of Mexico under Lázaro Cárdenas, and the University of Chile under Arturo Alessandri's first presidency. Thus, scientific professionalism, the key role of the state, and the existence of social struggles inside the university are three features of one type of university; a low degree of professionalism, the domination of a ruling class loosely linked to a restricted political power, and the subjection of students to an educational model stressing social integration define another type of university. American colleges and universities developed historically from the second type into the first.

This is the first level of sociological analysis of the academic world, defining it in terms of the model of knowledge, the cultural model, and the class relations of a society.

As we shall see, taking into account this level of analysis alone, the academic system in the United States, as established in the last third of the nineteenth century, did not play a central role in the society. The society itself played a limited role in the creation and development of the "historicist" model of knowledge, which owes much more to the English, the Germans, and even the French. The academic system's dependence upon the "civil society" was a direct one, which limited the professional autonomy of the teachers.

Things are very different in the middle of the twentieth century, when the cultural creativeness of American universities and their increased dependence on the state put them at the very heart of political conflict and social and cultural change.

In the in-between period, both creativeness and dependency were weak; the academic system was turned inward toward the problems of education proper. In defining the third level of our general analysis, we shall see that this type of functioning is related to a different type of link with the social-class system.

The second level of analysis   This level concerns the set of mechanisms, which we shall call institutions, by means of which a society organizes its change, that is, its adjustment to modifications occurring within itself or in its environment. The university is a political decision-making center. It sometimes happens that the university's participation in the decisions affecting it is reduced. In this case, the central or regional political authorities decide, through legislative or executive measures, what changes must be made in the university's organization to enable it to respond adequately to the so-called needs of the society. In other cases, the universities have a genuine administration, or at least there is a close interaction between the decision makers inside and those outside the university, so that the university itself takes important initiatives concerning recruitment and training, research and application.

The greater the society's mobility and the faster the change of its occupational pattern, the less important the transmission of the cultural heritage; the more important the training of new types of professionals, the greater we might normally assume the decision-making autonomy of the university to be. But these are not the only determining factors to be considered.

The greater the role of the national state and the more organized the academic system, the more limited is the university's internal decision-making ability. Rigidity and centralism can be very favorable to the propagation of changes decided at the top; but the faster the changes in the society and the more complex that society is, the less efficient is this kind of policy for effecting change. Strong submission to the ruling class rather than to the state is therefore usually associated with strong decision-making autonomy for the university. This is true provided that it is genuinely a ruling class and not merely a dominating class; in other words, that it is a class more concerned with developing the productive forces that it has the responsibility of managing than with maintaining law and order.

The French experience shows that the worst possible situation is one where a national state, imbued with centralizing traditions, lets itself be progressively colonized by special interests, particularly by economic and social groups. These groups need the state's protection to maintain their traditional position, and so oppose economic or cultural change. The university is then in danger of being managed by nothing more than a coalition of public administration bureaucrats and university dignitaries, acting from day to day and organizing general resistance to any organizational change.

Although from the point of view of cultural creativeness the American academic system of the nineteenth century seems rather weak, its capacity for adjustment, for organizational invention, and for adaptation to various and rapidly changing social demands seems exceptional. The importance of the presidents in American academic history proves the importance of the university's internal decision-making system. The preceding remarks would lead us to expect this political ability to diminish in the recent period because of a closer relation to the national state, and especially because of the introduction of political conflicts in the university. But despite these reservations, the flexibility and capacity for initiative of American higher education remain tremendous, so much so that they baffle the foreign observer, who can neither discover general organizational rules, nor determine the level of the various degrees, nor even identify the typical curriculum for a given vocational training course.

The latter part of the nineteenth century witnessed, within a few years, the creation or transformation of an unusual number of universities. During this period, the university's essential role was, no doubt, to follow and accelerate the social changes leading to national integration and to the constitution of a national elite. This political ability cannot, of course, be assumed to function in a vacuum. On the contrary, it is all the greater because it clearly fits within the limits established by class domination. But it is not confined to putting into practice a policy corresponding to the interests of the ruling class, an expression so vague that it does not, for example, account for the tremendous differences between the academic systems of various capitalist countries. The great flexibility of the American system is related to the fact that it was, at the end of the nineteenth century, and is again today, more an instrument for shaping a new type of society than the means of reproducing an established social order.

The third level of analysis   Lastly, a university is an organization occupying a territory, possessing a system of authority, and utilizing certain resources with a view to definite objectives and according to certain working regulations. But there are always two sides to an organization. On the one hand, it utilizes techniques and develops a more or less differentiated type of work organization. On the other hand, it possesses forces of integration that are rooted in the value orientations of a society and its system of class domination. This link between the academic system and class relationships is not the same as the one that is connected with the "productive" role of higher education.

At the first of the three levels of analysis, the academic system directly serves the ruling class, whether as the vehicle of its ideology or by its participation in the productive forces controlled by this ruling class.

Here, on the contrary, at the level of the academic system viewed as an organization, what is important is the reproduction of a social order, in other words the perpetuation of distances and barriers through selection, or even segregation. The content of the teaching is of little importance; what counts is the difference established between social classes. Let us take an extreme example: there existed in nineteenth-century France a school for the people and a school for the bourgeoisie. Even when both schools taught the merits of the fatherland, of science, and of progress, the educational system as a whole was based on oppositions—intellectual work versus manual work, humanism versus technology, verbal expression versus bodily gestures, prowess versus imitation—which reflect the separation and the hierarchy of the social classes.

This whole set of categories constitutes the system's ideology. It is not independent of the ideology of the ruling class but translates it into "disinterested," abstract, even technical terms. Much is said today, for example, about respecting the aspirations and specific cultural traits of the pupils, adapting education to their "needs." Thus is developed a model of order and distribution that reproduces inequalities.

The most general conceptions of the ideology of education usually imply a form of social hierarchy. This ideology, though not always explicit, cannot be unconscious. It is even less unconscious when the society is in a state of greater change and when the educational system must adapt to these changes—that is, when class segregation must be combined with the integration of the system as a whole.

But at this level, too, it would be a mistake to reduce academic behavior and images to the ideology of the class system.

The academic world today participates in a very fundamental way in the production of knowledge. As quite different forms of the "scholarly" world once felt close to other cultural models, so the academic world of today feels close to the cultural model of its society. It therefore tends to identify its own interests—those of the academic organization or profession—with those of the model of knowledge and the cultural model, over and above class relations and decision-making systems. Many university people who wish to be free from all interference by society in their work do not take this attitude in order to shut themselves up in an ivory tower, but because they feel they can serve society best by remaining as aloof as possible from its political controversies and its administrative apparatus. Even from the viewpoint of the university's educational role, rather than its role as a producer of knowledge, independence seems to work in favor of those who are changing the social order, either individually by their own advancement, or collectively—for knowledge is a factor of analysis and criticism.

This set of beliefs I call *academic rhetoric,* and there is no reason to think that it is merely an additional facet of the system's ideology. It may strengthen this ideology, conflict with it, or merely weaken its hold. Let us call it an internal opposition. It can have considerable significance in the absence of open, organized struggle over class domination and its political expression. The scientist can then loudly denounce the lies of the powers-that-be and the obstacles they raise against social progress or the progress of knowledge.

But this academic rhetoric loses its importance, and may play a more conservative role, when social conflicts become organized and the opposition challenges not only the power structure but also the ideology of the system and the mask of objectivity or high principles behind which it conceals its special interests. Academic independence feels threatened by this challenging opposition and this politizization. The university then tends to flounder in the midst of conflicting attitudes or to take refuge behind an established power that respects the academic rhetoric while imposing its own ideology.

Academic rhetoric has power of resistance only to the extent that it relies on the university's roles as a producer of knowledge and an instrument of social mobility. Conversely, it is "reactionary" when it is purely defensive, when it replaces the production of knowledge by disembodied and eclectic oratory, when it remains unconcerned by social and cultural barriers. Even when this rhetoric adopts a "left" tone, it is then no more than an agent of the prevailing ideology, an obstacle to the knowledge of social realities, an opponent of the social movements that reveal their contradictions and conflicts. Japan and France, in particular, are well acquainted with this type of liberal rhetoric. In my opinion, however, the United States—where the university's role as producer of knowledge is more important, at least since the First World War and especially since the Second World War—is more accustomed to an ambiguous type of academic rhetoric that is progressive and conservative at the same time and goes beyond a flat, abstract liberalism.

On the other hand, the American academic system has more often actively served the power structure's ideology. As we shall see, it played this role mainly in the first part of the twentieth century, when it developed themes such as general education, which are essentially instruments for strengthening the social order. More recently, however, with the increasing importance of the university's role as producer of knowledge, both academic rhetoric and the academic system's ties with the power structure were strengthened. During this recent period the ideological role of the universities and colleges was less important than before. Concern for education and the definition of a "spirit" of higher education lost the strength they had between the two wars.

Let me add that the greater the ideological role of the university, the more it stresses the importance of an educational model, and therefore the importance of its own integration, the more it represses "deviant" or oppositional behavior. On the contrary, when the university develops simultaneously its professional rhetoric and its ties with the power structure, it can open its doors more freely to controversy, since no unifying principle connects these two orientations.

Before describing the changes in the American academic system, it would be useful to summarize the above remarks in order to define what, in my view, is the general direction of these changes. Although my outline is not above criticism and will have to be qualified, supplemented, and amended, a distinction among three successive stages in the history of the academic system seems possible. The stages are successive, but they also partly overlap, and their overlapping contributes greatly to an understanding of the crises and conflicts that the system experiences at given moments.

During the first stage, roughly from 1870 to World War I, the main role of the colleges and the universities was to respond to the changes in American society, that is, to the development of its activity and to the formation of a new ruling elite. Adjustment to change was essential, but it cannot be isolated from the creation of a new cultural model and of new class relations. Of the three levels of analysis I have defined, the second seems to be the most important during this stage. This explains the search for new academic "policies" and the role of great presidents in the creation of new institutions and new curricula.

In the next stage, before the First World War, but particularly after it, the predominant concern was the consolidation of the ruling class, which resulted in the renewed importance of education, and especially general education. Organizational problems, and therefore the ideological role of the academic system, then assumed major significance.

Finally, in the most recent period, marked by the extraordinary expansion of research following the Second World War, especially after the launching of the first sputnik, the academic system has been characterized mainly by its role as creator of knowledge and of a new cultural model, and by its ties with the state and the big coordinated centers of political-economic decision making. Its autonomous decision-making power is weakening, its educational and socializing role is diminishing. The student revolt and the crisis of the system emphasized in a dramatic and fruitful way the significance of the changes undergone or desired, and confront the academic system today with new choices.

In other countries, the development of the universities could be summarized by saying that they progressed from the role of reproducer to that of producer of the social order. In the United States, which in the second half of the nineteenth century was a barely emerging nation in constant flux, the trend of development was more complex: before reproducing a social order the universities had to help integrate the society. These historical differences partially explain the differences in the way various industrialized countries have experienced the current academic crisis. After our attempt to identify several distinct stages in their development, it should indeed be added that universities, to a much greater extent than business enterprises and to almost the same extent as churches, are organizations possessing a vast memory. With all their modernism, they never completely escape from their task of transmitting the cultural heritage. Although it may be true that, as Robert Oppenheimer puts it, 90 percent of all the physicists in the history of the world are still alive, it cannot be said that 90 percent of all the books read in the universities are the work of living authors.

Every university is both a conservatory and a laboratory. And so the attitudes, the organizational forms, and the ideologies persist long after the reasons for their original appearance have disappeared. This is why the behavior patterns observed today cannot be understood independently of a history that is inscribed in the regulations, the human relations, and the curricula, as much as in the stones and the libraries. This is particularly true in the United States, a country that seems to have more of a past than a history — that is to say, where men and events of the past seem to exist in the present. European countries have a more detached attitude toward their history, which weighs upon them, and from which they strive to free themselves, treating it as an object of study. Concern for historical continuity is very much alive in the United States. Jefferson and Lincoln seem to be listening to what is said about them in the history classes. The appeal to civic spirit is perpetual, as it is in the Soviet Union, but no longer in Germany, France, or Great Britain. A Harvard student has a sense of the continuity of history from the college's founding in 1636 up to himself. A French student has the feeling that he is living in an institution without a past, without traditions, without any particular "spirit."

We should therefore avoid making too sharp a distinction between the stages suggested above. Yet, at the same time it is useful to break this sense of continuity, to reject a reduction of the university to the university spirit, and to take advantage of the fact that the author is not an American and is not trying to understand and define the American academic system in terms of its values—a hopeless effort in any case.

One more word of explanation concerning the voluntary limitations of the following analysis. It could be criticized for giving excessive importance to the best institutions, although they enroll only a small proportion of the students. To study a representative sample of establishments, it certainly would be necessary to give far more attention to the Catholic colleges and the junior colleges than to the 10 universities with the highest international and national reputation. It is no accident that I have constantly referred to the academic system, even though in describing its development I have recognized its low level of integration at the end of the nineteenth century. Regardless of its complexity, it has its own unity in each period, and this unity is most apparent in the largest institutions (this of course would be unthinkable in France or England). It is at Harvard or Chicago that the entire field of forces at work in 1900 can best be grasped, and it is at Berkeley or Columbia that the nature of the student movement can best be analyzed. By the same token, in an effort to understand the class relations or the political system of a society, we would not describe in the same way the big corporations and the small-town drugstores, or the federal government and the local courts. I hope the reader, as he proceeds further, will recognize the validity of this choice.

PROGRESS AND EDUCATION The American academic system was constructed along with the railroads. While the communications network that was to link all parts of the vast developing country was being built, a similar network of colleges was spreading across the land. From 1850 to 1890, the length of the railroads increased from 9,000 to 167,500 miles, that is, 25,000 more miles than for the whole of Europe. During the same period, the population increased from 23,200,000 to 62,600,000. Seventy percent of the population was occupied in cultivating the land. But the emergence of the nation was a slow process, even after the Civil War. The United States was a collection of communities, not a national state. Education, based upon the family, the church, the ethnic group, and the neighborhood community, strove primarily to maintain the group's values, to guarantee its ever-threatened cohesiveness, and also to enable it to play an active part in society's rapid changes.

Ethics was the main aim of the entire educational system. The first colleges, led by Harvard and other institutions that were founded before national independence, were inspired by the values of the Eastern bourgeoisie, which were primarily religious and moral. Education was in the hands of the clerics and its primary purpose was to train ministers. In the first half of the nineteenth century, the multiplicity of sects led to the creation of numerous seminaries and denominational colleges, a trend that continued with the development of the Catholic colleges, which were established to serve a new strain of immigrants. All these colleges, from the most famous to the humblest, subscribed to the same concept of education, centered on the group rather than knowledge, on education rather than learning. Since the first colleges created during colonial times were neither public nor private, no national educational system was then possible. As early as the eighteenth century, however, the training of a few scholars and gentlemen gradually began to be supplemented by more modern functions, such as the preparation of doctors and teachers. Benjamin Franklin went so far as to attack Harvard as a rich boy's refuge, and later, as one of the founders of the University of Pennsylvania, he gave that school the lead in this "modernizing" movement. Vocational training was still limited, however; the main role of the colleges was to keep up with the breakdown of the communities and, as Oscar and Mary Handlin (1970, p. 35) expressed it, "to train the nation's future leaders"— not the entire social elite, only that part of it concerned with the maintenance of law and order and of the established values. The same authors explain: "The college was charged with preparing its graduates for careers and also with transmitting to them a code of behavior not grounded upon religious doctrines, yet in some vague and undefined manner preserving Christian values" (ibid., p. 45). The high tuition fees payed by the social and cultural elite provided the essential resources of the colleges, which were, however, by no means wealthy, but often poorly attended and in financial trouble.

In the middle of the nineteenth century, while the West was being settled, the old Eastern colleges were still strengthening their moral and bourgeois hold. Because of the development of the mercantile spirit, Yale, under Noah Porter's presidency, and Princeton became fortresses of conservatism (Veysey, 1965, pp. 21–56). Their educational doctrine was based on mental discipline: they stressed such things as piety and memory exercises. Even after the reforms at Harvard, Yale endeavored for a long time to preserve this type of education.

The more modest colleges made no pretense of training a national elite. They were the mere expressions of a subculture. They answered the needs of a community. They ensured stability in a changing world (Jencks & Riesman, 1968, pp. 1–27). But the United States by midcentury was no longer simply an aggregate of communities, ranging from the high bourgeois circles of Boston and Philadelphia to the rural communities of the Midwest. It was also the new country to which people and capital rushed, where businesses and fortunes were built, where the robber barons reigned—whose economic success had nothing to do with community values, despite their strong religious ties. Andrew Carnegie, whose fortune was to play an important role in the development of the academic system, condemned the colleges and their education. And not without reason, for they did, in fact, serve the prevailing order better than the new ruling classes. Tocqueville had found more to admire in the United States than the spirit of freedom and equality. He particularly admired that bulwark of bourgeois society, the community spirit based on moral values and property—truly a bulwark against the rise of the people. The colleges, like the political and legal institutions, were indeed an answer to that fear expressed by this supporter of constitutional monarchy, who was to be so horrified by the 1848 Revolution in Paris. But just as the France of Tocqueville was primarily the France of Balzac, of the triumph of money, the United States of the colleges and seminaries was also, and above all, the place where commercial and industrial empires were developing, where technological inventions were proliferating, where social mobility was made possible by wealth. The colleges, in the meantime, rather than becoming part of this movement of economic development and social change, assumed the task of preventing the old elites from sliding down the social ladder.

This segregation of two societies, this isolation of communities entrenched behind their moral walls as the frontiers of the land and of the economy were constantly advanced by pragmatic conquerors, could neither be complete nor last indefinitely. The force of representative institutions, the series of populist upsurges, and the needs of industry and commerce—all called for a transformation of the educational system. It was carried out through the rapid development of two main types of institutions: the land-grant colleges, created by the first Morrill Act (1862) and reinforced by the second (1890), and the state normal schools, gradually converted into state teachers colleges, and more recently into state colleges and state universities.[3] During this whole period, technical, and especially agricultural, education was encouraged by the federal government. The Hatch Act of 1887 abetted establishment of experimental agricultural stations and the Smith-Lever Act of 1914 organized an agency for the popularization of agricultural knowledge.

But a sharp dividing line has been too readily drawn between the traditional and the agricultural and mechanical—or A & M—colleges, which were supposedly devoted exclusively to the progress of agriculture and the techniques required for the newborn mechanical industries. As David Riesman (1968–1969, p. 752) points out: "It is usually forgotten that the land-grant universities quickly taught the classics and adopted the collegiate style of residence; the usefulness of all but a few of them for actual husbandry is often overstated." It was less the role of the new colleges to create a technical education in the spirit of the special schools of the French Revolution than to bridge the gap between the two cultures, to link education and learning, moral values and vocational training.

These institutions were instruments of national integration and social mobility. That is why the hundreds of state normal schools that trained teachers at the semiprofessional level played a vital role in this movement. At that time, the most striking difference between the United States and countries like Germany or France was the weakness of American secondary education. Jencks and Riesman point out that while only 7,064 boys graduated from high school in 1870, 9,593 male students obtained B.A.'s in 1874. Obviously, a large number of college students could not have finished high school. This situation was to continue for a long time to come. "In 1914 male college graduates outnumbered 1910 high school graduates two to one. . . ." (op. cit., p. 29, footnote 3). And in the medical schools, when Abraham Flexner wrote his famous report (1910),[4] many students had completed not more than a few years of secondary education.

The strength of European secondary education reflected the strength of a bourgeois class that was completely isolated from the common people in the schools and was eager not just to take over

---

[3] Many of the state colleges have turned into comprehensive colleges, with both liberal arts and vocational programs.

[4] See Flexner (*Medical Education. . . ,* 1972).

the cultural heritage of the former ruling classes, but to prepare its own sons to become members of a new ruling class closely linked to the state. Hence the separation of technical education from a secondary and higher education closely associated with each other. In the United States such a separation hardly existed; the role of the new colleges was to link technical training to general culture rather than to set them apart. Consequently, when the United States became an industrialized capitalist society, it was less of a "bourgeois" society than the European countries. The idea that education is an instrument of social mobility has prevailed ever since. But higher education had a further role: it was not only an instrument of upward mobility or of participation in the shaping of a national culture. If that were its only role, the development of the land-grant colleges would not have affected the colleges that trained the Eastern social elite. The important fact, however, is that this new educational orientation not only prevailed in the medium-quality colleges created by the states, but profoundly modified the most prestigious institutions, governed the establishment of new universities, and was related to a deep cultural change.

According to David Starr Jordan, president of the new university established by the Stanfords: "The college has ceased to be a cloyster and has become a workshop" (Veysey, 1965, p. 61). The wealthy Ezra Cornell founded a university "where any person can find instruction in any study" (ibid., p. 63). Not only did the idea spread that technical training should be developed and that "vocational calling" and community service should be stressed, but the whole former conception of culture was put in question. History is progress; education should therefore look to the future, not to the past. The United States, a new nation, born of the rejection of colonial bondage, overflowing with energy, attracting the human resources neglected by an old Europe crushed under the weight of tradition and authoritarianism, was the social expression of progress, of confidence in the creative individual and the enterprising spirit, of the emergence of a new type of social solidarity—a social expression that Durkheim was later to describe as *organic solidarity.*

The most enthusiastic representative of this new conception of education and society was Andrew D. White, who became the president of Cornell in 1868. Hostile to traditions as well as to racial barriers, he stressed the importance of technical training, advocated an exacting education based on strict discipline, and was less interested in research than in the development of human energies. It was Cornell that exerted the strongest influence on the universities that were being established in the West.

White was a Darwinian, and Darwinism was the philosophy of nature espoused by these new educators, and especially of Charles William Eliot, who, between 1869 and 1909, transformed Harvard completely and turned the oldest American college into the most distinguished modern university. His work was so vital, his success so extraordinary, that it cannot be explained solely in terms of the new educational philosophy. Indeed, it was Harvard more than any other institution that was to combine the new cultural model, the German influence, and the development of a new national bourgeois elite.

Here we will consider only Eliot's principal reform: the introduction of the elective system that was to spread to most of the big academic institutions. Although inspired by the German *Lernfreiheit* (the freedom of the student to take whatever course he chooses at whatever university he selects), this concept is primarily American and has remained one of the guiding principles of the academic system of the United States right up to the present era of today's multiversity. It involves much more than simply allowing the students to freely choose the components of their education. It is a rejection of the old dogma of education as a set of moral values and as a conception of man and his virtues. The key word is utility: service not to the community but to society, to what is being created, not to what is being transmitted. Classical studies were supplemented by commercial and industrial ones without the former being considered noble and the latter menial. At that time the business administration schools were established. The first, the Wharton School of Finance and Commerce, was established by the University of Pennsylvania in 1881; similar schools were created in 1898 by Berkeley and Chicago, in 1900 by Dartmouth and New York University, and finally by Harvard in 1908. The movement continued spreading until, in 1970, 500 colleges and universities had business and administration schools or programs with a total enrollment of 100,000.

The new cultural model, that of progress, cannot of course be viewed as independent of the hold of the ruling class, as we shall see below. But while its success attracted endowments from the Rockefellers and the Carnegies, it also corresponded to the expectations of students and families of quite varied social backgrounds.

It is because of this cultural model that there was no sharp division between such universities as Harvard, Chicago, or Stanford and the land-grant colleges. The old image of the university, inherited from English colleges and codified by Cardinal Newman just as England was discarding it, was clearly rejected. The college or university was primarily the means of transition from a little-differentiated society to a more complex one, from communities preserving their values to a national society convinced of its historical role and superiority. We are dealing indeed with a conception of education and not with the replacement of education by technical instruction and vocational training. Yet many felt that chaos had been created by turning the universities into service stations. Flexner denounced American academic institutions that did not conform to his definition of a university, which, he felt should be "an organism characterized by highness and definitiveness of aims, unity of spirit and purpose" (Flexner, 1930, p. 178). Such a judgment is surprising. In his introduction to a 1968 edition of Flexner's book, Clark Kerr criticized the author, pointing out that Flexner had not understood how the multiplicity of the universities' functions contributes to their general development, their service role of persuading the communities to provide ample resources for basic research and disinterested studies. But this pragmatic criticism is inadequate. The most appropriate image for the new or renovated universities was that of an organism; hence Herbert Spencer's social organicism enjoyed widespread popularity in American universities. They did not change in the name of ideas and values, but of a natural evolution that they helped to accelerate by diversifying, by becoming multifunctional, and by acquiring the means of internal regulation. Darwinism encountered—and still encounters—strong resistance in many communities, where it was viewed as destructive of religious idealism. The universities did not merely sing the praises of Darwinism; they learned to see themselves as organisms subject to the laws of evolution.

The new education no longer spoke in terms of values, but of energies. At the same time, it contributed to the creation of a national consciousness. In the old nations of Europe, national consciousness seemed inseparable from the national state and its decision-making power. In the United States, on the contrary, the nation could be nothing other than an organism determined by its activity and its evolution. All these themes took shape gradually in the collective consciousness and developed fully during the Progressive Era, the

time of Theodore Roosevelt. They played an essential role in the
early development of the social sciences—first of economics, then
of sociology, which was basically an offshoot of economics—and
many social scientists gave a radical interpretation to this Progressivism. The themes also converged with the demands of the Popu-
lists, who were followers of Henry George and were hostile to the
universities "teaching rich lawyers' boys Greek with farmers'
money" (Otten, 1970).

The chaos image could be sustained only by those who saw a
threat to the former conception of education and to the social and
cultural domination of an aristocraticlike bourgeoisie. Resistance
was indeed lively, especially at Yale and Princeton (the latter being
closely linked to the Southern white high-bourgeoisie); but it sub-
sided rather quickly. At the beginning of the twentieth century, the
new type of university and college was solidly established. Within
a few years, the new or renovated universities, particularly the
University of Chicago, under William Rainey Harper, and the University of Michigan, under James B. Angell, became centers of
knowledge and education whose very dynamism proved that they
were in no danger of disintegrating.

The period that coincided with Eliot's presidency at Harvard
marked the birth of an academic system as well as of an organization that in many respects remained unchanged. Universities that
ranked highest in 1909 are still top-ranking today. The main features that characterized them then, and that continue to character-
ize the American system of higher education (although today's
universities are of a quite different nature), are the combination
of scientific and vocational training, the absence of any strict
boundary between higher education and technical education, and
the central role of the colleges and universities, rather than the
secondary schools, in the educational system. The very solidity
of this model might well explain why it is so difficult to draw up a
different one today.

**THE GERMAN
MODEL AND
PROFESSIONAL-
IZATION**
If the development of the colleges and universities was closely
linked to changes in American society, and at the same time corresponded to the creation of a cultural model reflecting a general type
of society, then it is clear that the central role in these changes cannot be attributed, as is so often done, to the German influence.
Moreover, ethnologists have long since pointed out the inadequacy
of the theories of cultural dissemination.

Historically, there can be no doubt about the importance of the German model. Its influence was felt primarily in England, which remained quite receptive to it. After 1870, its impact also became strong in France, where it was openly advocated, not only by those who, like Renan and Taine, explained the German victory by the superiority of German science, technology, and education, but also by the group of professors and administrators who launched the great movement that resulted in the half-abortive reforms of 1885, 1893, and 1896. The German intellectual and organizational model also strongly influenced most of the other European countries, as well as Japan. For nearly a century, the University of Berlin and its followers were without a doubt the most admired academic model.

As early as the first half of the nineteenth century, but even more from 1850 up to the end of the First World War, a large number of American professional and academic people visited the German universities. They admired the development of graduate studies and research institutes, the success of *Lehrfreiheit* (the right of the university professor to freedom of research and teaching) and *Lernfreiheit,* the academic ethics, the historical studies, and the great works of experimental science.

Johns Hopkins University was established in 1876 on the German model, marking the first time in American history that graduate studies were the keystone of academic organization. Its first president, Daniel Gilman, who had left Berkeley because he had felt it was threatened by its overly pragmatic conception of service and was too far removed from scientific discovery, became the advocate of an exacting conception of education that inspired enthusiastic followers. One of them was Flexner, who fought unceasingly for universities of the highest scientific standards, carried out effective action for the improvement of medical schools, and finally ended his intellectual career at the high seat of basic research, the Princeton Institute of Advanced Studies.

Harvard, under Eliot, was soon to institute graduate studies, and by the end of the century all the big universities, especially Chicago, Wisconsin, and Columbia, were following the German model.

But this brief historical review is misleading. Those universities that remained most faithful to the German model, Johns Hopkins, and especially Clark, were soon to experience failures and even serious crises. Paradoxically, if we attribute a central role in the evolution of American universities to the German influence, those institutions were the only ones not to maintain their relative rank on the prestige scale. In fact, it is inaccurate to speak of a German model, for the German universities were too dependent on national conditions for their organization and their spirit to be successfully transposed to a very different society. What did come to the United States from Germany was something more limited: the professionalization of the teachers. And even this encountered serious obstacles in the United States.

In other respects, the differences between the German system and the American were striking. Let us first mention the close ties of the German universities to the various states. Academic policy in Germany was set by the ministers of education, while in America it was set by the university presidents. More concretely, the great American innovation was the creation of the departments. They made their appearance at Cornell and Johns Hopkins as early as 1880, at Harvard and Chicago around 1891-92, and at Columbia in the late nineties. This creation was accompanied by the very broad and often autocratic authority conferred upon the chairmen. It also resulted in the combination of research and teaching within the same units, a situation that still largely exists today, especially where the technical research apparatus is not so extensive as to require a full-time staff.

All this was foreign to the German universities, whose basic unit was the chair, and therefore the individual professor, a system that long remained in force in most European universities. The *Ordinarius Professor* alone ensured the unity of teaching and research. Under him gathered two distinct units. The *Privat Dozent,* directly and personally attached to the professor, provided the teaching together with him, but did not have automatic access to the research units where the professor recruited assistants. Finally, so far as the "freedom" of teacher and student is concerned, it was certainly more solidly established for both in Germany, where political pressures on professors less frequently resulted in their expulsion and where students, as Flexner pointed out, had greater mobility than their American counterparts, who identified much more strongly with a given institution.

J. Ben-David and A. Zloczower, in a deservedly famous article (1962, pp. 45–84), carried this analysis further, pointing out the essential differences between the academic situations in the two countries, and showing how Americans who went to study in Germany often inadequately analyzed the German system, probably because they had too much admiration for it to fully grasp either its raison d'être or its weaknesses. The German universities developed in a society where the aristocracy had adopted French culture and where the national bourgeoisie was still weak. They were established and developed by the state, and first of all by the Prussian state. Monarchy was hailed by Hegel as the synthesis following the disruption and the progress brought about by the French Revolution. Marx explained the potency of German intellectual life by that country's economic and political backwardness, which forced it to experience theoretically what England and France had experienced practically. As Ben-David and Zloczower brought out, a determining cause of the greatness of these universities was also a cause of their weakness:

The status and the privileges of the universities were granted to them by the military-aristocratic ruling class, and were not achieved as part of the growth of free human enterprise. It was therefore a precarious status based on a compromise whereby the rulers regarded the universities and their personnel as means for the training of certain types of professionals, but allowed them to be this in their own way and use their position for the pursuit of pure scholarship and science (which the rulers did not understand, but were usually willing to respect). The universities had to be, therefore, constantly on the defensive, lest, by becoming suspected of subversion, they lose the elite position which ensured their freedom (op. cit., p. 61).

The combination of autonomy and a defensive position is clearly reflected in the concept of *Wertfreiheit,* which was upheld by Max Weber.[5] This concept was quite foreign to the intellectual climate of the United States at that time, for the professors there were much more deeply involved in the society, the majority of them in order to assume or seek a role of social integration, others to demand the role of social critic. The American visitors also did not bring back to their own country the more profound German concept of *Wissenschaft,* which denotes much more than scientific or professional knowledge and is closely related to an idealistic conception of knowledge and society. As I have pointed out, the close links between theoretical knowledge and the most varied practical training were quite important in America. These links, however, were bound to be foreign to German organization and thought, since in Germany higher technical education was developed in special schools.

---

[5] This was particularly the case in his famous Munich lectures (1918) on the two vocations, where he stressed the necessary separation of value judgments and scientific inquiry.

The contrast between the two situations is closely related to the one I described in my introduction. The German universities were more closely connected with the state than with a ruling class; they were oriented more toward pure science and an elevated conception of *Wissenschaft;* they also cultivated a specifically academic rhetoric. The American colleges and universities, on the other hand, were closely connected with the ruling elites and with social change. They were more imbued with various ideologies, emanating not so much from the professors as from university officials, especially the presidents.

These general differences, however, were not the only ones, at least at the time when Americans were looking at the German universities. Although in the first half of the century, the rapid development of the German universities had been related to their competitiveness and to the comparative weakness of the political power in a divided Germany, this situation no longer prevailed after 1870 and the establishment of the Reich. The strength of the imperial state, the Bismarckian autocracy, and the development of an aggressive nationalism made the position of the universities increasingly precarious and increased the conservatism of many academic people, a conservatism that was expressed during the First World War and even more so during its aftermath.

In general, the American system displayed much greater creativeness at the very moment when many of its most intelligent representatives were proclaiming the superiority of the German system.

There is no clearer evidence of the contrast between the two academic systems than the very critical spirit with which the most germanophile elements in American academic circles accepted the so-called German model. Here we must refer again to Flexner. He struggled all his life against the "dilution" of the university and tirelessly insisted that research be considered its fundamental task. He recognized only traditional higher vocational training, like law or medicine, and showed very little interest in the colleges. It is true that he had Eliot's ear and left his mark on Columbia Teachers College, but he always remained marginal to the academic world proper, spending many years on the General Education Board set up by Rockefeller before going to England to deliver his famous Rhodes lectures.

Flexner may be considered the spokesman for the demands of teachers, which he raised to the level of an academic philosophy. But this philosophy remained abstract because it did not involve an analysis of the close connections between the university and the society of which it is a product. That is why Flexner's sharpest criticisms, as is traditional among professors, were directed against the power of the administration and against the president, who, in his view, should be no more than *primus inter pares.* Flexner was often very mistaken in his judgments concerning the future of American universities (Kerr, 1968) and dealt in an astonishingly flippant way with the business schools, whose role was extremely significant. He was for the progress of science, but he showed little curiosity about the social conditions necessary for that progress.

The strength and failure of his protest are easier to understand in the light of the obstacles to the professionalization of the teachers in the United States. These obstacles were much greater than those that existed in the European countries. We should not forget that in France, one of the European countries with the weakest academic organization — a country where research functions were mainly carried out in the higher schools or big institutions like the Collège de France, the Muséum d'Histoire Naturelle, and the Ecole Pratique des Hautes Etudes — the formation of a body of professors largely responsible for the management of academic affairs could be observed as early as 1840 and had become an established fact in the first years of the Third Republic (Gruson, 1970).

The material conditions and the influence of the professors in the American academic world long remained inadequate. A general retirement scheme was made possible through a large grant by Andrew Carnegie, but for many years there was no generally recognized criteria for advancement within the academic profession. Toward the end of the 1800s, however, there was rapid progress. The first Ph.D. was awarded at Yale in 1861; by 1900 it had become an essential requirement in applying for a university post.

Most of the learned societies in every scientific field were established at that time and medical schools showed impressive progress. The first medical college had been founded in Pennsylvania in 1763, but it was not until the birth of the Johns Hopkins Medical School in 1893 that scientific training and research in medicine really began. At the turn of the century, however, many medical schools were still independent of the universities and directly linked to the medical profession. The intellectual level of the students was often low and the quality of the teaching inferior to that of the European countries, especially Germany.

Following the Flexner report of 1910, change came about very swiftly; many schools had to close. All medical schools were attached to the universities and their field of scientific research expanded constantly, raising them to an undisputed top rank in medical research. It is not easy to make an overall evaluation of the level of professional and scientific development of the American universities at the end of this period. But there is no doubt a large element of truth in the conclusion of Fritz Machlup (1962), who drew a parallel between the United States at the end of the nineteenth century and Japan at the end of the Second World War: both were better able to import discoveries than to make their own. The steam turbine, the electric generator, the automobile, the diesel engine, the wireless, x-rays, radioactivity, the discovery of the electron, nuclear transmutation, isotopes, catalysis, catalytic cracking, quantum theory, the discovery of the relations between mass and energy — all are European contributions to science and technology, in comparison with which the American contributions appear rather limited. During that period, and up to the end of the First World War, basic research was not carried out very actively in the United States. Germany and Great Britain were much more important centers of scientific production, as evidenced by the distribution of the Nobel prizes. Considering the United States' population, material wealth, and large number of academic institutions, its scientific progress at that time can legitimately be described as slow, a fact that the rapid progress of the past 40 years tends to make us forget.

The main feature of the universities and colleges of that period was not, therefore, academic professionalization, however important that may have been. Of the three groups that make up the academic organization — the administration, the professors, and the students — the first and the last played the main roles. The professors, crushed between the president, the trustees, and the donors, on the one hand, and a student world largely indifferent to their scientific concerns, on the other, felt isolated and mistreated. As we shall see, this situation helps to explain some of their reactions.

The colleges and universities were too closely dependent on society and its demands and pressures for the professors to enjoy much decision-making autonomy. They won it gradually at the department level alone, and, starting with Chicago, where Harper granted broader freedom to the teachers, they finally managed to obtain the right to elect the department heads, who had previously been appointed by the president. But, owing to the scarceness of research funds, they were more dependent on their university than on outside authorities or their own professional circle. Some of the senior professors were occasionally involved in administrative decision making, but the majority of the teaching staff was subjected to decisions made without their participation.

The professors' lack of influence in the colleges or universities was to remain a characteristic feature of the American system. More recently this has been offset only by their increased influence outside the university—in the federal agencies and private foundations that subsidize research, and even in public and private decision-making centers where academic people sometimes act as consultants. In the period under consideration, the professors played a very small role in national life. The definition of a university as a "community of scholars," so popular in academic circles, is never accurate; it certainly does not apply to American academic institutions before the First World War.

At any rate, the professors were not primarily responsible for the basic changes that occurred between 1880 and 1900. In many countries, this period was marked by a great development of scientific production, but this development does not explain the nature and organization of the academic system in the United States. Education continued to be a more important theme than scientific research. Yet in the very concept of education there was a change that explains the resort to scientific knowledge and to the development of graduate studies, as well as to the elective system and to the establishment of agricultural and mechanical colleges and state normal schools. Scientific knowledge was but the property of a culture, the instrument of a type of progress that continued to be conceived, formulated, and controlled by people outside the academic world.

By the end of this period, science had become so complete a part of the university that in the twentieth century few scientific discoveries were made in the United States outside the academic world. This is the cause of the basic change in the function of the universities in the contemporary period. But in 1900 the social elite was still thinking in terms of the college rather than the university. Academic ceremonies expressed the loyalty of the professors and students to the alma mater rather than the homage of the community to the creation and spread of knowledge. This helps us understand why American academic circles so enthusiastically created and perpetuated the "German myth," an indirect expression of their own demands, but a poor explanation of the changes they were experiencing and in which they would have liked to participate more authoritatively.

CREATION OF A MODERN ELITE The grievances and demands of the professors seem weak indeed in the context of the powerful movement that created and transformed academic institutions. Universities emerged suddenly, thanks to generous endowments, and within a few years rose to the highest international standing. The University of Chicago provides the most dramatic example, but the cases of Cornell or Stanford, not to speak of Johns Hopkins, are almost equally impressive. An increasingly urbanized America, whose cities were expanding with the influx of successive waves of immigrants, was building with incredible speed academic cathedrals whose style and campuses were more eloquent than any presidential oratory. The students had to be brought up on campuses completely cut off not only from their original environments but also from their immediate surroundings. The grand and even pompous style of the noble Tudor or Georgian buildings; the aristocratic charm of the lawns with their beautiful trees; the preeminence of the presidential mansions; and the isolation of the campuses, sheltered from the vulgar people and their hustle and bustle—all this goes to show that the main task of the colleges and universities was to shape the culture of a ruling class.

But it was not a traditional type of elite that was being reproduced. That is why the old educational methods to which Yale remained so faithful had to be replaced by a more modern and often more scientific type of training. The aim of this new training was to convert the new rich into a social elite, to give to money the nobility and patina of a civilization. Those who built the most spectacular fortunes could afford to despise the traditional world of the colleges. Their wealth once acquired, they reverted to the tradition of the Greco-Roman *evergetes,* or of the European monarchs, who, with the help of the Jesuits, consolidated the social order they had helped create and rose above mere mercantile considerations to build the seminaries of the new ruling class. These Yankees, the conquerors of new frontiers, wanted to display and enforce their domination just when waves of Italian and Slavic immigrants were sweeping into the country. American economic power was sufficiently established to reinforce itself by, on the one hand, becoming the base of a world imperialism, and on the other, by organizing its culture and surpassing the monuments of an old Europe, the object of both admiration and contempt. This elitism could easily be combined with the concept of a university at the service of social change and modernization. Thus, Ezra Cornell, whose quasi-populist declarations were recalled above, founded a university that immediately became an elite institution.

This explains the important place of symbols in academic life, and the introduction of rituals, ceremonies, costumes, and the widespread use of Latin or Old English inscriptions. The inauguration of a new president, commencement exercises, and graduation rites, all reveal the desire to thrust upon everyone, from the academic elite to the remote common people, the grandeur of a cultural and social order.

But these images must be clarified. When I speak of the establishment's culture, I am describing the objectives of the big colleges, particularly those of the East, between the Civil War and World War II; I am not describing the spirit of the period of development of the American academic system.

It is true that on the campuses of that time the rich sought to be recognized as the upper class and strove to acquire new marks of social superiority, those of the old aristocracy being unacceptable to American democracy. But it is also true that the campuses acted as pumping stations for the social elite and were therefore characterized by the social climbing of their students as well as of their benefactors.

The college is said to act *in loco parentis,* but this expression has two quite distinct meanings. The first can be applied to the English public schools or to the Jesuit colleges: The school's duty is to transmit codes of conduct so exacting that the family alone cannot assume this responsibility. The young man must be removed from his environment, and especially from the women's world, and learn to see himself primarily as the member of an elite. But there is a second meaning. The college also acts *in loco parentis* when it replaces the family in order to give the youth an opportunity to participate in a broader, not a more restricted culture. In view of the importance of community spirit in the traditional American society, and of the role of religious ethics in the determination and preservation of this spirit, the college is an agent of secularization and enlarged social participation. In fact, Riesman has repeatedly stressed the importance of the idea that colleges are never more innovative than when they play such a secularizing role, a role first played by the Protestant colleges, and then by a number of Catholic colleges. It is not paradoxical to say that some denominational colleges acted as agents of secularization.

Two complementary and conflicting trends are thus combined. The youth—the male much more than the female—is withdrawn from his community and put in contact with young men different from himself, with ideas and behavior patterns that were not permitted in his community. He listens—not always attentively—to professors who represent a world of knowledge no longer defined by its local and ethical roots, but by its power of long-distance communication. Yet, while being thus exposed to a vast world of varied and wonderful men, ideas, and books, he is at the same time carefully isolated from the urban world, social turmoil, and political struggles. For the aim of education is not to help him shift from particularism to universalism, however fond the ideologists may be of such expressions, but from a local community to the society of a class elite.

In reality,then, there is more than one type of education. Following Laurence Veysey (1965, pp. 342–380), we can distinguish at least three main types: the culturally homogeneous Eastern colleges, the heterogeneous Eastern universities, and the homogeneous Western universities.

It was in the Eastern colleges that social elitism was most in evidence and that education's role was most clearly that of reproducing the social order. In these colleges, which were really just the clubs of the bourgeoisie, emphasizing college loyalty became a way of instilling a sense of class roles. But the relative importance of these colleges was waning during the period under consideration.

In the renovated universities of the East, on the other hand—mainly at Harvard, Columbia, and the University of Pennsylvania, where enrollment was more varied and graduate studies more important—the paramount function became that of opening up pathways to the changing intellectual and social world. Owing to their lack of homogeneity, the students brought social stratification into the colleges and the universities, maintaining there the considerable social distance between the rich and the relatively poor and among students of various ethnic and religious backgrounds. Already at that time, nonconformist groups emerged, some of the café-society type, others composed of youths who, despite their upward mobility, were somewhat marginal, like many New York Jews; they at least partially escaped the hold of the academic world and reached out either to the private world of art and literature or to social and political criticism.

But the universities of the West were probably the most typical of this period, because they were its product. It is here that the two trends identified above—formation of an elite and secularization—were best combined; for the Eastern universities were characterized more by their outward-looking attitude and the colleges of the Yale and Princeton type were more shut inward upon a class culture.

Let us take a look at Berkeley, then the sole campus of the University of California, at the time of President Benjamin I. Wheeler (1899–1919) (Otten, 1970, pp. 18–76). Since they were geographically isolated on their campus, the students often retained the social conservatism of their small hometown communities, especially before the turn of the century. But they also discovered there a university open to the utilitarian spirit. During this period the prevailing force on the campus was the student subculture, with its hazing ritual, its initiation ceremonies in the Greek Theater, and its cult of the capital C dominating the campus.

Wheeler, who was more interested in the college and in education than in research, gave a tremendous impetus to this subculture and institutionalized it. The Associated Students of the University of California (ASUC) was founded in 1880, but it was Wheeler who developed student government and made it the instrument of institutional loyalty, equally treasured by James B. Angell at Michigan and Charles R. Van Hise at Wisconsin.

Wheeler reigned over the Golden Bear Senior Men's Honor Society, which consisted of the outstanding seniors in the student government, and even went so far as to name it the Order of the Golden Bear. The younger students had to submit blindly to the absolute power of their elders, a power preserved by the secrecy of their deliberations. A student's real social environment was his academic class. Studies were only a relatively minor aspect of the collegiate culture, which expressed its independence by preferring the "gentlemen's C" to the efforts of the "grinds."

As the campus at Berkeley expanded and the ratio of students to professors increased (4.5 to 1 in 1880, 11 to 1 in 1900), antieducation behavior patterns developed, and there, as elsewhere, the problem of cheating assumed considerable importance at the turn of the century. Political activity remained minimal, despite lively interest in the Progressive Party and in Theodore Roosevelt, with whom Wheeler had close relations.

This isolation of the subculture could also be observed in other universities or colleges, where it assumed various forms. In some cases it was expressed as club spirit, often represented by the fraternities and sororities; in others the student-professor conflict prevailed, sometimes becoming extremely violent, as in Virginia where a professor was killed by a student. This student culture existed in Germany and England, too. In France, the student agitation at the end of the nineteenth century also reflected the existence of a separate student world rather than any genuine political sensitivity.

In the women's colleges this student life assumed the most traditional forms and persisted longest. At Vassar (Bushnell, 1962, pp. 489–514), for example, the College Government Association, although it involved students, administration, and faculty in internal management, left the students a wide margin of initiative for the organization of their social life. Among the student associations at Vassar, the main ones, the "Big Five," were the Athletic Association, the Community Religious Association, the Political Association, the Weekend Activities Association, and the theatre group called Philaletheis. Participation in the social and cultural life of the country was obviously less significant than the integration of a community whose members still thought that what they should mainly expect from college was preparation for their future roles as wives, mothers, and notables. The peer group was more important than the institution. College sports were of course an outstanding feature of this student culture, but we are not dealing with them in this context because they had other, more significant functions that will be considered below.

Naturally, this picture does not describe all colleges, but mainly those that recruited the developing national elite. Indeed, there was not yet a complete break between the traditional community spirit and the ruling class, and therefore broad sections of the student population were not affected by this dominant culture. This is particularly true of the black colleges in the South. Although efforts were made to create in the South colleges and universities of the same level as in the North, the southern black student population remained confined to colleges that provided professionals and teachers for the black community. They thus contributed to the formation of a black bourgeoisie that neither expressed the problems of this oppressed ethnic and social group nor was an element of a national elite affected by the values of the new universities. The most interesting case is probably that of the Catholic colleges, which we will examine here by following the analysis of Jencks and Riesman (1968, pp. 334–405), without remaining confined to the chronological limits of this chapter.

At first glance, only a certain time lag distinguished Catholic colleges from the others. Founded to ensure the preservation of a community, mainly of Irish origin, they later slowly assumed the role of introducing immigrants to the national culture, while Catholics were still segregated in supposedly secularized institutions. These colleges exhibited a characteristic feature: "The Catholic system probably produced more ethnic and economic mixing than was common in Protestant institutions" (ibid., p. 336). The Catholic colleges were a means of upward social mobility, while continuing to play their role of community defense. These two functions, which, for the rest of the student population were increasingly performed by distinct institutions, could be fulfilled simultaneously owing to the greater unity of the Catholic Church and to the role of the bishops and the religious orders. It would be too simple to oppose "open," multidenominational institutions and "closed," Catholic Colleges. It could almost be said that Catholic education in America was in this sense closer to French lay education than to the rest of the American educational system, for the role of the Catholic schools was to train the lower ranks of the social elite. These characteristics were to disappear for the most part after the Second World War. But up to that time, the student culture was much less autonomous in the Catholic colleges. They had no student government, admitted no fraternities or sororities, and the student press was strictly controlled. This also explains the existence in these colleges, to a greater extent than in others of the same level, of a critical minority to which the Jesuits, in particular, paid special attention. But, despite their numerical importance, the role of the Catholic colleges in the academic system as a whole has remained limited, mainly because the Catholics have been progressively immersed into a national culture.

All the above remarks lead necessarily to the conclusion that at the end of the nineteenth century the three main features of higher education — "progressivism," professionalization, and the formation of a class elite — were so loosely interrelated that the United States did not yet have an integrated academic system. The institutions were numerous and of varying quality, no central authority existed to impose identical orientation upon all, and cooperative efforts were just beginning. The College Entrance Examination Board was established only in 1909 and the foundations, especially the Carnegie Foundation, were only starting to make their influence felt. Information on higher education was spread widely, and the presidents of universities and colleges were often national figures, some of whom, like Gilman, Eliot, and White, exerted considerable intellectual influence. It is difficult, however, to share the often-expressed view that there was a conscious and deliberate effort to combine the English college and the German graduate school with such a purely American creation as the service station. One might just as mistakenly assume that the traditional college model broke up under the impact of both the A & M colleges and the scientifically oriented universities.

But although the system was not the product of methodical creation, it did, nevertheless, establish a close link between higher education and the formation of a ruling class. Because it was a rising class, it enthusiastically adopted new values, the idea of progress viewed as impelled by the energy of the entrepreneur, of the market and of productive labor. Because it was already the dominant class, it was concerned with consolidating its power, giving it the ideological cloak of a type of civilization and an image of man, as well as with establishing continuity between its own achievements and the previous forces of cultural and social domination. The two faces of the upper class—the ruling class, creator and manager of the new forces of production, and the dominant class, guardian of the social order—were present in higher education. The professionalization of the teachers was not an independent phenomenon but the area where these two types of action overlapped and combined. Science was not the main concern of the American bourgeoisie, whose fortune was based on business and finance rather than on technology and investment in research and development. The professor was above all an educator whose knowledge was at the service of the triumphant young bourgeoisie, which he helped become aware of its identity as a national elite; but it was also he who expressed and developed the cultural model of the entire society. This gave him a certain amount of autonomy, which he was allowed to exercise so long as he did not make the impossible utopian attempt to build a predominantly scientific university.

It was not in one of the new universities that the unity of the academic system was to find its most concrete expression. As we shall see in the next chapter, the most spectacular creation of that period, the University of Chicago, was on the contrary, beset by the deepest doubts and went further than any other in an attempt to change the university structure. It was rather the oldest and most elite of American universities, Harvard, which had the extraordinary success of becoming the crossroads of all the new tendencies, thus acquiring among the big universities the exceptional luster it has retained to this day.

Harvard was not far behind Johns Hopkins in introducing graduate studies and the departments and was firmly oriented towards the development of new knowledge. At the same time, its name, more than that of any other university, was associated with the adoption of the elective system. Finally, its college, benefiting from the considerable financial resources of the corporation, remained one of the most prestigious seminaries for the training of an aristocratic-like bourgeoisie. Perhaps we can determine more accurately the reasons why Harvard was able to play these multiple roles. The bourgeoisie of the Midwest, once it had made its fortune, wanted to return to the East, to its traditions, and to the glory of its ruling class. In the same way, the British capitalists brought to Oxford and Cambridge, with all the richness of their history and their educational role, the resources and inducements that led them to become great centers of scientific knowledge.

But Harvard's success cannot be adequately understood without taking into account Eliot's personal role. A Tory democrat, an eminent member of the mercantile aristocracy, a conservative, a Unitarian, a foe of trade unions and of compulsory elementary education, he was also a rationalist and a Darwinian, concerned with the formation of a social elite with a high sense of social responsibilities. He was also, in the words of Laurence R. Veysey, "willing to give the lower class a kind of franchise in order to avoid revolution" (1965, p. 89).

Under the influence of Spencer, and his interpreter, Thomas Huxley, Eliot applied the evolutionary outlook to the whole field of knowledge. Knowledge must proceed from the simple to the complex, according to the experimental method that starts from facts to arrive at theory. Such is the natural way, as opposed to the artificial way that proceeds by the application of general principles to specific cases. As Metzger put it: "And the natural way, to these evolutionary naturalists, was doubly blessed: first, because nature was good and guaranteed human perfectibility; second, because control of nature was good and ensured competitive success" (Hofstadter & Metzger, 1955, p. 359). Science is much more than a professional ideal; it is the expression of the natural progress of nature and society.

Eliot did not fall into the trap of Gilman's utopia, whose praises Flexner was later to sing, and he was not carried away by the German myth. Harvard's solid financial situation gave him the freedom to exhibit a progressive attitude, encourage the education of low-income students, accept the token enrollment of a few black students, and at the same time develop a socially and intellectually elite institution. Finally, he was one of the most intelligent promoters of the integration of a national bourgeoisie that both served progress and knew how to use it.

THE EDUCATIONAL ENTERPRISE AND ITS PRESIDENT

After attempting to reconstruct the parts and the whole of the academic system that was getting organized in the last decades of the nineteenth century, how can we avoid crowning our edifice with the statue of the president? True, the president was already, in the preceding period, the central figure, the symbol of the college, and very often the real holder of all its powers. But as the role of higher education changed and its functions became more diversified, the role of the president assumed much greater importance, for he had to be the agent of both change and continuity, with the duty of combining education, science, and service. The history of many colleges and universities could be written on the basis of the biographies of their presidents alone. This was true only of the American academic system, and compared with its German, French, or English counterparts, it constitututed its most original feature. Is it not a fact that one of the most dramatic signs of the recent crisis was the impotence or inadequacy of the presidents of some of the most prestigious Eastern universities, and the downfall at Berkeley of the strongest personality of the American university world? The reign of the presidents over academic history lasted so long and was so absolute that their picture can be drawn without strictly confining ourselves to a definite historical period.

The college or university president is a stable authority. From 1900 to the early 1960s, the average length of his stay in office was 11.4 years, the tenure of the big university presidents being slightly below this average.[6] He is a man of experience, whose median age

---

[6] This average length seems to be shorter during the most recent period.

when appointed is 46 years in the recent period and a little younger at the turn of the century.[7] In the early years of American history, the president was generally a minister, but such a background is now increasingly rare. Also, at the beginning of this century, the president was not usually, as the majority of them are today, a scholar holding a Ph.D., but he did come most often from the world of education and had administrative experience. His selection has always been the responsibility of the trustees, who have increasingly tended to leave management in his hands, especially as the administrative apparatus of the university has developed. His selection is the result of prolonged deliberation. The trustees appoint a special committee and seek extensive advice, especially that of other presidents, and recently, of the big foundations, often headed by former presidents or academic administrators.

The president today derives his importance from his management of the relations of the college or the university with society, especially with those who finance education. He is less and less an educator, more and more an administrator, an entrepreneur, and the preserver of the conformity of academic work to the prevailing ideology. As one trustee has explicitly stated: "We do want to know that he subscribes to the basic economic, social and political thinking of our country" (Demerath, 1967, p. 53). He expresses this concurrence in his numerous speeches to clubs, businessmen's associations, colleges, etc. He is therefore a member of the social elite. He is often a member of Phi Beta Kappa, belongs to the Rotary or the Kiwanis, is more often a Republican than a Democrat, is a member of the Episcopalian, Unitarian, or Methodist Church, and is often a Freemason.

It would be easy—but mistaken—to draw the conclusion that he is selected for his ability to maintain law and order and the respect for established principles. If this were true, how explain the many crucial initiatives taken by presidents? The French *recteurs,* who were for a long time appointed functionaries, governing the university as well as the whole educational system of a region, were certainly not such public figures and had fewer contacts with the ruling circles. They were, nevertheless, the purest bureaucratic guardians of the established order, distrustful of innovation in the

[7] The source of most of the information used here is N. Demerath et al. (1967).

great majority of cases, and more responsive to administrative logic than to the demands for change expressed in the academic world.

The respect for established principles that the presidents loudly exhibit, often in the tritest terms, merely shows that in the United States, as elsewhere, the university is traditionally subordinate to the social and political power structure. But such a broad generality explains very little.

The special role of the American university president lies elsewhere.

It derives in the first place from the direct and nearly unlimited power he exerts on the professors. Some of them, like Jordan at Stanford, were real autocrats. Jordan declared that the president should keep the faculty at a distance and avoid meetings and committees that encouraged the formation of cliques. The best policy, he believed, would be to call the professors together once a year only, and prevent them from speaking by delivering a long speech.

But at that time such a conception was already an anachronism. The great presidents at the end of the nineteenth and the beginning of the twentieth century were those who succeeded in creating an administration. Two names are prominent here: Harper at Chicago, more flexible and enterprising, and Nicholas Murray Butler at Columbia, more authoritarian. Each of them set up a complex administrative organization. But this did not imply any increased power for the faculty, particularly at Columbia; rather it created a screen between strictly professional problems, partially left to the departments, and the general management of the university.

The power of the president also mainly derives from his role as a negotiator with external decision-making centers. Sometimes he even is an entrepreneur, often a very delicate role, especially if the university has owed its existence to the fortune of a single benefactor. Harper, who succeeded admirably in persuading Rockefeller to create the University of Chicago, certainly had an easier time as president because his benefactor refrained from trying to rule the university. Jordan, on the contrary, had his differences with Mr., and especially with Mrs., Stanford. The president also has to establish ever closer relations with the alumni, whose accumulated contributions must follow the first spectacular donations, and who, to quote a former university president "never cease to think of themselves as members of the family."

In the public universities, the financial fate of the institution depends on the relations with the governor and the legislature, which makes the president's political affiliation particularly important.

But the fact that tuition represents so large a share of the colleges' resources also leads the presidents to launch real commercial operations. They must attract students as well as contributors, and so we see the University of Chicago engage in advertising, and the University of Pennsylvania, in 1910, even establishing a bureau of publicity.

The development of university sports at the end of the nineteenth century was primarily a commercial operation, aimed mainly at those alumni whose enthusiasm about a Harvard-Yale or a Stanford-California match moved them to make generous contributions to their alma mater.

The university is indeed a business enterprise that strives to recruit the best technicians, produce what the public demands, and develop its capital and its current resources. Veblen was particularly violent in his denunciation of the university's willing submission to the interests and spirit of business. But such a judgment is more attractive than accurate. By the same token, Flexner criticized the universities by saying: "Their centers are the treasurer's office into which income flows, out of which expenditures issue, and the office of the registrar who keeps the roll." But he draws much too narrow a picture, which he himself amends by concluding that the president should be able to go beyond mere administration and have ideas (Flexner, 1930, p. 179). It is hard to claim that they had none and that they have gone down in history merely as good administrators and good fund raisers.

It is just as inaccurate to try and explain the history of the university by the ideas of its great men as by its direct subjection to a kind of education market. The parallel between the university and a business enterprise has obvious limitations, a fact of which a Rockefeller or a Carnegie was perfectly aware.

The president's importance lies in the fact that he is the coordinating agent of the incoming, the internal, and the outgoing demands on the university, in a situation where these three types of demand are formulated and presented independently of each other.

The incoming demands—whether those of students or donors, both of whom express their desires through financial contributions—are different from those expressed by professors and administrators, especially as there is an increase in the professionalization of the teachers and the bureaucratization (in the Weberian sense) of the academic administration. The danger of a direct correspondence between incoming and outgoing demands is greater. This is what happens, for example, when the students expect vocational training from a college or a university. That is why a president has much less freedom of action in a college oriented toward vocational training directly linked to the local labor market, as is the case for many of today's community colleges. This situation exists, in an extreme form, in the Soviet system, where the political power structure determines the openings in each type of training in accordance with the estimated needs of the economy, as well as with ideological and political options.

The American system, precisely because of the important ideological function of the university, whose role it is to form a social elite and serve a given cultural model, is characterized, on the contrary, by a lack of correspondence between educational demands and the needs of the economy in terms of professional, technical, or scientific personnel. The president, with increasing help from the deans, has the task of preserving or establishing a balance between demands that are not directly related to each other. That is the source of his autonomy and his importance. The objectives he must achieve are so hard to define accurately that it is almost impossible to reach a short-term judgment of his success. That is why he keeps his position for a long period of time (theoretically he is appointed for life), and why only a very serious crisis can force him to resign.

But his role is possible only insofar as the demands arising inside the university do not conflict with those originating from the outside. Until recently, the students had never put forward such demands and the presidents had always tried to exercise strict control over the public activities of the students. This went so far sometimes that in the case of the University of California at the end of the nineteenth century, for example, an entire class of sophomores was expelled.

But as the teachers increased their professionalism and intellectual authority, they started to express a social criticism that sometimes jeopardized the authority and influence of the president. These incipient crises assumed dramatic proportions once they combined with the students' active criticism of the university and with outside groups' violent criticism of colleges and universities that did not satisfy their demands. But such a situation, though it exists today, could not even have been imagined at the turn of the century. At that time, the agreement between the university and the society, in the context of the prevailing values and the strengthening of the dominant class, was contested only by a few professors.

REBELLIOUS
PROFESSORS

Of these professors, some were intolerant of the expansion and diversification of the academic world, an elitist reaction that sometimes harked back to the virtues of the English college as being superior to the pedantry of the new universities. For example, William James, who played an important role in the history of psychology and philosophy in the United States, denounced "the Ph.D. Octopus" in a famous article. And George Santayana eventually retired from the university at 48 to lead an independent intellectual life. In general, colleges and universities did not care to welcome and shelter men with talent and high intellect, or with an individualistic way of life. Charles Peirce, for example, had to leave Harvard, was excluded from Johns Hopkins, and was forced to carry on his work in semidestitution. Veblen's quarrels with the academic world, on the other hand, were not merely intellectual: he was dismissed from Stanford for his life of adultery. The university, wanting to present a reassuring image to the dignitaries, was more concerned about social achievement than intellectual creativeness.

Aside from these personal conflicts, the teaching profession resented its mediocre material conditions. The professors witnessed the erection of luxurious buildings and the strengthening of the administration, while their job security remained tenuous and their salaries low. They felt they were the mere tools of the university rather than its raison d'être. But these conflicts took on significance only to the extent that some professors invoked the prevailing cultural model and gave it an interpretation opposed to the interests of the ruling class (Hofstadter & Metzger, 1955, pp. 412–467). Economists and sociologists, in particular, tried to use their knowledge to promote social reform in the very name of progressivism and utilitarianism. They frequently engaged in political controversy, and at the time of the great debate between supporters of monometallism and bimetallism exhibited the same intolerance toward whichever of these factions was in a dominant position.

The universities reacted quite violently against these deviants who threatened both the established order and their own good relations with the bourgeoisie. Edward W. Bemis was dismissed from Chicago, John R. Commons from Indiana State, and Richard T. Ely from Wisconsin. The greatest stir was created by Edward A. Ross, who, in his opposition to coolie labor, came into conflict with Stanford's president Jordan and, through him, with Mrs. Stanford.

Nothing was more dangerous than to turn against the ruling class the culture with which it identified, for this represented a direct challenge to its class interests. Hence the violence of Veblen's attacks as well as of those directed against him. Each time a crisis broke out, conservatives had no trouble questioning the character of the rebels, pointing to their eccentricities and their blunders. But psychological factors do no more than emphasize the minority position of, and the pressures exerted upon, a small group confronted by the academic and social establishment.

With the development of a professional body, the nature and treatment of the conflicts gradually changed, and the theme of the business conspiracy or the incompatibility between two ways of using knowledge was replaced by an attempt to set up deontological rules, to allow a professor to be judged by his peers, and to obtain guarantees for the profession in the face of pressures exerted mainly by the administration.

A more massive but less radical action, whose target was no longer the ruling class but the academic authority, thus developed. The American Association of University Professors (AAUP) was created in 1915 at Columbia on the initiative of a few great professors like John Dewey and James Mckeen Cattell. Roscoe Pound participated in the committee that drew up the association's charter and its General Declaration of Principles and the committee itself was chaired by the Columbia economist, E. R. A. Seligman. This outstanding role of the Columbia professors can be attributed mainly to the administrative authoritarianism of President Butler, who was to become even tougher after the declaration of war.

For a start, the AAUP had to defend Cattell, who was forced to resign after coming into violent conflict with Butler. This crisis also led to the resignation of Charles Beard, an independent who had even refused to join the AAUP. The association, however, was far removed from the radical positions of Commons, Ely, or Veblen. It defended academic freedom on professional grounds as the guardian of high-standard intellectual research. It also tried to invoke utilitarian values, but only to assert that the professor should enjoy freedom in the university because his work must serve the public and not merely an institution. It was therefore the principle of institutional loyalty that was attacked.

The responsibility of the university teacher is primarily to the public itself, and to the judgment of his own profession; and while, with respect to certain external conditions of his vocation, he accepts a responsibility to the authorities of the institution in which he serves, in the essentials of his professional activity, his duty is to the wide public to which the institution itself is morally amenable (Hofstadter & Metzger, 1955, p. 409).

This appeal to the public responsibility of the professor is so vague that it defines no specific principle of action. The appeal to judgment by the profession and to independence from the administration, on the other hand, has a very clear meaning. Better than any other, perhaps, this text marks the end of the period I have been discussing. At its outset, great presidents proclaimed a general conception of the university, that is, its links with culture and society. When it ended, the narrow administrative spirit of a Butler had replaced the broad views of a Gilman, a White, or an Eliot. The professors had acquired increasing importance and were beginning to withdraw into a professional world fortified by the progress of their work. For a rather long period, this world could entertain the illusion of independence from a society whose only duty was to provide the necessary resources for disinterested scientific research. The academic world, at first open to the cultural model of progress, but at the same time subjected to the ruling class, now withdraws to devote its efforts to the formulation of a professional rhetoric. This rhetoric, however, did not fully prevail until the rapid development of research work that occurred much later.

Between the triumphant period just described and the glory of a professional rhetoric linked to the production role of the universities, higher education was to go through an intermediate stage. During that stage, although more concerned with asserting its own values than in the previous period, it still remained concerned with education rather than production. This was the stage for the creation of academic ideologies, making the reproduction of the social order the main function of the academic system.

CONCLUSION I have stressed in this chapter the loose integration of the academic system. During the period we have covered here, roughly from the 1870s to the first decade of the present century, administrators, professors, and students, though they interacted, seemed to belong to distinct worlds: the first launched a policy of "progress" tinged with utilitarianism; the second began to organize their professionalization; the last began to develop into a social elite.

We must now try to go further and inquire whether, of the three levels of analysis indentified at the beginning, one should be given central importance or whether they combine here in a special way.

It seems to me that the second of the three levels of analysis is the most significant, provided we keep in mind that each of the levels, from the first to the last, determines the next and that adjustment to change occurs within a cultural model and class relationships.

The academic system does not represent an important force of production, for the role of science and technology in economic growth is much less vital than the accumulation of the classical factors of production—namely, capital and labor.

Nor is the ideological role of education, and therefore its role of reproducing the social order, a central one, since the problem is more to construct a new social order than to preserve preexisting social relationships and ideologies. That is why initiatives are much more frequently taken in the name of progress or usefulness than in the name of education. Before Eliot and Gilman, higher education meant the college. At the time of Lowell and Hutchins, the college became again the center of attention for the reformers. At the end of the nineteenth century, however, the key word was university and the great innovation was the introduction of graduate studies. The elective system broke down the unity of the college and tended to make of it a center of preparation for an intellectual or professional activity rather than a place for the shaping of the personality.

The universities' most manifest role was to organize change; that is why the presidents were so important. Their role was primarily "political"—they were the decision makers.

It would be a mistake to think that this change can be defined in the purely evolutionary terms of modernization and differentiation, or even of quantitative extension or improvement of educational standards. The academic system was a decision-making center, but the decisions were made in the context of a cultural model and class relationships.

I have stressed the class role of higher education, which shapes a national elite, in other words, a ruling class. But this role was then less influential than it was to become in the following decades. Education was not the only access to the ruling class and businessmen had not yet been replaced by executives. Moreover, although they were certainly not open to all, the best colleges did not have very selective admission policies, indicating that the academic system was not in itself a further instrument of social selection.

The academic system plays the same passive role for the maintenance of the cultural model. The academic system was inserted in a cultural framework closely combining evolutionism, historicism, and utilitarianism. The organization of change was at no time separate from the defense of these cultural orientations against the moral philosophy of the preceding period. We could speak here of secularization, but I prefer to call it the replacement of one cultural model by another. Again, however, higher education did not play the central role in the creation of the cultural model. The world of progress was the field where energies were exerted, while in the following period, our own, the cultural model has been dominated by the concept of system, and therefore by the capacity to organize communication systems. American society at the end of the nineteenth century was one of industry, entrepreneurs, manual labor, the market, and the conquest of the frontier. In the second half of the twentieth century, it is a society of computers, programs and planning, management, and white-collar workers. In a civilization of energy, the academic system cannot have the same importance as in a civilization of information.

The university's "political function," that is, its role in the organization of change, also derived considerable autonomy from the fact that, owing to the scarcity, and therefore the high price, of labor, and an abundance of free space and of capital, the emerging ruling class did not have to disorganize the previous social and economic system and impose strong restraints upon the emerging proletariat. There is no question that it was a capitalist society and that the working class was dominated by the employing class that derived profits from its labor. But this new and conquering ruling class was able to attribute more importance to its role as entrepreneur than to its task of repression and domination. It relied more on money to establish its power than on political and ideological restrictions. The academic system, therefore, existed within a class society that was also an open society.

By the same token, the cultural model was not the monopoly of the ruling class and its ideology. It was by no means independent either, but it was sufficiently autonomous to be grasped directly by the large number of people who were drawn into this rapidly progressing society.

This is why I do not regard the work of the great creators of the academic system as the direct expression of the ruling class ideology. It is undeniably linked to it—as I pointed out in portraying the figure of Eliot and in referring to the role played by the colleges in shaping a national elite. But these colleges were not linked to the cultural model exclusively through the ideology of the ruling class. As I have stated, utilitarianism also assumed forms of expression opposed to the interests of the ruling class—as in Wisconsin and California. To think that the university was exclusively concerned with values detached from all social interests would be as much of a mistake as to see it as a mere instrument of ideological control in the hands of a ruling class.

It was this openness of the society, together with the secondary role played by scientific knowledge, both in the cultural model and in the mode of social domination, that gave such crucial importance to the institutional initiative of the presidents.

This idea corresponds to my original one concerning the low level of integration of the academic system, for that integration is greater either when the university's essential role is that of social production or when its main function is to reproduce the social order. At the end of the nineteenth century, the academic system played neither an economic nor an ideological role, or at least neither of these roles was predominant. It is for this reason that its great achievement was its self-creation rather than the promotion of scientific research or the transmission of a cultural heritage.

The American academic system, at the stage we have reached in our survey, did not possess the splendor or glory of the German or even of the British universities, but its dynamism and its capacity for initiative were probably unequaled. The British system had shown its ability to adopt new ideas rather than to initiate planned changes; Germany had already experienced the weight of political conformism and the limits imposed upon the development of research by the power of great professors; France, despite a striking academic reform movement, had failed to give genuine autonomy to its universities. But the United States, driven forward by the rapid development of its power, and especially by the meaning society attributed to education, built, within a few decades, an academic system that, despite its low level of integration and strong internal and external tensions, was extraordinarily dynamic.

It is understandable that, in the years following this creative phase, the American academic system became more concerned with its own integration, the control of its functioning and growth, and the internal definition of its roles. The relation between university and society was reversed. The theme of general culture superseded that of social usefulness.

3. The Consolidation of the Social Hierarchy

INTRODUC-
TION Every academic system participates to a greater or lesser degree both in the production and in the reproduction of the social order. The first role is the more important when a new type of society is being set up, for during that time the society is being defined by a new model of knowledge and a new cultural model, as well as by a new type of accumulation and thus a new type of economic organization. This tie between the university and the creation of a social order greatly enhances the importance of intellectual innovation within the university, which is, however, thereby subjected to the influence of the ruling class. On the other hand, under conditions of consolidation, not to mention when the social order is becoming outmoded or is in crisis, the driving force no longer comes from above. The educational system then often enjoys the illusion of being more independent; it closes in on itself. But in reality, if it is less subject to a conquering ruling class, this is above all because it fulfills an ideological function: reproduction of the social order. Education maintains or increases social and cultural distances, not reducing but actually reinforcing and extending the inequality of opportunities between students from different social backgrounds. The emphasis that colleges and universities like to give to their role as agents of social mobility is no more than an ideology belied by the facts. Thus, it is superficial either to draw the dichotomy between a university that is dependent upon the powers that govern society and another, supposedly independent, university, or to contrast concern for education with submission to functions defined by the ruling elites. It is more accurate to distinguish two contrasting types of relationship between the university and the social organization.

In the first, the university shares directly in the ideology of the ruling class, but also, through it, in a cultural model. It is at once

59

culturally creative and directly related to power. In the second, the university claims above all a role in social integration. It speaks, in this case, less of knowledge than of education, and the education it speaks of is tied to the class system in that it takes different forms depending on the social level to which it is addressed, preparing the future members of the social elite under the sign of excellence and general culture, and the future dependent workers under the sign of pragmatism and of a narrowly occupational function. Along with this goes a certain independence in regard to economic needs and the possibility for nonconformist tendencies to crop up.

Submission to the class system is always present—at least unless the university takes up a position of social criticism, which it cannot, in any case, adopt entirely without risking the loss of its resources—but such submission does not mean that this function accounts fully for its activity. The university, in the two cases considered, maintains a link with the orientations that define what I call the *system of historical action.* I am only saying that this link is never direct enough nor strong enough to suppress the class function of the university. This elementary fact must be recalled especially whenever the university most stresses its educational role, speaks of general culture rather than of production, and tends to endow itself with illusions in talking about its independence.

It is necessary to add right away that the cultural role of the university, serving the ideology of the system more than the ideology of the dominant class, is not to be confused with the professionalization of the university and the rhetoric that goes along with it.

The latter develops insofar as the link with the cultural model of the society, in the present case with science, is directly connected with the integration of the academic organization itself around its professional independence; it even takes extreme forms when that professional independence becomes an end in itself, the alpha and omega of a "liberal" rhetoric.

The currents of ideas that developed within the American academic system just after World War I did not lean on that professional rhetoric. The colleges did not cut themselves off from society as did, for instance, the French university of that period, which enclosed itself in a "petty bourgeois" rhetoric. Quite the contrary, they stressed such themes as general education and excellence, which have, as we shall see in a moment, a very distinct ideological content and which play an active role in the consolidation of the social order; the rhetoric of professionalization was only to develop later, when the progress of research would provide a solid cultural and social base for the theme of academic independence. This theme was to have an ambiguous influence, perceptible in the mixture of liberalism and conservatism of most professors.

The situation that we are about to examine was dominated, on the contrary, by a lively awareness within the university of its role in the service of society. This is why the professors, as in the period before World War I, do not play an important role. It is still the presidents who define the functions of the university. Certainly there is, as ever, an academic rhetoric. We have even seen that it amounted to a force of opposition during the preceding period— that of Eliot, Harper, and Jordan. It shows up also in the era that we are now considering, situated symbolically between the arrival of Lowell at Harvard and the launching of the first sputnik. (We should keep in mind that there is no clear break either at the beginning or at the end of that period and that we are dealing here with a mixture of historical periods and sociological types rather than with a pure chronology.) But it is scarcely visible, for the professors, faced with the administration, do not yet have the financial means to provide them with any great influence in the running of the university. That is why it seems to me justified to consider in this chapter only the educational role of academic institutions and to follow their functions of consolidation of the social order on two levels: first that of pedagogical ideas, then that of the actual part played by the colleges in social selection.

It may be expected that the students will behave differently depending on whether the university plays a greater role in the production or in the reproduction of the social order. Not that it can be said that they are conformist in the one case and oppositional in the other. Rather, the forms of conformism and opposition vary from one situation to the other. In a "production" university, a ruling elite is formed, but there also appears an opposition to the influence exercised by the ruling class on the new culture and the new society. In a "reproduction" university, student conformism is more likely to take the form of a desire for limited social advancement, for good job opportunities in what Dahrendorf has called "the service class"; opposition forms only to the extent that such opportunities do not exist, that an economic crisis or a political paralysis threatens the future of bureaucrats and professionals.

In other words, in the second case both opposition and conformism are more "internal," whereas in the first they more directly find support in external forces—whether in the ruling circles themselves or in forces of social opposition—to which a portion of youth and faculty attach themselves.

The American academic situation described in the preceding chapter corresponds clearly to the production of a new social order. Its creativity is explained by its close ties to the main cultural themes of evolutionism, historicism, and utilitarianism, which are summed up in the key word: progress. It was at the same time directly attached to the formation and integration of a new ruling class, as was well understood in Veblen's passionate criticisms. But this function is not of central importance in a society in which science and technique do not yet play an essential role—in a nation still in formation, rapidly expanding, and where there exist many paths to social advancement other than education. In the contemporary period the role of colleges and universities is analogous. But now knowledge is an essential element of the system of accumulation, an important factor in economic growth and thus in social change. The universities are closely tied to the new cultural model and to the new ruling elites. The novelty is that this time, for reasons that will be examined further on, the university becomes the scene of social conflicts and political confrontations.

The general idea of the present chapter is that between those two eras, each corresponding to a structural social change, there was a long period during which there developed a system whose main function was reproduction of the social order. During that period, the three levels of functioning that we distinguished at the beginning of the preceding chapter became hierarchized in such a way that the functions of social integration took on the greatest importance, dictating the role of the universities in change and in mobility and reducing to least importance the role of cultural creation.

This period is less rich than the one that precedes or the one that follows both in terms of taking significant initiatives and of making spectacular changes. At the moment when it begins, most of the elements of the present university organization are already in place, but what is to be the new feature of the following period, the development of research and its financing by the federal government, was only dimly foreshadowed. Let it suffice to recall that in 1938 the budget for all research in the natural sciences was only $28 million.

The years between the two world wars were marked neither by any great personalities—with the exception of Robert M. Hutchins—nor by any great institutional creations. They were characterized rather by pedagogical initiatives, by major discussions around the theme of education, by a considerable material expansion (at least at the beginning of the period), and by an absence of internal crises that foreshadowed the listlessness and mediocrity of the silent generation.

As a consequence, some dramatic changes occur in higher education (see Table 1). The number of students involved in higher education jumped in the 1920s from 2.5 to 4.8 million of the corresponding age group, that is, from 32 percent in 1920 to 51 percent in 1929. As shown in Table 1, the number of students doubled in 10 years and caused a somewhat smaller increase in the number of faculty.

TABLE 1   *Growth of the academic system, 1900–1940*

	1900	*1910*	*1920*	*1930*	*1940*
Population U.S. (millions)	75.9	92.0	105.7	122.8	131.7
College age (18–21) (millions)	5.9	7.3	7.3	9.0	9.8
Institutions conferring doctorate	25	32	44	70	88
Academic employees in higher education (thousands)	29.0	45.0	62.0	105.4	146.9
Enrollment in colleges (thousands)	237.6	355.2	597.9	1,100.4	1,494.2
Enrollment—graduate (thousands)	5.8	9.4	15.6	47.3	105.7
Degrees:					
Bachelor's and first-professional level (thousands)	27.4	37.2	48.6	122.5	186.5
Master's and second-professional level (thousands)	1.6	2.1	4.3	25.0	26.7
Doctor's (thousands)	0.25	0.44	0.62	2.30	3.29

SOURCE: B. Berelson (1960, p. 26).

This expansion implies an increase in resources. Private donations to higher education go from $7.5 million at the end of World War I to $25 million just before the Depression of 1929 (these figures do not include donations earmarked for construction). Above all, the state and local governments enormously augmented their contributions, which go from $21 million in 1909–10 to $62

Expenditures for institutions of higher education as percentage of GNP

Year	Percentage
1900	0.26
1910	0.29
1920	0.24
1930	0.69
1940	0.75
1950	0.94

SOURCE: F. Machlup (1962, p. 78).

million in 1919–20 to close to $152 million in 1929–30 (still not counting funds earmarked for construction, which increase just as rapidly). During this period, the value of the physical property of colleges and universities increases from $750 million to more than $2 billion (*Report of the Assembly . . . ,* 1970).

During the 1920s progress was especially rapid. It picked up again at the end of World War II, when, thanks to federal aid under the GI Bill, there was a massive influx of veterans into the universities.

Along with this development there went an important shift in distribution of students among fields of specialization. For instance, as Table 2 indicates, the traditional professions, law and medicine, lost a large part of their relative importance more rapidly in America than in Germany.

The relative loss of ground of the older professions in the United States in the first two decades of the century was due, above all, to the rise of technological studies and the social sciences, and in the following period to the increase in the number of students in education.

The shift in flow is directly tied to an institutional transforma-

TABLE 2
The relative decline of the traditional professions in the United States and Germany

	United States			Germany	
	Medicine	*Law*		*Medicine*	*Law*
1901–1905	26.6%	11.2			
1911–1915	14.7	10.7	1914	26.3	14.5
1921–1925	7.8	8.2	1925	11.8	22.0
1931–1935	5.0	6.1	1933	30.9	14.8
1941–1945	4.9	2.4	1951	17.1	11.2

SOURCE: J. Ben-David (1968, pp. 39–40).

tion: the growing importance of public colleges and universities, a movement that will become more and more marked.

In 1900, two-thirds of the student population is in private establishments; that proportion drops to 44 percent in 1953–54 and to about 25 percent today. The proportion of public funding out of the total expenses of higher education is already at 40 percent by 1930. A notable number of public universities rise to the first rank during this period: for example, Wisconsin, Illinois, Minnesota, Indiana, and Iowa, without mentioning the University of California, already near the top but still strengthened by the opening of UCLA. Public education is especially oriented toward practical and professional training that responds to the needs most readily perceived by state and local authorities. Little, if any, selection is used in admitting students to these universities and the differences between the good public and private establishments are slight: the average IQ in 1920–30 is roughly the same at City College of New York (CCNY) and at Harvard (Jencks & Riesman, 1968, pp. 257–290). Selection develops only after World War II.

It thus seems easy to conclude that this period is dominated by the reinforcement of the middle levels of higher education. There is no longer a small elite of traditional colleges and new universities far removed from the rank and file of the denominational colleges, the A & M colleges, or the teachers colleges. The university system is more integrated. The work of the College Entrance Examination Board contributes to this integration, as does the multiplication of the number of Ph.D.'s and the resulting advance in the professionalization of the teaching staff.

The academic world is getting organized. It depends more on public authorities than on the initiatives of a few donors. It seems to be becoming an important element in a society in which large organizations, public and private administration, technical specialization, and secondary education are all rapidly developing, requiring a numerous and ever more highly qualified personnel. Certainly, the material condition of professors is mediocre, since their real income by 1959 is even less than it was in 1904; but their career is now well structured and their professional role is recognized.

The university system has specific functions that it fulfills well and even brilliantly. American science rises little by little to the top rank and there is rapid growth in the number of students.

But this picture is quite incomplete and remains limited to material expansion. In fact, going along with this material expansion there is also a new conception of the relationship between higher education and society. This time, that conception springs less from the development within society of a new cultural model than from reflections and initiatives that are born in the universities and colleges themselves.

GENERAL EDUCATION AND SOCIAL ELITISM

One might, in looking at the Eastern colleges in particular, come up with the notion that the most celebrated of them were the refuges of the upper bourgeoisie. Fond of tradition, holding membership in clubs or fraternities, spending their college years leading an agreeable social life, the students of these colleges formed friendships and made connections there that reinforced the social elite. Later on, they met with other members of this elite at the Harvard and Yale clubs, in the prestigious Wall Street law firms, and on the governing boards of the big corporations. But if these class attributes of the best Eastern colleges are a lasting reality, the influence brought to bear by the great colleges on their students surely did not aim at the preservation of such an aristocratic way of life. On the contrary, Woodrow Wilson at Princeton waged a relentless struggle against the eating clubs, and if he introduced the tutorial system, it was to bring students and faculty closer together, to socialize the students to university norms. However, one must be careful not simply to trade one distortion for its opposite.

At a time when a more technical and professional training was being developed in the expanding state universities, the aim of the great colleges and universities, especially the private ones, was indeed to form a ruling elite. But is not that the meaning that we already gave to the reforms of the preceding period? Yes, but then it was a matter of getting the universities to take part in the same general movement of change and development being undertaken by American society as a whole. Between the two world wars attention was directed more specifically toward the students and thus toward the great ideological themes that would enable them, as members of a solidly established ruling class, to set themselves up as heirs to a long cultural tradition.

Thus the socialization to university norms is inseparable from the creation by the university of an ideology of continuity and tradition. This new ideology is quite different from the theme of progress and thus from the intention to break with the past that had characterized the progressivism or utilitarianism of the end of the nineteenth century.

But there was no possibility here of a complete about-face. The United States continued to conceive of itself as a modernistic, dynamic society, especially just after World War I and during the "roaring twenties." This confidence in the future weakened during the Depression, precisely when economic and social reforms, and consequently a critical view of society, appeared necessary. Self-confidence built up again during and after World War II, with the return of prosperity and the more or less conscious assumption by the United States of the role of leader of the free world, first in the fight against fascism and its allies, then defending the "free world" against Stalinist totalitarianism.

The Search for an Ideology

It is thus during the two postwar periods that we see the strongest development of the movements for educational reform. Americans proclaim the necessity for young Americans to consider themselves the active defenders of cultural traditions born in the eastern Mediterranean and carried on by the great countries of Western Europe, now worn down by internal strife, paralyzed by social barriers, or sunk into dictatorship.

There are two sides to every pedagogic initiative taken during this period. On the one hand there is the question of constituting a modern or even modernist culture, animated by the scientific spirit and by a sense of professional achievement. On the other hand there is the question of consolidating the power and superiority of a social elite that is threatened by the rise of immigrants, especially in New York, where Jewish families spur their children on to an intellectual success that might make up for the difficulty of crossing certain social barriers.

It is, in fact, Columbia that becomes the birthplace of the great movement for a return to general education (Bell, 1966). That it was Columbia is explained in particular by the vigor with which President Butler, advised notably by the historian and jurist John Burgess, had fought the spirit of the liberal arts colleges, defending the idea that two years of college would be sufficient for most pre-professional study.

Against this policy, two kinds of opposition took shape at Columbia during the war. The resistance, in the name of humanism, was first led by John H. Van Imringe, dean of the School of Arts, and later of the college. In 1917, John Erskine proposed the creation of a general honors course, including the study of one great book per week and stressing the need to reestablish a humanist orientation in order to repair the harm done by an overly exclusive professionalism. But another group of professors, including Harry J. Carman, was creating courses on war issues, then on peace issues, thus forming a program of instruction in contemporary civilization.

The compromise consisted of establishing a two-year course in contemporary civilization, the first year dealing with the cultural and intellectual history of the West, the second analyzing recent changes and socioeconomic problems of Western society. Later, other basic programs were instituted, first in the humanities, then only later, and in fragmentary fashion, in the hard sciences. All this culminated in the most characteristic creation of the era, a lower college that focused on general programs. Juniors and seniors, on the contrary, were already oriented toward more specialized studies.

Eventually, the Carman Committee in 1946 tried to go still farther and prepare a general four-year program — an attempt that met with little success. In 1954 Columbia put restrictions on general education by introducing the major system.

The ideas launched by Columbia played a central role in the thinking of people concerned about higher education between the world wars. Certain of them show up in the thought of Hutchins, which will be examined separately because it had a particular ideological importance and because Chicago College exercised a direct influence on a number of liberal arts colleges. They show up again, much later, in the Harvard report, *General Education in a Free Society,* commonly known as "the Redbook." Drawn up at the end of World War II in an elitist university, it is, much more than the post-World War I Columbia declarations, inspired by the sense of tradition that is inseparable from the search for unity in education. "The supreme need of American education," it says, "is for a unifying purpose and idea" (Hofstadter & Smith, 1962, vol. 2, pp. 958–959). The report does not deal with graduate education, for its main concern is to create a general education capable of replacing secondary education, which is in the process of breaking down. If one recalls the role played by elite secondary education in Germany and France, the class ideology that inspires this document is readily visible; in fact, it is more explicit than it is in European texts. A defense of Western culture and its values and a concern for continuity are central to all these writings. Certainly, respects are paid in passing to the pragmatism of William James and John Dewey; the important thing, however, is not to insist on the novelty of a cultural orientation, but to assume the heritage of the past. It is worthwhile to pay attention to this text, whose principal authors are an historian, Paul H. Buck, and a Hellenist, John H. Finley. It is fairly natural that it should be the work of professors in the humanities and not in the natural or even the social sciences.

Insofar as our culture is adequately reflected in current ideas on education, one point about it is clear: it depends in part on an inherited view of man and society which it is the function, though not the only function, of education to pass on. It is not and cannot be true that all possible choices are open to us individually and collectively. We are part of an organic process which is the American and more broadly the Western evolution. Our standards of judgement, ways of life, and form of government all bear the mark of this evolution, which would accordingly influence us, though confusedly, even if it were not understood. Ideally it should be understood at several degrees of depth, which complement rather than exclude each other. To study the American present is to discuss at best the aims and purposes of a free society animating its imperfections; to study the past is immensely to enrich the meaning of the present and at the same time to clarify it by the simplification of the writings and the issues which have been winnowed from history. To study either past or present is to confront, in some form or another, the philosophic and religious fact of man in his history and to recognize the huge continuing influence alike on past and present of the stream of Jewish and Greek thought in Christianity. There is doubtless a sense in which religious education, education in the great books, and education in modern democracy may be mutually exclusive. But there is a far more important sense in which they work together to the same end, which is belief in the idea of man and society that we cherish, adapt and pass on (ibid).

The text is so extreme that one must be careful not to hold it up as more exemplary than it really is. It would be more precise to say that it is the supreme expression of the ideology of general education at the very moment when it begins to decline. Indeed, shortly thereafter, the Presidential Commission on Higher Education, named in 1946 by President Truman and chaired by George F. Zook, published a report in an altogether different spirit. Insofar as it defends general education it is as a means of acquiring cultural tools that allow the student to understand and evaluate the world in which he lives. But this text, like the preceding one, bears the stamp of its era and of the dominant American values. Far more innovative is the effort, undertaken especially by Jerrold Zacharias of MIT and Jerome J. Bruner of Harvard, to discern, behind professional specialization, the general principles of scientific knowledge and the structure of science. This tendency won out at Harvard. A general knowledge of the sciences based on their history was replaced by a more analytic approach. In any case, the resistance to general courses had always been and remained strong in the hard sciences, so that general education programs were, in fact, limited to the humanities and the social sciences.

More recently, new efforts have been undertaken to revive such general education programs at Harvard. Freshman seminars, created thanks to a donation from Edwin Land of the Polaroid company, have sought to bring young students into contact with some of the greatest teachers in the university, particularly in areas of general significance in the social sciences.

But this extremely costly solution could not be widely copied. In fact, general education has not been able to hold out against what J. Finly calls the "departmental take over."

With the start of an era of organized scientific research, the search for a general education was weakened, or rather it took a new form. During the preceding period, as we have seen, the spirit of general education was upheld by a small number of intellectuals who were ill-at-ease in the university and drawn more toward European traditions than to American progressivism. But between the world wars the idea of a general education became the doctrine of at least a part of the university system, and in particular of the better colleges. Finally, more recently, the call for a general education has been taken up by radicals like Paul Goodman and Herbert Marcuse and has been used to criticize a university that is too closely tied to the military-industrial complex. This critical theme was already sounded by Hutchins in his vehement reaction to the publication of the Zook report: "It is filled with the spirit of brotherhood and the sense of American superiority. It has great faith in money; it has great faith in courses. It is anti-humanistic and anti-intellectual. It is confident that vices can be turned into virtues by making them larger. Its heart is in the right place; its head does not work very well" (ibid., 1962, vol. 2, p. 990).

From the first Columbia program on Contemporary Civilization up to that reaction by Hutchins, the whole history of a major theme in American higher education unfolds. It starts out being closely tied to the conquering historicism of the nineteenth century, then is taken up as the cultural tool for the shaping of the young American elite (fighting in the name of the heritage of Western culture), and finally is claimed by the critics of the university system.

But to understand the historical importance of this theme during that period, we should examine how it was linked to the reorganization of the colleges, and thus how the union of a university education and a social education was managed in the elite colleges.

Excellence and the Elite   Once more Harvard offers the most rewarding field for observation. Just as one could symbolize the era ending early in the century by the long reign of Eliot, the start of the presidency of Lowell, scion of a great Boston family, marks an important turning point in American academic history. Jencks and Riesman define well the twin aspects of his undertaking. "If we take Lowell's original schema for an honors college as an indicator of his motives . . . we can say that he was driven by the same Puritanical quest for excellence that had animated both his Boston Brahmin ancestors and the Harvard tradition. But he believed excellence ought to be academic and intellectual, and his problem was how to offset the idolatrous claims of social and athletic pretenders" (Jencks & Riesman, 1962, p. 739).

The key word *excellence,* which plays such an important role in university thinking in that period, shows better than anything else the search for an elitism at once intellectual and social, distinct from the "chaos" of the preceding era.

This search for an internal selection of good students was marked especially by the creation of honors programs. Harvard's was one of the best known. So too was Swarthmore's, which was created in 1922 by Frank Aydelotte following the model of Oxford, where he had been a Rhodes scholar. The separation of honors students from pass students does not bring an early isolation of future specialists. Rather, it sets apart a university elite, which, thanks to the tutorial system, is put in closer contact with professors, or more precisely, with excellent graduate students. Using a particular discipline as a point of departure, these graduate students, whether as resident or nonresident tutors, see to the general intellectual formation of the better students.

Thus is created in another form the equivalent of the French system, in which many of the best students are isolated from those who go directly into the university and are put in classes of preparation for the Grandes Ecoles. There they are subject to a strict academic discipline, but at the same time enjoy both closer relations with their professors and the emulation of their peers.

In colleges like Harvard, where the proportion of honor students is already high and is increased still more by programs of advance placement for entering students, veritable French-style Grandes Ecoles are formed, except that at Harvard there is greater emphasis on individual work and in particular on the honors thesis.

This type of education corresponds fairly well to the analysis made by P. Bourdieu and J. C. Passeron (1964 and 1970) of the education methods proper to the reproduction of the dominant culture. What is needed, first of all, is an emphasis on rhetoric, general concepts, and the ability to express ideas. Secondly, the culture must be one of communication and representation rather than one of production, and must put greater value on literary than on scientific culture. Such a value emphasis would implicitly affirm the separation between "the two cultures," since these educational methods are more easily applied in the literary domain. It is a type of education especially useful in training a teaching profession whose members are thought of as transmitters rather than as creators of knowledge. This is why very often a university turned in on itself and its own reproduction serves the reproduction of the social order just as effectively.

This interpretation corresponds better to the situation that we are studying than to the one that preceded or the one that follows. During the preceding period, it was a matter of the universities not so much reproducing as producing a ruling elite and a new culture. During the following period, which, as we shall see, is dominated by the triumph of research and professionalization, the academic system asserts its autonomy and its attachment to the values of rational knowledge, of which it considers itself a repository. It thereby develops what I have called an academic rhetoric, which confuses the service of science with the defense of the special interests of institutions and professions, forgetting the links between the university system and the dominant social order.

General education and the practice of the elite colleges are much more clearly ideological creations linked directly to the ruling class, whose children and successors are educated by these elitist institutions. It is definitely a matter of a class education. The only observation that needs to be added to this evaluation is that these excellent colleges produce an intellectual elite that, thanks to its education, possesses a certain autonomy, to the extent simply that many of the best students there turn not toward business but toward academic life itself for their careers. But this professional orientation can not yet lean on a strongly constituted rhetoric, because it is still education, not the production of knowledge, that is considered the principal function of these colleges.

Moreover, the university milieu is all the more dependent on the dominant values in that it is not contributing to the creation of new values. This type of education seeks, above all, to give a particular consciousness, a particular language, to a well-established social elite. Harvard and Yale see to the education of a considerable part of that elite, from economic and political leaders to eminent figures of the bench, philanthropy, and belles lettres (Pierson, 1969).

The nonconformity that occasionally shows up in this milieu is still of an elitist type and closer to that of the preceding than to that of the following period. These observations deviate from those of Bourdieu and Passeron.

Their analysis seems to me to assert in an unconvincing manner the fundamental identity of two aspects of academic life: its submission to the dominant order and its "abstraction," which allows it to present in the form of rules or general principles what is in reality only the interest of the ruling classes in their own preservation. But in fact the defense of the establishment, as we have seen, is more direct and not so abstract. The avowed aim of the elitist colleges is to assure the defense and development of a certain type of culture, functions which, in contrast to the French system, are not glossed over by dissertations on equality. No one has ever seriously thought of Harvard or Cornell as democratic institutions.

The rhetoric of equality and freedom never merges entirely with the elitist ideology. The rhetoric of professionalization is always distinct from the ideology of general education. What is combined at Harvard is the theme of university excellence and a class ideology, a combination that is, in reality, a relationship that amounts to including the former in the latter.

At Harvard this submission to university excellence and to social elitism is easily assured by the social origin of the students and is reinforced by their way of life. Many students come from private preparatory schools, especially from the little core of "Saint Grottlesex" formed by St. Paul, Middlesex, and Groton. At Harvard itself, after their freshman year, they live in houses that are meant to bring back to life the spirit of the English colleges, following the wish of their creator Edward Harkness, who, having amassed a huge fortune in the oil industry, first proposed building such houses for Yale. Yale having hesitated, Lowell accepted with enthusiasm.

One can agree with Jencks and Riesman, when they say, in the article already cited, that the houses "have done something to break down parochialism of all sorts, making today's Harvard undergraduate more cosmopolitan than his father" (1962, pp. 792–793). But the same authors recognize that the houses are dominated by the humanities, by virtue of the simple fact that good graduate students in the sciences easily obtain research grants whereas graduate students in English or history are happy to live as residents in these houses as a way of financing their studies and the preparation of their thesis. Above all, despite the precautions taken by the administration, the houses acquire a certain spirit—more highbrow at Lowell, more aristocratic at Eliot, more bohemian at Adams. Even if these stereotypes are artificial, their very existence and persistence point up the importance of the community to the student. Work and social milieu are thus united, like the department and the house within the university, and the acquisition of techniques of work and expression is placed in the framework of belonging to an elitist social and cultural milieu.

Obviously, the higher the tuition, the more firmly a social selection is installed that dictates the submission of excellence to elitism. It is therefore fairly difficult to define the role of methods of education in the formation of a social elite within the colleges. It seems as inaccurate to say that the programs of excellence are independent of an elitist milieu as to say that they are the direct agents of its formation or of its reinforcement.

It seems to me preferable to pose this question: In a system materially and ideologically dominated by the ruling class, under what conditions does the search for excellence reinforce elitism or isolate a group of university professionals, or on the other hand prepare a counterelite, more open to change and to social criticism?

This question, it seems to me, is impossible to answer with any precision. Simply asking it, however, may help us to better understand the ambiguities of the renaissance movement among liberal arts colleges that developed during this period.

The Liberal Arts Colleges In reality we cannot speak of a single movement, for the diversity of tendencies that I have tried to sort out in the case of Harvard becomes more striking as we extend our observation to a larger number of colleges.

This diversity can be grasped by comparing the ideas of Dewey and of Hutchins, classically regarded as opposites. But this opposition needs to be defined less simply than it often is when the progressivism of the one is held up to the conservatism, or even the reactionary tendencies, of the other.

There is no need here to recall Dewey's familiar ideas — expressed, for example, in *Democracy and Education* (1916) — which had greater influence on secondary education and on the teachers schools than on the colleges, even though such colleges as Black Mountain, Bennington, Sarah Lawrence, Goddard, and St. Stephen's were formed or transformed according to his principles. The insistence on the experimental method, on the connection between study and work, on the importance of conceiving the educational process as a series of ever more difficult problems to solve, falls directly in line with the conceptions on education that marked the preceding period and its utilitarian climate.

But one cannot define the meaning of that pedagogy in purely technical terms. That education is also one that leads to the staffing of the medium ranks of society, which trains people to think and act within a given social and cultural framework. By concentrating on the means, it assumes that the ends are defined and accepted. This empiricism is progressive in the sense of refusing traditionally accepted ideas and in giving education aims other than the transmission of established values; but we have here, if one can use the term, a conformist progressivism, that is, a progressivism in the service of a democracy sufficiently confident of its principles to define itself entirely by its mechanisms of change. Democracy is defined here as a set of types of behavior and of institutional mechanisms, not as a criticism of power.

The thought of Hutchins deserves greater attention, as it is more ambiguous than that of Dewey (Hutchins, 1936).

Hutchins' criticism is aimed first of all at "vocationalism," in other words at the role of money and its influence in the university. Readily referring to Yale Law School, where he achieved a brilliant career at a very early age, he denounced the overly tight link between the training and the profession. This relationship, he felt, gives the advantage to the practice of law over a broader and more theoretical training and leads to anti-intellectualism and to the universities' lack of interest in research, which, according to him, is kept alive thanks only to the foundations. He expresses indignation at the extravagant expenditures of the universities, guided by "the self-interest of professors, the vanity of administrators, trustees, and alumni, and the desire to attract public attention" (Hutchins, 1956, p. 165). He is even more profoundly indignant at the way the university submits to the ever-changing demands of society in the name of a false conception of democracy, according to which "education should be immediately responsive to public opinion" (Hutchins, 1956, p. 165). These criticisms of the role of money and of a consumer democracy are completed by attacks against the ideology of progress, which naïvely holds to the belief that civilization can be improved by technology and consequently turns attention away from the content of education.

Hutchins' proposals for reform thus aim at organizing education around a content and consequently at making it an end in itself. His desire was to create a four-year program, lifting the two final years from high school and attaching them to the first two years of ordinary colleges. This was accomplished in part by Chicago College, even though the proportion of those who entered after only two years of high school never exceeded 20 percent (Bell, 1966, pp. 26–38). Since this training is supposed to be terminal, it should be conceived of as a general education, with a program that must be prescribed and not elective. Knowledge should be organized in three main areas: humanities, social sciences, and natural sciences. The college should have an autonomous faculty and the end of each year should be marked by a comprehensive examination administered by staff members other than the student's teachers for that year.

Hutchins claimed that this organization of study would help to unify the realm of knowledge, and, for this reason, he crowned the three main areas of knowledge with a general course called at first "Methods, Values and Content," and later, "Observation, Interpretation and Integration." The course played a central role at Chicago until the college went back to the classic formula of four years of study, partly under pressure from the universities, which did not want to accept the Chicago B.A. as the equivalent of a B.A. granted after four years of college. This intellectual unity gives a central role to philosophy, especially if that word is taken to mean a system of knowledge, the meaning it had until the era of Descartes and Newton. Hutchins defines it almost in the same terms as the Trivium and Quadrivium of the medieval universities. A society should have an intellectual unity. The Middle Ages got theirs from theology; the Soviet Union gets theirs from Marxism; American society must find with its own, for "it is impossible to have a social order without intellectual order" (Hutchins, 1936, p. 105). The Hundred Great Books movement, to which Hutchins' reform is sometimes incorrectly reduced, is a logical continuation of it, and when St. John's College at Annapolis came to make it the base of their program it was with Hutchins' support.

These ideas and the reforms they brought with them ran into many forms of resistance, in particular on the part of young instructors who did not want to cut themselves off from graduate schools and thus from research. Hutchins left the presidency, to which he had been named in 1929, in 1945, but he remained chancellor until 1951. After his departure his project underwent profound transformations: the lower and upper colleges were separated and more usual divisions were reinstated, up to the point when the 1964 Levi Plan brought together Civilizational Studies in one of the five divisions of the college.

Many attacked what they called the return to a metaphysical tradition—for example, Harry D. Gideonse, who criticized Hutchins for placing himself "within the framework of the traditional metaphysics of rational absolutism" (Hofstadter & Smith, 1962, vol. 2, p. 943), and Dewey, who accused him of being "authoritarian," for who is to choose the great authors to be studied, who is to decide whether to study Aristotle rather than Marx?

Singular thought indeed. Yet this man, considered a reactionary, influenced by neo-Thomism, eventually became chairman of the Center for the Study of Democratic Institutions, where he earned the reputation of a "left-wing liberal."

There is no doubt that Hutchins' philosophy and reforms push to the farthest point the will toward consolidation of the social order. During the twenties this consolidation seemed to be assured naturally by the development of the deepest tendencies of American society, an open, pragmatic society, confident in its resources and values. During the thirties, however, that optimism fell by the wayside. American society was in deep trouble, grappling with a basic crisis. The ideology that united order and progress, change and integration, fell apart. On the one hand, the rise of a mass workers' movement led to a strengthening of the role of the state, which set up, with the support of the Congress of Industrial Organizations (CIO), the framework for collective bargaining. As a consequence social relations were created that limited the personal power of the great entrepreneurs, who were indeed already being shoved aside by the evolution of industry itself and by the triumph of the General Motors mentality over the Henry Ford mentality. On the other hand, the idea of social order stopped being natural. In response, some people tried to reestablish some sense of social order by embracing the beliefs of right-wing extremisms, others were drawn toward socialism or communism.

The thought of Hutchins, however, did not try to create a wide social base. It was a reaction born in the heart of the university world, in elite institutions, and proclaimed the need for intellectual order. Similar movements were to be found in other countries. In France, for instance, a group of Catholic intellectuals who gathered around some Dominicans made an effort to elaborate the principles of a new social order, taking up the spirit of right-wing social Christianity—a far cry from the ideas of other Christian intellectuals who, around Emmanuel Mounier, adhered to the social movement that led to the Popular Front.

Hutchins' criticism of the power of money stopped short of being a social critique, and this product of Yale returned quite naturally to an elitist conception of knowledge. However, the influence of his thought cannot be summarily dismissed as reactionary. Let us say, rather, that he created a liberal elitism that was proper to a university world sure enough of itself to want to detach itself from the interests and ideologies that bore it. He advocated a movement that turns first toward the past, toward the "permanent studies" and the great books of philosophy, but that also bears within it a freedom of mind and a concern for the unity of knowledge that are at least to have beneficial effects on the programs and the organization of a certain number of elite colleges.

Hutchins refused to accept the submission of a purely technical and professional university system to society, to its dominant interests and ideology. He recognized, like the generation of the great founders, that the university must place itself on a higher level. That insight is probably more important than the "reactionary" image of his proposed intellectual order. The modernism and instrumentalism advocated by many, the concern for a narrow professionalism justified by service to social ascent and by a contribution to the general progress of society are, in fact, instruments of social conformism. The thought of Hutchins marks the movement by which the upper-class intelligentsia refused any longer to serve society as the purveyors of efficient and optimistic functionaries, and, while turning toward the past, created the conditions that would make it possible for a later generation to imagine a different future. With Hutchins, a part of the liberal elite broke loose from the wave of the present, to which they were pressured from all sides to adjust. Their response may be only to enclose themselves in an aristocratic culture, or to attempt an impossible return to the past, a past that is largely a myth. In spite of all that, the movement headed by Hutchins indicates that it is possible, in the very heart of one type of society, to bring into question its social and cultural orientations. But there would have to be other conditions, other ideas, and other figures before the expression of a doubt and an uneasiness could become a critical action.

During the 1920s and 1930s, the academic system indeed appears to be dominated by two principal tendencies, both of them complex. The first, reinforced by the growth and progress of the state universities, carries on in more or less routine forms the inspiration of the preceding period and contributes to the formation of a new social order, no longer only at the top but especially at the middle levels.

On the other hand, the colleges, or at least those that are secularized and are detached from the pressures of local communities, train a social and intellectual elite that at times becomes a ruling class as sure of itself and as arrogant as any aristocracy, and at other times fosters a spirit of intellectual inquiry and of critical doubt that did not exist previously.

The role of certain colleges should not be exaggerated. But one cannot speak of consolidation of the American social order without recognizing its contradictions and limitations, primarily because that social order itself was not always of a reassuring solidity, and its failures could cast doubt on the short-range optimism of capitalism's loyal employees. The elitism of the best of the liberal arts colleges was not in the service of the leisure class, but, on the contrary, of young men who accepted and even sought the rigors of intellectual effort, tempered by an oligarchic democracy. Antioch organized student participation in decision making long before the call for student power was so much as formulated in the academic world as a whole. And it was also in certain of these colleges, such as Oberlin, that the "radical humanism" of the Students for a Democratic Society (SDS) was to find its strongest support.

Perhaps one can more precisely place the influence of Chicago College in the history of the liberal arts colleges, of which it constitutes the central phase. The first phase is that of secularization, when students coming from a semirural and often lower middle-class background transferred to the service of education and science the puritan rigor of their parents. As they became hothouses for the development of future scholars, the colleges, at the same time, were concerned with working out new teaching methods.[1] As this highly demanding academic environment, located especially in the Middle West, broadened its intellectual horizon, it became equally receptive to the most liberal teaching methods and to the most exacting curricula. But the development of university colleges and the growing role of the great universities as training centers for research are today causing these smaller colleges to lose a lot of their old drive. Their population is changing, and the new colleges studied by Riesman and his associates (Riesman, Gusfield, & Gamson, 1970) run into difficulties that force them to stray from their original intentions. Oakland College, created by Michigan State, was meant to maintain a high intellectual level, but its faculty, intent on following Eastern models, finds itself colliding with students whose goals are less ambitious. Monteith, created by Wayne State, was meant to carry on the spirit of Chicago College, and the faculty have gone out of their way to establish close personal and working relationships with the students. But the students resist the community spirit, and their plagiarism and cheating are a big disappointment to their generous-spirited instructors. This model of college has not managed to work outside an elitist milieu. It is therefore not surprising that a very elitist climate has been the setting for such new attempts as the Santa Cruz campus of the University of California, with its specialized residential colleges, its tiny classes, and its geographic isolation.

The percentage of graduate students recruited by the better universities from these elite colleges is getting smaller all the time, and those who speak for the great universities, even if they are

---

[1] See D. Riesman (1959), who cites in particular Robert H. Knapp and H. B. Goodrich, *Origins of American Scientists,* University of Chicago Press, Chicago, 1952; and Knapp and Joseph J. Greenbaum, *The Younger American Scholar: His Collegiate Origins,* University of Chicago Press, Chicago, and Wesleyan University Press, Middletown, Conn., 1953.

themselves products of elite colleges, are more and more of the opinion that they no longer meet the needs of contemporary education. James Perkins is very hard on them: "After all a liberal education is the objective of a lifetime. Why assume it should be crowded into the first two post-secondary years?" (Perkins, 1966, p. 44).

The progress made in secondary education—at least in the schools reserved for the children of the rich and the well-to-do—robs of its point Hutchins' project of setting up college as the pivot of the educational system, between a shortened, mediocre high school and a graduate school reserved for a limited number of high-level researchers and professionals. On the contrary, college is steadily losing its autonomy. The major system is a preparation for entrance to graduate school, which is considered more and more as a matter of course; at the same time, the faculty are turning their attention still more firmly toward research, leaving most lower-division teaching to young teaching assistants. Only a few great liberal intellectuals, faithful to the Chicago spirit, go on playing their part in teaching undergraduates.

The setback of the independent colleges in favor of the university colleges marks the transition from one phase to another. From now on the main objective is no longer the education and consolidation of a social elite, but the active participation of the academic system in a production of knowledge that appears more and more to be an essential factor in economic development and national power. Between secularized puritanism and the liberalism of small elites, Chicago College marks an intermediate stage, the most brilliant and influential, but all in all no more than a countermovement of limited scope that does not negate the main movement — a systematic consolidation of the social order through training an elite in the best colleges, the middle and upper ranks of society in a growing number of good colleges and state universities, and finally, as we shall see in a moment, lower-ranking personnel in the junior colleges.

The lively interest in college in America has most often gone along with a certain confidence in the effects of education. Is not college the place where students break away from their home background to come into contact with a more varied intellectual and social world, where they become citizens of a country defined by its ability and will toward progress and change, where they gain broader interests, greater tolerance, and a well-rounded education? Whether one is talking about the virtues of pragmatism and adjustment to change or about the need for general culture, it seems that one is always conceiving of college as the meeting ground between a young man or a young woman and the universality of modern values, the spirit of a civilization.

That idealistic conception is not supported by an examination of the effects of college on students. Theodore M. Newcomb[2] who has played a central role in the study of these effects, arrives at much more prudent conclusions. The impact of college is rather to reinforce those characteristics that the students arrived with: "The degree and nature of different colleges' impacts vary with their students' inputs—that is, entering students' characteristics, which differ among types of colleges in patterned ways" (Feldman & Newcomb, 1970, p. 317). That effect is strongest in the small four-year colleges, where the student population and even the faculty are more homogeneous.

Moreover, outside their special fields, professors have little influence on the social and cultural attitudes of their students. One can even say, "The maintenance of existing values or attitudes which, apart from certain kinds of college experience, might have been weakened or reversed, is an important kind of impact" (ibid., p. 329).

This conclusion is not to deny that college years affect the student. Rather, it is a matter of recognizing that the effect in question amounts less to a transition from a particularist experience to universalist values than it does to a reinforcement, especially from the peer group, of characteristics present at the time of entrance, especially when those characteristics are consistent with the dominant orientation of the college itself.

College plays a socializing role, but it is risky to define it according to the supposedly general characteristics of American culture. Education reinforces particular social milieux and types of participation in culture.

Stratification takes an organized form. Or is it an illusion? Is not that supposed pyramid more a whole set of ways to rise on the so-

---

[2] Feldman and Newcomb (1970). Certain themes of this major study had been presented by Newcomb, "Research on Student Characteristics: Current Approaches," in L. E. Dennis and J. F. Kauffman (eds.), *The College and the Student,* American Council on Education, Washington, D.C., 1966, pp. 100–116. Philip Jacob, in *Changing Values in College,* Harper & Brothers, New York, 1958, had earlier cast doubt on the oft-proclaimed idea that college exercises a liberalizing influence.

cial scale, in other words, a means of social change rather than of maintaining the established order?

Does not the rapid swelling of the ranks in higher education (especially public) mean that democratization is basic and inevitable? Whereas Europe reserved its universities for a small number of students coming from the upper strata of society, is it not the distinctive feature of American society—particularly during a period when it is not especially hard to get into a good college—to provide great possibilities for social advancement, allowing each to receive the education that suits his aptitudes? The reality is in fact rather different.

**MASSIFICA-
TION OR
DEMOCRATI-
ZATION**
The material growth of colleges and universities went on throughout the whole period between the world wars, first taking advantage of the new wealth and modernization of the 1920s, but continuing also during the Depression, when studies were an attractive refuge for white-collar workers, who seemed less affected by unemployment than blue collars. The moment is approaching when more than half those of college-entrance age will in fact be enrolled, and that proportion is already exceeded in California. Such proportions put the United States very far ahead of all other nations. How is it possible in such circumstances not to speak of democratization of a system of higher education that may very well not be open to all, but that is open to the majority? Do not the forecasts say that 75 percent of the appropriate age category will soon be going to college?

The rapid rise in figures and percentages (see Table 3) is even more impressive than the level achieved at any given moment. That rise has quickly gone beyond most forecasts; it amounted to 53 percent between 1962 and 1967.

As this rise is due, above all, to the growth of public institutions, it should also be a democratizing factor by reducing the importance

TABLE 3
College entrants

Year	Percentage of high school graduates			Percentage of eligible age group		
	Total	M	F	Total	M	F
1955	45.9	56.5	36.1	28.6	33.9	23.4
1960	49.6	60.1	39.8	34.3	40.1	28.6
1966	53.0	64.7	46.7	41.0	46.4	35.5

SOURCE: Folger et al. (1970, p. 151).

of the liberal arts colleges, symbols of social elitism. In 1965, enrollment in selective and very selective institutions was distributed as follows:

SOURCE: Folger et al. (1970, p. 163).

TABLE 3A
Number of entering freshmen in selective and very selective institutions

Bachelor's-degree-granting institutions	47,000
Master's-degree-granting institutions	71,000
Doctorate-degree-granting institutions	237,000

One can deduce from this table that entrance into the upper level professions has opened up socially, as is maintained by Talcott Parsons and Gerald Platt (1968, p. 502) when they compare the social origins of those who entered the professions before and those who entered the professions after World War II (see Table 4).

Inequality of Opportunities

But I only cite these figures to show just how little concrete proof there is for the deep-rooted belief in democratization. These figures simply point to well-known shifts in patterns of employment in the United States, that is, to an overall growth in the worker and white-collar class, a reduction in the numbers of independent entrepreneurs, farmers, businessmen, and industrialists, and an increase in the number of professional people and managers. As a result, the chances of getting into the professions are just the same after World War II as they were before, if one is willing to take into account, as indeed one must, the size of the categories from which recruitment takes place.

The existing inequality of opportunities is a relatively simple fact to observe. Here I first present it in its raw form, then examine its evolution, and finally try to find its causes.

Inequality exists not only between students and nonstudents, but between different categories of institutions as well. The social origins of students in private universities are clearly higher than those of students as a whole. The American Council on Education—

TABLE 4
Changes in students' social origins

	After World War II	*Before World War II*
Working and white-collar class	27%	23%
Entrepreneurial background	28	38
Professional and managerial background	45	39

SOURCE: N. Kaplan (1964, p. 863).

ACE (1970)—has presented detailed evidence, based on a vast inquiry, which we shall refer to here only sparingly. As Table 5 shows, the social differences between types of institutions show up also in the student's source of support. For women, whose social origins are in general a little higher, the results are similar, with the exception of the source of financial support.

The student populations of predominantly black colleges—which will be treated separately—show markedly lower social origins. It is hardly necessary to recall that the great majority of these colleges are located in the South, have low academic standards, and obviously do not open the gates of entry into the national elite.

It is almost possible to tell the intellectual quality of a college or university by looking at its social composition, just as one could ascertain the quality of housing and planning in a city by knowing the income of its residents. For example, Martin Trow cites the social composition of various California schools (see Table 6).

An SDS document points out that only 4 percent of Harvard freshmen come from families whose income is less than $7,500—the national median.

TABLE 5
Social origins of male students

Father's education	Mass		
	All two-year colleges, %	All four-year colleges, %	All universities, %
Grammar school or less	16.7	9.1	5.4
Some high school	21.7	15.6	11.1
High school degree	32.6	30.5	27.2
Some college	14.5	17.2	18.4
College degree	10.5	17.6	24.1
Postgraduate degree	3.9	10.0	13.8
High school students characterized as			
Upper class	3.5	3.6	4.3
Upper-middle class	20.0	27.4	31.6
Middle class	60.3	56.9	54.1
Working class	14.7	11.2	9.4
Lower class	1.5	.9	.6
Parental or family aid			
All students	37.2	51.9	65.1
Women only	50.3	64.4	74.3

SOURCE: ACE (1970, pp. 21, 23, 24, 32).

TABLE 6   *Socioeconomic background of students attending selected California colleges and universities*

| | White collar | | Blue collar | | | |
Private institutions	Upper %	Lower %	Upper %	Lower %	Other %	Total
Private institutions						
Stanford	61	37	1			100
University of the Pacific	42	37	6	4	11	100
Public institutions						
University of California, Berkeley	46	37	9	4	4	100
San Francisco State	31	33	15	15	7	100
San Jose State	38	17	29	16	4	100
Diablo Junior College	40	14	26	16	4	100
San Jose Junior College	23	15	45	17		100
Contra Costa Junior College	18	23	39	12	8	100
State population	29	29	18	20	4	100

SOURCE: Trow (1962, p. 256).

As in most Western countries, that social inequality is especially pronounced in certain parts of the university, particularly in the medical schools—where studies are long and expensive and assure entrance into a very high socioeconomic bracket.

As Table 7 shows, students entering medical school come on the average from markedly richer families.

The income level of recruitment for the best private schools is even higher than for the best public institutions. In the former more than three-quarters of the students come from families whose income is over $10,000, and 36.8 percent come from families whose

TABLE 7
Comparison of characteristics of freshmen physician aspirants with total freshmen, 1966

Parental income	Percentage of freshmen in medical schools	Percentage of total freshmen
Under $10,000	37.4	53.7
$10,000–$15,000	26.8	25.2
$15,000–$20,000	12.7	9.4
$20,000–$30,000	10.8	7.0
$30,000 or more	12.7	4.7

NOTE: Based on a representative sample of the entering class in approximately 250 undergraduate colleges and universities in the United States in 1966.
SOURCE: Fein and Weber (1971, p. 96).

income is over $20,000. In these schools the proportion of sons of doctors, other professional people, and independent businessmen is more than 80 percent.

There is no point in multiplying such examples. No doubt considerable inequality of opportunity exists; but does it not tend to diminish as higher education becomes more widespread? Jencks and Riesman are among the first to have looked into this subject (see Table 8).

If one considers the whole of the school system, it is possible to speak of a general trend toward equalization of opportunity. There is sharper progress from the first to the second generation than from the second to the third, since this progress is due mainly to the spread first of primary and then of secondary schooling. But the authors stress that the change does not prevent an increase in the difference between the upper third and lower third in absolute numbers. The difference has gone from 5.8 years for the 1910–1914 generation to 7 years for the 1930–1934 generation.

Surprising as it may seem at first glance, higher education's social transformations appear very slight in the course of such an extraordinary period of expansion.

The data just presented already lead to the observation by Jencks and Riesman that the distribution of resources devoted to education for different social categories has scarcely been modified, since the years of higher education are more costly to the community than the years of primary or secondary schooling.

If we consider only the chances of entering college, we see that inequality between social categories has not decreased: in fact, in absolute terms, the gap between those who start from a high level and those who start from a low level has increased. According to the same authors (1968, p. 96), an individual whose father had less than eight years of schooling had 8 chances out of 100 of entering college in the 1915–1925 generation (years of college entrance) and 14 chances out of 100 in the 1945–1955 generation.

On the other hand, an individual whose father went to college

Year of birth	*Top third*	*Middle third*	*Bottom third*	*Total*
1930–1934	43	35	22	100
1910–1914	46	34	20	100
1875–1885	53	34	13	100

TABLE 8
Percentage shares of total years of schooling obtained by best- and worst-educated thirds of U.S. males, 1875–1934

SOURCE: Jencks & Riesman (1968, p. 82).

had 47 chances out of 100 of entering college in the years 1915–1925 and 78 chances in the years 1945–1955.

As to entrance into graduate school, the son of an elementary school dropout sees his chances of entering graduate school go from 5 to 6 percent between the 1920s and the 1950s, whereas the chances of a son of a college graduate increased from 28 to 52 percent.

It is necessary to accept the conclusion of Jencks and Riesman (ibid., p. 95) that "the increase in enrollment among upper-middle-class children seems to have been even greater than among lower-middle and working-class children." The upper social categories, even if educated themselves, did not always send their children to college, for there were other paths open to social mobility. More recently, on the contrary, the advance of the meritocracy makes it impossible to look forward with confidence to social success if one is obliged to confront professional life without a college education. But this interpretation should not be carried too far. It describes a fairly recent trend and applies only to very high-level jobs.

The overall picture to keep in mind is that of a general rise in the level of education rather than of a redistribution of opportunities because of education.

Data on social inequality cannot, however, suffice to define the social mechanisms in action. An academic career also depends upon intellectual aptitude and the correlations between various tests of intellectual aptitude; in particular the correlation between mathematical aptitude and academic performance is always strong. A study of a group of high school seniors in Wisconsin (Sewell and Shah, 1967, pp. 1–23; see also Wolfle, 1954) shows that the effect of intellectual aptitude is stronger than that of socioeconomic status for men, whereas the opposite is the case for young women, both in regard to entrance into, and graduation from, college. The idea has been put forward that social origins count especially in regard to entrance into higher education, whereas afterward it is intellectual aptitude that determines the academic career itself. A variety of research supports rejection of that idea. The effect of the original social background continues to make itself felt at the highest level. Lower-class students are likelier to obtain a Ph.D. from a low-ranking university, which decreases their career opportunities. And even when lower-class students have obtained their B.A. in a major university, they still have less chance of getting a position in a major university, especially a private one (Crane, 1969, pp. 1–17).

Inequalities in aptitude do not explain all academic inequalities, especially if one considers the best universities:

> When only the most selective colleges were considered, socio-economic background was an important factor in attendance for the students who had sufficient academic talent to be admitted. When we compare attendance patterns of the students in the top fifth of ability we find that a boy from the top fifth group in socio-economic status was about ten times as likely to attend a highly selective college as a boy from the bottom fifth in socio-economic status (Folger et al., 1970, pp. 164–165).

For socioeconomic reasons, a considerable proportion of gifted students from secondary schools do not enter college. Table 9, used by Folger, Astin, and Bayer is enlightening.

Even at a high level of aptitude, the difference in the odds between the various social groups are still considerable. It is particularly noteworthy that among lower-class girls only those with a very high level of aptitude have one chance in two of going to college.

It must be added that scores made on aptitude tests are not independent of social origin. But in the studies used here the correlations are only on the order of .30. The relative weakness of that correlation allows us to conclude that a significant segment of stu-

TABLE 9
Percentage of high school graduates who went to college the following year, by academic aptitude, socioeconomic status, and sex — 1960

Academic aptitude		Socioeconomic Status					
	Low	Low middle	Middle	High middle	High	Total
Boys							
Low	10	13	15	25	40	14
Low middle	14	23	30	35	57	27
Middle	30	35	46	54	67	46
High middle	44	51	59	69	83	63
High	69	73	81	86	93	85
TOTAL	24	40	53	65	81	49
Girls							
Low	9	9	10	16	41	11
Low middle	9	10	16	24	54	18
Middle	12	18	25	40	63	30
High middle	24	35	41	58	78	49
High	52	61	66	80	90	75
TOTAL	15	24	32	51	75	35

SOURCE: Folger et al. (1970, p. 310).

dents qualified for higher education are kept away for social reasons. Even taking into account the considerable development of junior colleges during recent years, it can be maintained that access to the higher levels of education remains very unequal.

The first explanation for these inequalities that comes to mind is an economic one. In the good institutions, tuition is high and has risen rapidly in recent years. In fact from 1950 on, tuition in private colleges has been rising faster than per capita disposable income (Carnegie Commission, 1971a, p. 80). But these arguments are less convincing than they seem. In the first place, disposable income has risen much faster than the price index, and the strong elasticity of educational expenses normally allows acceptance of a rapidly rising tuition. Furthermore, in public institutions the tuition has been rising at about the same rate as disposable income, which ought to facilitate access to education in the public colleges and simply reduce the share of the private colleges. Since many must rapidly raise their tuition to maintain or achieve acceptable standards of quality, they are finding themselves in greater and greater financial difficulties from which they show no sign of being able to extricate themselves. The evolution in tuition rates tells us something about changes occurring in academic organization; it only very inadequately explains the continuing fact of social inequality.

The way in which tuition is calculated, however, plays an important role. In general, institutions arrive at tuition figures by dividing the number of students into the whole of their expenses — or at least that part of their expenses that cannot be covered by other income. The result is that a university with considerable expenses at the graduate school level imposes a high tuition on its undergraduates. Now, the cost of teaching undergraduates is low, given the large number of instructors and teaching assistants who carry the burden of teaching at that level. Thus, from the start the poorest students are discouraged from entering those institutions where they would have the best chance of continuing their studies to a high level. The material obstacles confronting students are in part removed by various types of financial aid, but there is reason to think that at the college level the role of scholarships is not necessarily designed to encourage the democratization of recruitment. Scholarships seem just as likely to enable a certain number of middle-class students to choose certain colleges rather than others. Moreover, scholarship aid has on the whole been limited. At Harvard in 1962, 1,400 out of 4,737 undergraduates received scholarships averaging $1,125 each, that is, about one-third of the actual annual cost of their education. The rest of the students mostly had loans or college jobs, which provided smaller amounts of assistance. At Stanford in the same year, the average amount of scholarship money granted to 1,505 out of 5,600 undergraduates was $900, the average loan was $374, and the average income from college jobs $561. The expenses are comparable to those at Harvard. In 1959–60, at a typical state university such as the University of Illinois, the students derived their support from the following sources: family, 36 percent; student earnings, 20 percent; reduction of assets, 18 percent; scholarships and awards, 14 percent; miscellaneous, 10 percent; and loans, 2 percent. These figures describe the situation prevailing in the "classic" period, which, although it does not have precise chronological boundaries, may be defined as the period prior to the massive intervention of the federal government in the functioning of the universities. That is why we have not yet mentioned the GI Bills and more recent measures whose effects will modify appreciably the situation that has just been described. The role of federal aid will be examined as a whole further on.

Aside from economic barriers, an essential role in student selection is played by family background. It is, in fact, very superficial to imagine social mobility as a sort of horse race, with all the runners equally vigorous and determined, but having to leap greater or lesser hurdles. Numerous inquiries have shown that a student's academic career can best be predicted from knowledge of his intentions (Folger, et al., 1970, p. 147–150)—and his intentions are formed in the family and school milieu. Several writers have suggested that not only does the economic and cultural level of the parents make a difference here, but also that any disparity in educational level between parents may be important. For example, a mother who has reached a higher educational level than the father may push her children to acquire an education that will enable them to reach the level she would have liked to attain herself. But the study of Sewell and Shah already mentioned does not confirm this hypothesis and shows that it is indeed the general family level that plays the main role (see also Sewell & Shah, 1968). The difference in educational level between parents has an effect, but that effect depends upon the child's sex and level of aptitude, and it is less significant than that of the educational level of the family as a whole.

Family influence is reinforced by the school milieu. Certain high schools, send unusually high proportions of their students to college, a fact that is linked to the students' social level and to the reinforcement that they exercise on each other.

The influence of the original social background makes itself felt not only at the time of entrance into college but all through the course of academic life. It explains a large part of the drop-out rate.

The proportion of college drop-outs generally is considerable. Various inquiries place it around 50 percent of each college class. The median proportion of graduates at the end of four years is around 37 percent. These figures do not seem to have changed much in the last 40 years (Summerskill, 1962, pp. 627–657). The distribution of the university population is summed up in Table 10.

The differences between the various types of institutions are considerable, with rates going from 12 percent to 82 percent. The most selective institutions are those with the lowest attrition rate (see Table 11).

The drop-out rate is higher for the lower-level professional careers, in business, secretarial work, and engineering. It depends

TABLE 10 *A generalized model of success and attrition in American colleges and universities (by percent of entering students)*

	Entering	Terminating before securing degree	Securing degree	Securing degree and terminating
Entering college	100			
Undergraduate attrition		47		
Earning bachelor's			53	
Terminating education				23
Entering graduate school (and studies for first-professional degrees)	30			
Master's attrition		11		
Earning master's			19	
Terminating education				11
Entering doctoral program	8			
Doctor's attrition		4		
Earning doctor's			4	
Terminating education				4
TOTAL		62		38

SOURCE: The Carnegie Commission (1970*a*, p. 9).

TABLE 11 *Variations in graduation rates according to selectivity of institutions*

Types of institution	Percentage of students graduating within 4 years at initial institution	Percentage graduating within 10 years at some institution	First-time full-time enrollments, fall 1969	Percentage of first-time full-time enrollers
Fifteen most selective private institutions	80–85	90–95	20,000	1
Large state universities	35–45	60–70	239,000	15
State colleges	15–25	35–50	322,000	21
Public junior colleges	20–25	15–30	457,000	29

NOTE: For junior colleges, the first column refers to those who receive their diploma in two years, and the second column to those who receive a four-year B.A. after transfer.
SOURCE: Report on Higher Education (1971, p. 2).

also upon the type of institution and is lower where cohesiveness is greater and where the faculty shows greater interest in the students.

As indicated in Table 12, surveys taken on why students drop out show the importance of psychological reasons, principally a clash between expectations formed in prior social milieux and college experience. Dropping out is explained by economic reasons in less than a quarter of the cases. But specifically professional reasons are just as rarely cited. In the last analysis, it is less a matter of academic failure than of choosing to leave an academic environment. This abandoning of the academic milieu is understandably less pronounced in highly selective institutions and in those where

TABLE 12
Reasons for dropping out

	Male, %	Female, %
Changed career plans	22.1	20.7
Dissatisfaction with college environment	26.7	27.0
Scholarship terminated	2.8	1.4
Wanted time to reconsider interests and goals	16.4	17.7
Marriage	7.8	29.0
Pregnancy	1.1	8.2
Tired of being a student	11.3	6.0
Could not afford cost	23.6	17.8
Academic record unsatisfactory	15.5	5.8

SOURCE: Panos and Astin (1967, p. 19, table 2).

there is the greatest continuity of milieu between campus and family background.

In Table 13, the researchers of the American Council on Education have summarized the various odds for academic success for students of high aptitude but of different socioeconomic levels.

To remind ourselves of the weight of social inequality—and especially of the fact that it has not decreased despite the massification of higher education during the 40 years following World War I —is obviously not to say that education does not play an important role in social mobility.

It is now necessary, within the limits imposed by the figures analyzed, to try to specify the role of education in mobility and in consciousness of mobility.

Does the wider and wider opening of the gates to higher education mean that attending a university is perceived and felt as an experience of social ascent and of access to a superior cultural world?

In a brillant article, Ralph Turner (1960, p. 855–867) has contrasted two types of mobility: sponsored mobility and contest mobility. In the case of the former the members of the future elite are chosen very early. "Upward mobility is like entry into a private club where each candidate must be 'sponsored' by one or more of the members." Hence the significance attached to signs indicating that one belongs or wishes to belong to the elite. Contest mobility, on the contrary, is an open race in which there is the attempt to keep as many competitors as possible in the running right down to the wire. Symbols of belonging to the elite cannot matter here,

TABLE 13
Patterns of academic life for rich and poor students

Out of 100 male high school graduates with HIGH socioeconomic status and high ability	Out of 100 male high school graduates with LOW socioeconomic status and high ability
9 do not go to college	31 do not go to college
9 go to junior college, of whom	17 go to a junior college, of whom
3 go on to a senior college	5 go on to a senior college
82 go to a senior college, of whom	52 go to a senior college, of whom
63 graduate	32 graduate
36 continue immediately in a graduate or professional school	15 continue immediately in a graduate or professional school

SOURCE: Folger, Astin, and Bayer (1970, p. 322).

where selection must be gradual. The first type of mobility corresponds best to English society, the second to American society. This distinction explains, in particular, the high rate of dropouts in America, since no early selection intervenes to stop a large number of students who will give up only through exhaustion along the way. It explains also the stress placed on "social adjustment" in America, since that society has no preestablished elite code of behavior, whereas the English bourgeois, unmistakable thanks to his accent and his manners, can more easily allow himself to be bohemian or eccentric.

In fact, the ruling classes in England or France, upheld by a previously established order, are more accustomed than those in the United States to actively absorbing new elements, whether foreign or of other class origin, without thereby modifying their own code. This could not be the case in the United States, the "first new nation," as Seymour M. Lipset has described it.

But these notions, which contrast a closed society to an open society, are not very far from being stereotypes and fall a long way short of a thorough description of reality. One is almost tempted to play at turning the picture around, for American society has long been and, to a certain extent, still is based on communities defined by their values. Schools and many colleges were long connected to local communities. Because of this connection and because membership in the elite class required not only certain manners but a religion—not to mention attributes by definition impossible to acquire—entering college by being sponsored was more difficult than entering the elite in European countries.

Aside from these somewhat marginal reservations, what seems questionable is that one can properly define the American academic system in terms of contest mobility. To simplify further, it is appropriate in order to answer such a question to distinguish between various historical situations. I have mentioned several times how much, in the first of the stages that I have identified, and to some extent in the second, access to higher education is associated with entrance into a social elite that is not very numerous—or rather, into a still relatively limited segment of the social elite. I have also noted how the development of a student culture lends importance to mutual sponsorship. Students are and must be gentlemen; they strive to re-create the signs of an upper class that European students had to start with and were perhaps trying more to get rid of. The liberal arts colleges were infused with a spirit of mobility, but that mobility was not at all experienced as an open race. The students, basically inner-directed, committed themselves to knowledge in a way that does not seem to me to be fundamentally different from that of German or French or Italian middle-class students, who are sustained, however, by another type of puritanism. In France, service to the nation, progress, and science—all related to the laicist spirit of the Third Republic—played the same role as the religious morality of the Middle Western communities, which made of certain liberal arts colleges the great lycées of America.

Turner's image seems much more suited to the state universities and colleges that were developing especially after World War I, starting perhaps in Wisconsin and Illinois, then spreading to a larger and larger number of states. At this stage the academic world is already vast: its link with particular communities is broken and it cannot claim identity with the national elite that is educated in such great private colleges of the East and the Middle West, as Harvard, Yale, Columbia, and Chicago, which are renovated but still elitist.

The race is open because it is a matter of filling the intermediate ranks of society, less strictly defined than the narrower framework of the elite. Certainly many students climb all the way to the top of the social ladder—and many nonstudents get there too. But is this so different from the situation of the English students of the "Red Brick Universities" or of French students whose number has increased much more rapidly in the last 20 years? Has contest mobility become widespread in the United States in the most recent period, when it is becoming more and more usual for young people to be students and when junior and community colleges are multiplying and decidedly no longer have any contact with the social elite? Most observers reach the opposite conclusion.

To a large number of students, college appears as a way of asserting their personal independence and of taking part in a particular kind of life (Donovan & Kaye, 1962, pp. 199–224). Many women students find there a sort of sublimation of the sexual role; many men consider it a necessary and usual step toward finding an ordinary job.

Yet McDill and Coleman (1963, pp. 905–918) have shown, to their own astonishment, that high school seniors have a low achievement orientation even when they are intending to go to college. The following table sums up their findings:

College plans	Achievement orientation		
	High	*Low*	*Total*
Yes	54	84	138
No	27	115	142
TOTAL	81	199	

The intention to go to college goes along with a stronger achievement orientation, but the striking fact is that even in this category the achievement orientation of most young men finishing their secondary schooling is low.

This kind of attitude has often been described:

Our Mid-western students, although frequently from homes of moderate means and meager education, exhibit no such eagerness. They happily take it for granted, as does our society, that there are no social hurdles to learning. Our students, in entering the university, cannot feel that they are overcoming ancient restrictions and embarking upon a new way of life. For them education spells advancement rather than change, improvement rather than transition. The fixedness of their viewpoints thus is a counterpart to our equalitarian ethos (Pinner, 1962, pp. 954–955).

In regard to this change, linked both to the spread of higher education and to more general cultural causes, Trow draws this overall conclusion:

I suspect that college aspirations reflected mobility orientations more commonly in the past than they do in the present or will in the future. . . . While the extension of mobility orientations would account for steadily rising college enrollments, the growth of mass, and eventually near universal college attendance is a product of changes in what the great mass of non-strivers—those who are satisfied just to "get by"—expect in the normal course of events (1962, pp. 236–237).

For parents to send their children to college is seen as a "prerequisite for a decent, reasonably secure life."

This is a faithful portrait of the silent generation, which entered mass education as a means to take, not to change, one's place in society.

We are a long way here from contest mobility. Higher education had first formed a national elite, which it then consolidated, organizing at the same time the middle echelons of the social order. Now in becoming more widespread, it draws into its system considerable masses of students who are seeking for the most part simply to do what is required in order to participate, under conditions that are acceptable, in the great social machine.

Minorities But we might go still further and ask if the massification of higher education does not actually have a reverse effect, reducing more than it enhances the possibilities of ascent for people in certain social categories.

1 At first, women were for the most part isolated in women's colleges, where the sororities were even more active than the fraternities in the men's colleges. At least some of these colleges, such as those comprising the "Seven Sisters," were often centers of feminine emancipation, just as the liberal arts colleges in general served to emancipate a social elite from community constraints. But in this case isolation has also amounted to marginality. Only Bryn Mawr reached a high level. In the end, it took coeducation to open up broader perspectives to women students. Little by little, fusion has taken place, whether practically complete, as between Harvard and Radcliffe, or by a partial integration, such as unites Columbia with Barnard.

One might think at first glance that there is not much discrimination against women. After all, 43 percent of all freshmen are women, and the medical schools accept the same proportion of men and women applying for entrance (Folger et al., 1970, pp. 280–304). But these initial impressions are deceptive. First of all, the inequality between women and men becomes more pronounced at the graduate level. Furthermore, the relative equality that is supposedly established upon entrance to university life is in fact discriminatory.

Actually, women make better grades in high school than men. Yet only 41.5 percent of those who obtain their B.A. or first professional degree are women (*Report on Higher . . . ,* 1971). Women who apply to graduate school are as a group more highly selected than male applicants; thus, if there were not discrimination, more women than men would be admitted. Inequality is reinforced by the fact that a large proportion of women go into so-called feminine professions, which happen to be relatively poorly paid, often subordinate, and limited to personal services: education, health, secretarial work, etc. In their own employment policies, the universities themselves practice obvious discrimination: slower advancement for equal scientific productivity, lower salaries. The idea prevails in the United States, as in other countries, that women frequently do not practice the profession for which they have been trained. This is fairly inaccurate, since among married women the proportion of those working full time is about 65 percent in psychology, 70 percent in the social sciences, 60 percent in the natural sciences, 70 percent in the humanities, and 80 percent in education. If we add those working part time, we find that around 85 percent of married women Ph.D.'s are employed either full time or part time. Single women, widows, and divorcees are obviously much more fully involved in professional activity. In spite of these figures, educational equality for women is tending not to increase, but, on the contrary, to decrease. Women represented 40.4 percent of M.A.'s in 1930 and 38 percent in 1968; they were 15.4 percent of Ph.D.'s in 1930, only 12.6 percent in 1968.[3]

Alice Rossi (1965) has indeed shown that the discrimination practiced corresponds to a lower level of expectation on the part of women, an inferiority of expectation that is a product of family background and is further maintained by the ambivalent attitudes of women students, torn between a conjugal and maternal role on the one hand and a professional role on the other. This is not the place to examine the cultural and social justifications for that strange situation by which women become a minority. But the example of women makes it clear that the academic system does not have an equalizing influence, but rather contributes toward stratifying those who enter along the lines of the dominant ideologies.

2   The case of black students is more extreme, but it is not entirely different, for women constitute the majority of students in the Southern black colleges.

The major development of Southern black colleges dates from the Reconstruction period, when about 200 colleges were created, many of them denominational. White philanthropists played a prominent role in their creation, and their administration passed only gradually into the hands of the blacks themselves.

Here I shall limit myself to the role played by these colleges in the functioning of the American academic system, since the role of

---

[3] The most detailed study is that of Helen S. Astin (1969).

the black movement in shaking up that system will be considered further on.

Three main facts deserve attention.

The first is the inferiority of the black colleges. Although blacks represent around 12 percent of the total population, the proportion of blacks in the student population is so far only half that figure. Between 1964 and 1969, however, the proportion rose from 5 percent to 6.6 percent.[4] The quality of the vast majority of these colleges is certainly mediocre. The low average scores of blacks on national aptitude tests are a direct result of their lower economic and social level. Until recently, it could be said, along with Jencks and Riesman, that many black colleges were caricatures of white colleges, complete with an authoritarian atmosphere, stress on sports, importance of fraternities and sororities, and sometimes even dishonest practices. The greater part of the graduates of these colleges make up a black bourgeoisie that F. Frazier (1957) severely portrayed.

In the second place, many of these students hope to leave the South at the end of their studies (Jaffe et al., 1968). But if two-thirds express the desire, only half of them go, and then not immediately after graduation. The attraction of the junior colleges that are spreading rapidly in the South also comes from this desire to escape segregation.

In reality, these attitudes are very complex. Whereas the good Northern colleges have a great power of attraction, the blacks' feelings of distrust and hostility for the Southern social system create attitudes unfavorable toward white Southern colleges, especially among black women. The individual and collective will to get ahead cannot be reduced to a desire for fusion; on the contrary, it is attached to a strong loyalty toward black institutions. When judging the civil rights movement, "the graduates put a much greater emphasis on achieving equal job opportunities than they do on educational desegregation" (Fichter, 1967, p. 242).

The students are at the same time desirous of rising in the hierarchy of academic establishments and aware that they run into racial barriers. As a result, the majority of them support the strug-

[4] In 1970, 21 percent of the black population between 18 and 21 went to college, as compared with 36 percent of the whites. The proportions are 7 and 15 percent for the 22–25 age group. The gap between whites and blacks is wider for the graduate-student population.

gle against segregation, but as an instrument of social change rather than as an effort at integration.

Thirdly and lastly—and here is the most interesting fact—the double movement of imitation and integration does not halt the financial deterioration of a large number of black colleges, even though their enrollments are expanding numerically.

In 1950 the black colleges spent four-fifths of the national average per student; in 1960 that proportion was down to two-thirds. The proportion of black students choosing a natural science major dropped from 29 percent in 1930 to 25 percent in 1940 and 20 percent in 1965. More broadly speaking, as A. J. Jaffe notes, the most rapidly developing colleges are the ones with the lowest intellectual quality; they are also the ones where the students' family income is lowest and the proportion of dropouts is highest.

The more psychosociological study by Patricia Gurin and Daniel Katz (1966) arrives at analogous conclusions. The professional goals of students in black colleges remain traditional. Those who are of a higher social level have higher aspirations, but they remain essentially within the professions and occupations that offer the most traditional type of social advancement. There is no progress to be seen when it comes to participation in the most modern activities with the most promising future.

This isolation seems, on the other hand, to be diminished by the success of the black movement in the Northern universities ("Record Number of Black Students . . . , May 15, 1969, p. 2). The number of blacks accepted by the good universities has grown considerably. For the Ivy League, the increase between 1968 and 1969 is 89 percent: in 1914, out of 12,929 students, 1,135 were black. For the best women's colleges, the Seven Sisters, the increase in one year is 120 percent, with 428 blacks admitted out of 5,430 students.

But that sudden opening at the summit should not obscure the fact that the position of the black colleges encompassed by the Southern Regional Education Board (SREB) is not getting better. On the contrary, the share of degrees granted by the states of the SREB dropped from 25.3 percent in 1959–60 to 24.5 percent in 1965–66. Perhaps the new federal programs—Upward Bound, Talent Search, and Student Special Services—will manage to improve the chances of low-income black students. It is still too early to judge.

Thus, there is a growing tension between the ever-stronger desire for education and the fact that job opportunities are in teaching at an increasingly low level, between the desire for mobility and the fact of being stuck in isolation and in an inferior situation. This movement of involution shows once again the limits of the academic system's capacity to integrate its various parts.

In these conditions it is difficult to hang on to the optimistic image of a competitive society in which, of course, not all succeed in the long run, but which poses no barriers at the very start.

Nor must one underestimate the power of this system, a power linked to the expansion of the American economy, especially in the period following the Second World War. An image of society is imposed by the educational system, which stratifies itself and contributes to fixing the social hierarchy—a hierarchy that involves both an internal stratification and exclusions, that serves the economy but that also introduces an ideological conception linked to the dominant forces of society, and that can be dysfunctional in its rational use of manpower and talent.

Thus it is appropriate to close this description of the educational system with a look at the junior colleges, since they represent one of its newest and probably most dynamic factors, and at the same time offer one of the best opportunities to evaluate the system's strengths and weaknesses.

Junior Colleges

The history of the junior colleges appears, at first glance, to be the most direct expression of the broad movement of contest mobility that runs throughout the American educational system. In contrast to the liberal arts colleges, they, at least, seem to be both anti-elitist institutions open to all (since they are community colleges that do not impose on students and their families the high cost of residence) and also the place where technical and general education come together. They thus avoid a separation that is characteristic of European countries, where the bourgeoisie erected barriers around access to the higher professions.

Moreover, the junior colleges have developed most rapidly in the Middle West and the West. Although the first two-year colleges are much older, and private (Monticello College, 1835; Susquehanna University, 1858), the real birth of the junior colleges dates from the creation of Joliet College in Illinois in 1901, a creation encouraged by Harper. But it is California, where the first junior college was created at Fresno in 1910, that took the lead in the movement, passing in 1917 the law that organized this kind of

education in the most ample way. Missouri and Minnesota established junior colleges in 1915, Kansas and Oklahoma in 1919,
Arizona and Iowa in 1920, and Texas in 1921 (Blocker et al., 1965).
Today, California alone accounts for one-third of all junior college enrollment, and six states—California, Illinois, Michigan,
New York, Florida, and Texas—account for two-thirds. The movement has thus partly spread from the West throughout the country,
but it still remains very unevenly implanted. The rate of growth,
already strong between the world wars, has recently picked
up. Enrollment was 748,619 in 1961; 1,292,753 in 1965; and
1,954,116 in 1968, distributed among some 1,000 institutions.
The American Association of Junior Colleges forecasts that the
number of students attending such schools will rise to 3 million in
1980, and the number of colleges to 1,200. At present, a new junior
college is opening every week.

These are community colleges attached to local communities.
Most often they start out as extensions of high school and are situated in the high school building itself. But little by little they gain
their autonomy, insofar as they carry out different functions. In
the first place, there is college preparation, which allows the students of these two-year colleges to follow a transfer program that
will admit them to a four-year college. In the second place, there
is professional training, especially related to the local job market.
Thus, Berkshire Community College of Pittsfield, Massachusetts,
specializes in electrical engineering, what with the presence in
Pittsfield of a large General Electric plant. But often the training
offered is extremely diversified, as, for instance, at Brooklyn Community College, where there are courses in electronics, dentistry,
nursing, and hotel management. Finally, there is adult education
that is both professional and general. Junior college courses in civic
and public affairs, general education, home and family living, and
recreational skills accounted in 1957 for half the adult education
enrollment in the country.

Junior colleges are attached to the community by their organization and even more by their students, not only because they live in
the community, but because they often work there as well; 57 percent hold part-time jobs. Work and studies are combined or alter-
nated by many of these students, who are frequently older than the
average and take advantage of evening courses rather than going to
school full time. These colleges are almost always public. The
private ones are of slight importance, and their share of student

enrollment is constantly diminishing. Expenses are low and sometimes tuition is free; in any case, it does not exceed $400 to $500.

The evolution of these colleges, which initially developed around transfer programs, confirms the preceding observations. They are more and more comprehensive, responding to the community's most diverse demands. It follows that they readily express an ideology replete with democratic optimism: "The basic function of public education should be to provide educational opportunity by teaching whatever needs to be learned to whoever needs to learn it, whenever he needs to learn it" (ibid., p. 32).

These words recall those used by Ezra Cornell almost a century earlier.

Throughout an entire century, the same enthusiasm has led first to the creation of a few high-level academic centers; then, between wars, to the development of many state universities, infused, particularly in Wisconsin, with the same modernist and democratic spirit; and finally, in the contemporary period, to the widespread growth of junior colleges, which bring two million students, more or less young, into active participation in the academic system and in the economic functioning of a highly modern society.

This dynamism, which seems to meet nothing that might stop it or slow it down, is the most important fact, bearing witness as it does to the central role of education in the culture of American society. Progress in education appears, not as the result of the work of an administration, but as the responsibility of everyone and of all representative institutions. State and local governments have thus generously and most often enthusiastically poured out immense sums for colleges, which are their pride and joy. It is indeed the local community that runs the junior college, controlling it professionally and socially. Its teachers, whose work load is heavy, do not form a community of scholars; they are civil servants of education, and the local authorities take a very dim view indeed of any ideas or behavior in conflict with the standards favored by community leaders.

But it is not enough to speak in such general terms of the tight links between the junior college and the community, nor simply to recognize that the class composition of the vast majority of junior colleges contrasts sharply with that of the elite institutions (Clark, 1960*b*). At Stanford 87 percent of the students come from upper white-collar families, at San Jose State College 45 percent of the students come from blue-collar families, and at San Jose City College 62 percent of the students come from categories below the white-collar level. At Henry Ford Community College, 67 percent of the students come from families of skilled, semiskilled, and unskilled workers. But students who come from the lowest strata are also those who receive the poorest education, so that these colleges are not an instrument of social mobility.

In reality neither the overall optimism displayed by politicians and administrators nor the pessimism suggested by that last remark seem acceptable. The reality is more complex. Examined more attentively, junior colleges appear not as a unified and integrated milieu, but rather as the meeting ground of opposing tendencies that indicate that the links between the college and society are not what they appear to be at first sight. In fact, the transfer program, the first to have been created, attracts two-thirds of the students, especially those who in high school followed an academic rather than a vocational program, as Blocker, Plummer, and Richardson show in the following table (1965, p. 116).

Junior college program	General academic program	Vocational program	Total
Transfer	74.8	25.2	100
Terminal	56.1	43.9	100

There existed in 1958 only 144 colleges that were purely technical institutes. Between the two types of curricula there is a sharp difference in prestige. Often vocational training is reserved for students who seem the least promising (*Report on Higher Education,* 1971, pp. 57–60).

On the whole, the students belong to the group oriented toward transfer and want to identify with college students in general. The students who do transfer into four-year colleges do just as well in relation to their aptitude as students who did their first two years in the four-year colleges (Knoell & Medsker, 1965). The difference between the two is thus not to be defined by the students' scholastic characteristics, but by their respective degree of participation in the ideology of the academic system.

Actually, the intended transfer often fails to materialize. At Everett Junior College in Everett, Washington, about 80 percent of the students choose the transfer program, but only about 47.3

percent carry it out. Whatever the program, there is a significant proportion of dropouts. The attraction exercised by the four-year colleges and the bachelor's degree—which are much more highly regarded than the junior college degrees of Associate in Arts or in Sciences—indicates the hold of the dominant model over the junior colleges, a hold that is ideologically reflected in the theme of social advancement. Technical occupations are socially inferior. The prestige of a profession is related to the extent of its involvement, real or symbolic, in decision making. The state of the market and union organization may see to it that many skilled workers reach a salary level higher than that of employees adorned with B.A.'s. Nevertheless, students are still attracted to the administrative professions, mainly because they are more directly attached to the ladder leading to the most stable and remunerative positions, which offer the finest possibilities for promotion. It is significant that the working class is not taken into consideration by this predominant vision of society. Vocational training is carried on largely outside of the school system: approximately 50 percent of the expenses for vocational and technical training are covered by the trainees' firms themselves. The educational system is relatively unconcerned about what Georges Friedmann has called "the humanism of work." The society to which the educational system tries to correspond is not the entire society, but rather the upper part of the pyramid that goes from the rulers at the top down to the subalternate ranks of the service class.

What is more, the academic system exercises its direct influence with an eye toward that limited role. With the increasing production of Ph.D.'s, a growing number come to teach in junior colleges and have a tendency to disseminate there a diluted version of the academic culture produced at higher levels. State colleges and state universities are afraid of the competition that the junior colleges might represent and thus are interested only in the transfer programs. Many observers go further and suggest that these forces tend to turn junior colleges into buffer institutions whose general purpose is to maintain the selectivity and excellence of the higher levels. This is what Clark has called the "cooling-out" function of these colleges (1960a). Essentially this function prevents the formation of a pedagogic environment capable of devising aims and standards that are different from those of higher institutions. The students of these colleges are kept on the bottom level of a system that thereby defends itself against controversy.

Jencks and Riesman (1968) go further still. They note that junior colleges are a lesser burden to public treasuries than residential colleges, that the social level of their students is often no lower than in state colleges, and that consequently the role they play is as much that of a brake to descending mobility as an aid to rising mobility. The higher standing of the transfer programs is reinforced by the desire of middle-class families to provide their least brilliant children with a roundabout way back to the royal road of the B.A.

Jencks and Riesman conclude, "It is not primarily an alternative model for other colleges or an alternative path to the top for individuals but rather a safety valve releasing pressures that might otherwise disrupt the dominant system (ibid., p. 492). Thus, the junior colleges represent the tail, "lacking in much if any aliveness," in what Riesman calls "the snakelike procession" of the academic system (1956, pp. 241–262).

Imaginative pedagogy is in fact fairly unusual in junior colleges, although not altogether nonexistent. In part, the instruction fulfills the function of preparing a certain number of students for further studies and thus for greater independence from their original background. On the other hand, in the name of this liberal pattern, it accepts a definition of itself only in terms of its low level of participation in the cultural system, and thereby drops the possibility of becoming a place that could foster sensitivity and generate new demands on society.

The links that bind the junior colleges to the local community, or rather to local community leaders, thus do not have the effect of giving to that kind of instruction any real originality. On the contrary, it is the state, and especially the federal, government that has taken on the defense of technical and vocational training, otherwise extremely neglected. The Vocational Education Act of 1965 and its completing amendments in 1968 greatly increased the subsidies to vocational schools. Unfortunately this brought about the rapid development of technical and vocational schools by sector, setting them apart from the community colleges, who then abandoned their all-purpose curricula and often entered into competition with them.

To this transformation is added another, which also reduces the power of local authorities: In a number of states—including Colorado, Massachusetts, Virginia, Minnesota, and Oklahoma—there has recently been a marked tendency to organize the administration of junior colleges on the state rather than on the local level.

In all probability, however, junior colleges will continue to develop. The time is past when they aroused the suspicion of the four-year colleges (Medsker, 1960). They have taken their place in a general stratification of education, first significantly exemplified by the California Master Plan. Their success appears to most as proof that the large majority of young Americans can have access to higher education (Carnegie Commission, 1970*b*). But that rise in the "academic standard of living" is readily—and wrongly—taken for democratization. In reality, democratization is much better served by a number of bolder initiatives—by the creation of open-door four-year colleges, which, in endeavoring to suppress social barriers at the entrance to college must transform themselves in order to adapt the transmission of knowledge to students of diverse social and cultural backgrounds.

The junior colleges, far from being a democratizing force, are on the contrary the best example of extended participation in a system defined by its summit and by the needs of the social elite.

Is one to say that one's society is becoming more democratic because a growing number of its inhabitants now have the "right" to work in large corporations or to live in big cities?

Reproduction of the Social Order

This chapter seems to have gone beyond the chronological limits that I set for it at the beginning, since in considering the colleges I have not hesitated to follow them right up to their most current situation. But the unity here is not chronological. My aim has been to define an educational system that, as Riesman has said, has a unity—a unity in the sense that there is no essential difference between the best university colleges and the most mediocre junior colleges. The main function of the system is the fusion of society and the reinforcement of the social hierarchy. At its head the theme of general education aims to consolidate the ruling elite; at its tail the community colleges must above all release the pressure that could build up against the medium-level institutions and assure, not just the transfer of the best students, but the maintenance of the system as a whole. The ties that bind the academic system to society are not of the same nature here as in the major centers that were formed and transformed in the final decades of the nineteenth century. They are also different from those established by the development of research. American society, in the imprecisely delimited period that we have just examined, does not invent a new social and cultural model. It is already constituted as a national society. The cultural model of progress no longer has the creative force that it had in the preceding period; it is more and more an ideology in the service of the established order rather than a factor in the creation of a new social order.

The formation of large corporations is already far advanced, certainly, but the importance of science and technology has not yet transformed academic activity. What unifies the various aspects of academic life brought together in this chapter is the central importance of education, which in reality amounts to the reproduction of the social order. Elitist colleges as well as junior colleges belong to a system of education that puts everyone in his place: it makes rulers and leaders out of young men from the upper strata and employees out of those who come from a lower background, and at the same time maintains the vast majority of blacks in a limited and subalternate vocational and social existence.

The educational system that we have just studied is first of all an ideological system. It is defined by its aims of social integration much more than by its innovative role, at once dominating and critical. The three functions that I pointed out in the beginning, instead of forming a hierarchy from the first to the last—from cultural creation to adaptation to change to integration of the social organization—seem to rank the other way around: social integration dictates adaptation to change, which dictates a cultural creation that is no longer anything more than an ideological creation.

Within this system there are important differences between various types of colleges and students. The best-known analysis of these differences is that of Clark and Trow (1966). Their typology is defined by the crossing of two variables: strong or weak identification with the college and strong or weak involvement with ideas. Four main types result:

Type of institution	Involvement with ideas	Identification with college
Academic	Strong	Strong
Nonconformist	Strong	Weak
Collegiate	Weak	Strong
Vocational	Weak	Weak

But the authors hasten to add that it is not a matter of purely individual differences among students. Each campus favors, often quite consciously, one or several of these behavior types. But then the kinds of variables used appears inadequate and the very nature of the typology ambiguous: do the definitions apply to situations or behavior? A choice must be made between a psychosociological approach and an analysis of the functions of the academic system.

The observations presented in this chapter can be summarized by a typology of student behavior considered as a response to an academic system. The analysis of the latter should start with two principles of internal differentiation.

On the one hand, the academic system distinguishes and separates the mass from the elite. The unity of this system is not based on equalization or fusion, but rather on ranking. The latter is both social and academic. Elite is excellence: those who occupy ruling positions must also have general ideas; those who will have particular jobs to carry out should receive a more narrowly vocational training.

On the other hand, the system sees to both the production and the reproduction of the social order. The mass, like the elite, participates in the functioning and in the changes of a system of production, and, more generally speaking, in the changes of social activity. At the same time, the academic system assures the maintenance of a social distance between the two classes.

This leads us to propose the following typology:

	Elite	Mass
Production of the social order	Creativity	Integration
Reproduction of the social order	Elitism	Exclusion

The students who come from the mass are incorporated into the lower levels of the system of production. They are given a vocational training. While in college they are like people who must walk fast on a conveyor belt moving in the opposite direction just to stay in the same place and not fall behind. This situation often imposes on them a hyperconformism, a desire to participate in a campus culture that they meet only in an inferior form. At the same time, the academic system must eliminate the pressure that the mass could exert. Thus, one of its functions is repressive, showing up first in the limitation of the perspective offered to the mass of students, but also, more brutally, in the expulsion mechanism. Dropouts are not a psychological category; they exist because of a social mechanism, for it is not by chance that the colleges where teaching is at the highest level—the best private colleges—have the lowest drop-out rate. The aim is not to eliminate a part of the elite but to lessen the pressure from the mass.

For the elite, the college fulfills a function of socialization. Fraternities have traditionally been important in this respect, although their influence has been on the wane since Woodrow Wilson attacked the eating clubs at Princeton early in the century. Nowadays, social elitism is increasingly combined with a serious attitude toward work. Nevertheless, it remains distinct from the call to creativity; the social elite should be capable of innovation, which assumes an ascetic upbringing and the constraints of competition. The best American colleges, like the French Grandes Ecoles and their preparatory classes, combine insistence on effort and on an innovative capacity that implies a certain degree of deviation in relation to established conduct; at the same time, symbols of belonging to the elite must be maintained.

At the two extremities of this schema, the forces of rupture can appear. On the one hand, when exclusion is stronger than integration it can lead to revolt. We have seen that black students were torn between these two tendencies, but that as victims of segregation and other forms of discrimination they were led to reintroduce their desire for integration inside a revolt against the exclusion that oppresses them.

On the other hand, the call to creativity can break off from elitism and turn back against the academic system and against the social system as a whole. I shall examine closely this line of conduct when I analyze the student movement and the role of radical groups.

The Clark and Trow typology is not without interest, for it usefully describes types of behavior whose differences seem indeed quite clear. But it seems to me dangerous to consider the academic system as the meeting between intellectual life and an institution. The academic system can only be defined, especially in regard to its educational role, by its function in a society that is at once both a system of production and a system of social relations.

To analyze the system on the basis of this definition is all the more indispensable in that the system itself is unwilling to undertake such an analysis. It likes to speak of its values and its "spirit" and thus to consider only the relationships between those values and their institutional expression, the college. Clark and Trow are disturbed at the triumph of vocationalism that seems to them to weaken the importance both of collegiate culture—a development they welcome—and academic culture. But the American academic system has never been dominated by vocational culture. Moreover, the silence of the universities in the period after World War I was not due to narrow professionalization but to the triumph of an ideology that saw the university not as a critic of the social, but as its recruiting sergeant.

The silent generation is the final product of this system. American society, self-satisfied, concerned with defining itself by its values rather than by the nature of its class relationship, its power, and its exclusion, readily identifies order with progress, essence with existence. Its dynamism and power develop its academic organization, more vast and diversified than that of any other country, but its universities and colleges are only one element in the overall system by which the society functions. It is only in a few elite institutions that discordant voices are raised, and the counterprojects that they put forward seem linked more to the past than to the future. The majestic campuses remain for all intents and purposes isolated from urban problems, from working-class life as well as from conditions of the minority ethnic groups. Academic liberalism is also a kind of submission to the social order, in a more direct and narrow way at the bottom of the pyramid, in a more complex way at the top.

Alumni and political and economic figures contemplate with satisfaction an education that is primarily defined as a socialization process and that brings to a young America the conspicuous consumption of the ruling classes. Confident enough of their leading role to trouble to surround it generously with symbols, ceremonies, and rites, these classes present themselves as the heirs to the history of Western civilization. The decline of the great European nations lends still more luster to the American success story. After having been attached to the rise of modern capitalism, the academic system becomes the guarantor of bourgeois culture and society.

This conclusion contradicts the academic ideology that insists on the equalization of opportunity, the continuity between stratification and social mobility, the absence of barriers. In closing, however, we must take care to avoid a misunderstanding. The academic system, even during this period, did not superimpose a system of castes. Assuredly, at the summit social recruitment is very selective, and the educational conceptions are elitist. One may wonder what would be the real value of a caste education in a rapidly changing capitalist society. But at Harvard or at Yale it is by no means a matter of caste education, and the rapidly growing importance of scarcely selective state universities during this period is a reminder that American society is "open." The academic system is obviously much more open than in Europe, for secondary education does operate as a social barrier, and right in the colleges is to be found quite a variety of educational levels, as was mentioned in the preceding chapter.

But why should one have to choose between two equally extreme and equally unacceptable conclusions: the system is open or the system is closed?

The point lies elsewhere. The academic system, I repeat, not as a whole, but from the point of view adopted in this chapter—that is, considering mainly the dominant traits of academic ideology during the first half of the twentieth century—functions as a mechanism for the maintenance of social distances. The fact that the content of each element is transformed and the relations between the elements are themselves modified does not alter that fundamental function. This proposition does not imply the establishment within the academic system of an airtight compartment reserved for the elite and another reserved for the masses, without communication between them. There is no such form of separation.

But the unity of the system is not that of a harmoniously concerted organization, defined, above all, in terms of the interests and ideology of the dominant class. Liberal pragmatism often gives the impression of being an ideology opposed to that of the elite. Actually its role is merely to define the system's middle ground, a level occupied by the bureaucrats who carry out policies that emanate from the decision-making centers. The system as a whole is not the scene of any debate between opposing interests or ideologies. The system is open, diversified, and somewhat flexible; but that is not in contradiction with its class function. Is economic growth incompatible with the domination of a class?

What I cannot accept would be the reduction of the academic system to the single function of social reproduction. Even during the period under consideration, the presence of the two other levels of reality and analysis should not be forgotten. The professionalization of the faculty promises to stir up new problems, creating a distance between many of them and the dominant pedagogic ideology. Moreover, the themes and the realities of the era of "progressivism" have not entirely disappeared.

Above all, I think that the functions of social production are more and more important and that for all intents and purposes they are what explain the recent academic crisis. But, for all that, it would be a mistake to underestimate the sharpness of what can be called the "academic reaction" of the great colleges of this period, the solidity of social inequalities, and finally, most of all, the job of hierarchic differentiation carried out by the academic system.

4. *Power and Professors*

THE ACADEMIC SYSTEM

The aim of this chapter is to show the deep change in the academic system—at least in its main centers—that resulted from the appearance and rapid development of organized research. The massive influx of research funds, especially in the natural sciences and the medical field, accelerated the professionalization of the majority of professors and consequently diminished the importance of their educational role. The orientation of the preceding period is now reversed: The academic system is less concerned with the reproduction of the social order and participates much more directly in its production. This is due to the central role played by science and technology in the economic development and the political power structures of the great contemporary societies.

Introduction: Growth and Integration of Higher Education

Before expanding on these general propositions, mention should be made of an objection that comes naturally to mind. Aren't we going too far in establishing a qualitative difference between two stages of the academic system? Should we not stress instead the continuity of its development, and assume that any new aspect of its functioning should be reinserted in the general trend of higher education toward progress and universalization? This objection does serve to remind us of some important points. First of all, it is worthwhile to recall once again that the expansion of the academic system is not a new development, and above all that it cannot be explained solely by the progress of research. It is useful to look at the overall picture of the recent years to better understand the context in which research efforts develop.

The number of students increased from 1.6 million in 1940 to 3.7 million in 1960 and 7.8 million in 1969.[1] From 1953–54 to

---

[1] Rivlin and O'Neill (1970). The figure for 1970 is 8.5 million. This does not include 1.5 million students in technical or professional schools that didn't receive accreditation.

1966–67, while the population in the 18 to 21 year age group increased only by 55 percent and the number of high school graduates by 94 percent, the number of undergraduate students working toward a degree increased by 155 percent, the number of graduate students by 200 percent, and the number of nondegree students, enrolled mainly in the junior colleges, by 380 percent.

This expansion of the student population corresponds to an increase in the size of the colleges and universities, although the actual number of institutions grew only from 1,871 in 1953–54 to 2,382 in 1966–67. The number of colleges with less than 1,000 students has, in fact, decreased (1,424 in 1953–54; 1,167 in 1967–68), but there was an even more significant decrease in the proportion of the total student population represented by these small colleges of good or, more often, mediocre quality. The average size of academic institutions is growing: The average student population of public institutions was 5,556 in 1969, 78 percent more than in 1960, and 1,438 for the private sector, 29 percent more than in 1960. The public universities, keystone of the academic system, had an average student population of 23,000 in 1969.

The growth of the public sector, as I have already pointed out, is three times as great as that of the private sector, but this rapid growth is due mainly to the junior colleges, which represent one-fourth of the total enrollment. In 1966–67, the private sector represented no more than 34 percent of the student population but was still using 41 percent of the resources. The influx of private donations increased considerably, thanks to the launching of large-scale campaigns, engineered with particular success by Harvard. But we should not be misled by these results. Some elite institutions can still devote their energies to running a good college, with high tuition fees partly offset by scholarships. Others, thanks to their high intellectual standards and their prestige, receive both considerable funds for education and sizable federal grants for research. The remaining private institutions survive with difficulty or are gradually driven from the market.

Except for a few liberal arts colleges with very high standards and respected traditions, it can be said that the quality of education is closely related to the amount of research activity, or, more generally speaking, that the educational system is guided less by ideas about education than by the requirements of production and of the labor market.

The figures reported above show clearly both the lively growth of the demand for education at every level and the ability of the American society to answer this demand. Figures, however, are not enough to bring to light the main phenomenon whose background I have described in detail: the organization of an academic system which, in a relatively well-coordinated manner, assumes the responsibility of preparing students to participate—at various levels, within the framework of a culture and of a system of class relations—for the roles that are characteristic of a technological society.

This observation should indeed head this chapter, for its importance equals that of the spectacular progress of research. Other industrialized nations have also experienced a considerable development of research. This is especially true of the Soviet Union, and, to a lesser degree and rather belatedly (except in the case of Great Britain), of the main European nations and of Japan. But nowhere (again except in Great Britain) was the unity of the academic system preserved and even strengthened.

The case of the Soviet Union offers the greatest contrast with that of the United States. First, the Russian tradition of an academy of sciences was preserved and led to the constitution of a huge research organization essentially distinct from the universities. The other European countries ruled by Communist parties conform to the same pattern. Second, there is in the Soviet Union a much clearer boundary than in the United States between full-time students and those, much more numerous, who, in various patterns, combine work and study.

Separation of higher education from research is also an outstanding feature of the French academic organization, which is the least integrated of all. Indeed, it consists of four elements, more or less loosely interconnected, depending on the field of knowledge: the universities, which are responsible for training members of the traditional professions, teachers, and supervisory personnel (especially for administrative functions); the higher schools and all the engineering schools, which train executives for technical, economic, and administrative management, as well as technical supervisory personnel; the great higher education institutions, such as the Collège de France, the Museum d'Histoire Naturelle, and the Ecole Pratique des Hautes Etudes, which combine high-level education with research; and finally, the research organizations, of which the main one, the Centre National de la Recherche Scientifique, is rather closely linked to the universities, while others, of civilian or military status, are largely independent of higher education. A peculiar form of organization, where the universities play a relatively minor role in the research effort, especially outside the fields of natural science and mathematics.

This extreme example brings out all the more clearly the originality of the American system. Regardless of the importance of non-academic agencies of research and technological development in this country, the universities are indeed at the center of the research apparatus. Higher education and research are closely linked.

In this sense it would be a mistake to say that the development of research broke down the previous academic system. In many respects it rather strengthened it, as we shall see concretely when we study the use of federal funds.

My purpose, therefore, is not to describe a specific sector of intellectual and scientific activity in the United States; it is, rather, to understand the changing place of the academic system in American society at a time when a type of production is developing in which science and technology play the central role. This change does not represent a break in American academic history. In fact the rupture is even less marked than that between the first and second periods I have described, since, at the time of the First World War, there was a genuine upsurge of criticism against the earlier state of the colleges and universities. A qualitative change did occur, however, that is closely related to a new state of the American society.

Knowledge and Social Use of Knowledge

When an academic system is loosely integrated, each of its elements may seem to be determined by its own logic. While one of these elements answers the demands of the labor market, another transmits a cultural image, still another is subjected to the requirements of scientific research or the demands of the state, and so forth.

Consequently, tension tends to develop between each of these elements and the sector of social life to which it is related, for the academic system has no dynamics of its own, no internal power to manage or make decisions about its relations with its environment. For example, vocational training appears outdated, and scholastic culture is outdistanced by the culture transmitted through the mass media and the peer group. In the most extreme case, the academic or school system ceases to exist, and education can be analyzed entirely from the outside. The school is merely the place where a society and a culture—and especially class relationships—are reproduced.[2]

The American case is quite different. In France centralization and state control actually conceal the breakup of the system, but in the United States the decentralization and diversity are the means of unifying the system. As a result, the problems of American society are not directly reflected in higher education. They are reinterpreted by the academic system in its own terms. It would be just as mistaken to assert that this system is isolated and rationally organized around its own values as to break it up into parts assumed to correspond to given social categories or special social interests. In the following analysis I will examine successively:

1   The place of knowledge in society, particularly the role of knowledge as a productive force, and the dependence of the pattern of research activities on the cultural model of the society and on the role of the state.

2   The tensions between the various elements of the academic organization, the tensions that reflect the antagonism between the various cultural and social orientations of the society.

3   The reasons why the academic system occupies an increasingly central place in the society.

4   The forces of integration of the academic system.

The academic system, especially scientific knowledge, plays a double role in society, the confusion between the two roles being a cause of great misunderstanding. Today, the academic world has a singular opportunity to develop a new model of knowledge. But it is also an organization—or a set of organizations—or, as it is sometimes described, an institution that fulfills various social roles. Thus its functioning presents problems similar to those of other big organizations. The professors often think that these two roles are really one, that there is no difference between the scientist and the professor, and that the entire university is inspired by the superior value of the development of rational knowledge.

[2] The most recent book on the French school (Baudelot & Establet, 1971) provides an extreme and very interesting example of this type of analysis. According to the authors, the French school system has no other reality than that of preserving the existence of two totally segregated schools—one for the bourgeoisie and one for the people—whose function it is to maintain the domination of one class over another.

Conversely, when political protest spreads in the universities, these professors often feel, quite rightly, that the specific problems of the production of scientific knowledge are being neglected.

Knowledge as "infrastructure" of society

It should therefore be kept in mind, first of all, that the production of knowledge is not comparable to the production of marketable goods and services. This reminds us particularly of the fact that scientific "ideas" are not the property of the scientist and are not protected by any patent.

Every society constructs what Serge Moscovici has called a "state of nature," that is to say, it organizes its knowledge in terms of certain categories.

Any mode of scientific construction always plays a unifying intellectual role. When a society is not firmly established in a "state of nature," the concern for method seems to be less important than the concern for content. Today, on the contrary, we are witnessing a lively upsurge of methodological research as well as the integration of a large number of different contents within the same general approach. The General System Theory, for example, is an attempt to define such a general approach, embracing many of the human sciences, from biology and linguistics to the behavioral sciences and economics. This work toward the unification of knowledge progresses more easily in an academic world that is itself integrated, where interdisciplinary relations are facilitated, and where a concern for general methodological training exists. But there is no proof that such integration can be more easily achieved in an aggregated and planned academic system. Experience seems to show, on the contrary, that integration is facilitated by the existence of ill-defined marginal sectors, more conducive to intellectual encounters not anticipated in previous patterns.

We should not, therefore, accept too readily the image of a world of knowledge with a pyramidal organization, where the basic research carried out at the top results almost automatically in applied research and development.

A model of knowledge goes together with society's ability to act upon itself, which is inseparable from the type of accumulation and the type of representation of this capacity for change, and is also inseparable from conflicts for the control of the production of change.

Any society, once it attains a given level of accumulation and therefore possesses some capacity for self-transformation, is inspired by a particular image of this creative capacity. If the action of the society upon itself is weak, if most of its productivity is used to reproduce its own conditions of existence, this creativeness is grasped only as a principle, as a potentiality that is never realized. It is represented as a transcendant logos. Conversely, a society that withdraws from consumption a significant part of its resources and devotes them to accumulation, grasps its own creativeness as a praxis and not as a logos. It is no longer oriented toward a model of order but toward a model of movement. The god of our society is not the creative principle of the natural order, but economic and social development, and, even more concretely, growth. Science is then no longer only a model of knowledge, but a cultural model, a set of social directives for the use of accumulated resources. One society builds research centers and universities as another builds cathedrals or palaces.

The role of the state
The main condition for this development is the existence not only of a modernistic ruling class but also of a state capable of enforcing the application of this cultural model. The upper class is the social category responsible for the management of the cultural model and identifies its special interests with its materialization. But those who are dominated struggle against this identification, and in doing so invoke the same cultural model that they are trying to wrest from the hands of the ruling class. This complex struggle may lead to the weakening of the cultural model, torn between these conflicting private interests.

We can easily imagine a postindustrial society where the ruling class is more concerned with the accumulation of its own power than with scientific development and where the formerly dominated class strives, above all, to maintain its position against the consequences of development. The Stalin-type society, for example, displays many features of this kind. There are numerous political and ideological obstacles to scientific development, and the bureaucracy, the brakes, the extreme viscosity of the labor force are so many defense mechanisms.

For science to become a principle of development and of social change, the opposite tendencies must prevail. In other words, there must be a new ruling class that is primarily concerned with the promotion of the cultural model upon which it relies in its struggle against the old ruling class it is trying to replace. At the same time, the lower classes must have enough confidence in the future and in their political influence to oppose the barriers raised by private interests (including those of public agencies) and to demand the development of science or of another cultural model.

But such a condition, which guarantees the greatest possible autonomy for the cultural model, implies the existence of an area where the positive claims of the ruling class and of the people can be integrated—that is, a state apparatus both closely linked to the ruling class and open to the demands of the lower classes.

This is essentially what happened in the United States, and it is the real meaning of the unity established and maintained in this country between scientific research and education. The progress of research is inseparable from the authority of the great industrial, administrative, and military apparatuses that turn it into profit or, more generally speaking, into power. At the opposite end, the popular demand for participation in development is expressed through the importance attributed to education, which opens the doors to scientific and technological knowledge.

In the United States this unity between research and education was expressed by the significant fact that the influx of federal funds, first used to support research as an element of military and economic power, was also and increasingly directed to the improvement of education at all levels. But research and education can be separated from each other. The classical capitalist class, seeking profits on the market and perpetuating a particular type of economic functioning, can act against the interests of research. In fact, many of the biggest corporations use a significant part of the national resources to increase their profits, either failing to promote technological progress or diverting it from its main objectives. At the same time, political or trade-union demands can also put the brakes on economic changes that threaten vested interests.

Such obstacles may become much greater if the hold of the ruling class on the scientific and technological apparatus provokes a violent defense reaction. In that case consumption, equilibrium, and individual and community welfare prevail over an investment effort apparently aimed exclusively at strengthening the apparatus of economic, political, and military domination. Such a description fits at least one meaning of the current academic crisis. We shall return to it later.

Tensions Between the Orientations of the Academic System

We have just examined the first aspect of the production of knowledge, perhaps the most basic because it is the most "conscious" — the aspect concerning investment in scientific knowledge and the social relationships that determine it.

But the academic system participates in society in many other ways. Various social and cultural orientations are expressed within it, as within any big organization. Any society, as it produces, must determine the forms of work organization or decision, the ways it will distribute its products, and its models of consumption. It is not my intention here to make a general analysis of these four sectors and their interrelations. I merely wish to point out that they are sufficiently differentiated for their basic orientations to be quite distinct.

Our society is oriented toward development, but also toward consumption; toward flexibility and pragmatism in decision-making, but also toward new hierarchy principles that create new social barriers. To the extent that it is integrated, the academic system experiences internal problems born of the combination of these various functions, and therefore of the interdependence of different, if not conflicting, orientations. Let us then examine briefly not only the nature of the "consumption," the forms of hierarchy, and the modes of organization as they are manifested within the academic system and within the entire society, but also the tensions that exist among them.

Tension between development and identity

In the society of liberal capitalism, oriented toward a future that can be built by the productive forces, "needs" are expressed in terms of social mobility, which Balzac, in the sociological analysis that opens his novel *La fille aux yeux d'or,* called the money spiral. Consumption is experienced as a standard and as the effort to maintain and improve this standard.

This behavior pattern found its most complete expression in the United States, where the previous consumption models — to live according to one's "status" — did not have the same strength as in Europe. But in a society whose experience is no longer being built according to the evolutionist and historicist cultural model — where the future no longer gives meaning to the present, but appears, on the contrary, to be the result of decisions made in the present — this transformation of temporality finds expression in a radical change in consumption. In the face of development, and therefore of change, consumption is primarily a search for and a defense of identity; spending for enjoyment takes precedence over saving. This can be expressed either in a conservative way—by the defense of a petit bourgeois balance and of a local community spirit that is concerned with the integration of a homogeneous group and inclined to resort to segregation—or by a more exacting demand for personal and collective identity lodged against the ruling forces, their social power, and their capacity for cultural manipulation. Youth is particularly responsive to this search for identity and consequently opposes to the power structure and the apparatus linked to it the theme of education—the development and expression of the personality, conceived in its wholeness, that is, with the full depth of the unconscious.

It is primarily in the university, therefore, that the conflict is most manifest between the scientific and technological creativeness associated with the big technobureaucratic machines and the youth's personal and collective search for its identity.

Tension between education and meritocracy

To these two opposite poles of contemporary culture, others are added. For hierarchy in the new type of society can be based only on participation in the new type of accumulation and in the new growth factors, and therefore on learning and knowledge rather than on the ownership of capital. It is increasingly difficult to reach high positions in the big production and management apparatuses without the ability to deal with complex information—to compute, to organize, and to use study and programming techniques. Every higher technician becomes an analyst. The professionalization of every type of management reveals this necessary union of technological knowledge and the administration of the apparatuses. The students are not only increasingly trained to become the new mandarins of whom Noam Chomsky speaks, but they also become accustomed to finding within the university a production and training apparatus functioning as a big organization —this is true at least in some of its aspects, and especially in the sectors where organized research assumes the greatest importance.

The United States, however, is not the country where students, especially graduate students, are most completely incorporated into the production and management apparatus. The process has gone further in Japan, where the proportion of students preparing to enter the large corporations is much higher, and in the Soviet Union, where the close connection between the university and the political and economic apparatus is officially proclaimed. It is in the United States, therefore, that the tension between the instrumental and hierarchy-building function of the university and the students' search for personal and collective identity and expression is most strongly felt.

A last characteristic of this new society was analyzed long ago by its sociologists: The organization of work takes the shape of complex communication networks that are determined by objectives rather than rules. This is far removed from the Weberian model of bureaucracy, which corresponds in fact to an earlier situation, older even than industrial capitalism, and is related to the formation of a state bureaucracy in the mercantile societies. This bureaucratic model was replaced in the liberal society by the model of competition, of striving for maximal personal and group interests, and particularly by the constraints that capitalism and its executive agents imposed on productive labor.

In the postindustrial society, the organization of labor assumes the new form of the coordination of relatively autonomous elements within the framework of a complex strategy defined in terms of its objectives. In this case, as in that of the state bureaucracy, it was the army which first developed the new model of organization: Operation Overlord—the landing of Allied Forces in 1944—was the first spectacular application of methods that the English had begun to develop during the war.

It is not easy for this type of organization to make its way into the university, which is more comparable to the old state bureaucracy, because the university is based on principles (such as a curriculum and grades) and functions the access to which is controlled by examinations or by degree requirements. Thus the academic organization finds itself under attack from the "modernists," who would like to imitate the big firms and replace management through rules by management through objectives, as well as from those who oppose to these rules their own desire for free expression and community self-management.

The Central Place of the Academic System in the Society

In the preceding society—that of liberal industrialization—the university was not at the center of the cultural and social system. In that society, as in every other, contradictions and conflicts existed between the elements of the system, but they found their main expression in the area of the prevailing cultural model, that is, the area of the productive forces of the market and industrial labor. The university was linked to that cultural model (as I emphasized in my discussion of the major transformation of American universities at the end of the nineteenth century), but its place was only a marginal one in a society whose progress depended more on business than on knowledge, more on entrepreneurs than on managers. That is why the university could be so loosely integrated, and the respective worlds of students, professors, and administrators could coexist without really merging.

In the new society, the place of the university is a much more central one, because the production of knowledge is a much more important factor of social development. As a result, the university cannot avoid experiencing the tensions that arise among the basic orientations of our present society: scientific and technological creation, the search for identity, meritocracy, and management through objectives. To reduce these tensions, student life could be focused outside the university; flexible management through objectives could become the organizational principle of the research centers; the hierarchy-building function could find expression in separate institutions devoted to the preparation for various levels of participation in the technobureaucratic society; and scientific and technological creativeness could conceivably be concentrated in para-academic or extra-academic centers.

The American academic system has succeeded in avoiding these pseudosolutions and derives its greatness from the preservation of its unity. True, the United States, as we shall see, has established research and development agencies that, officially or in practice, are outside the university; moreover, a very clear differentiation is being created among institutions by the fact that a small number of them control most of the research funds. It is no less true that the geographic unity of the campus community has broken down and that an autonomous student life has taken shape outside the university: around Telegraph Avenue, next to the University of California at Berkeley; in Venice, somewhat farther from UCLA; or in Greenwich Village. But however significant these tendencies might be (and I shall try to describe them more accurately), the tensions analyzed above still manifest themselves mainly within the university. This is why the university in the United States, probably more than in any other industrially developed country, has become the seat of significant and lasting conflicts — a political arena.

The Integration of the Academic System What causes the actual unity of the academic system? What unifying forces integrate such diverse functions and orientations into an organizational whole? It might be assumed at the outset that this integration is limited, and that the only role of the university authorities is to manage necessarily unstable relations between inherently conflicting demands. I will discuss this idea, put forward by Kerr in particular, in the last part of this essay. But whatever our judgment about the role of the administration in contemporary universities, we are dealing with the subject in a different form now—since, because in the United States, no central apparatus for the management of the academic system exists. The unifying forces, if they do exist—and their existence can hardly be denied— must be sought out not at the level of the decision-making system of the colleges or the universities, but at a higher level, that of the power centers of the national society.

The academic system as a whole is driven and determined by its summit, by its head, to use Riesman's image. Indeed, the crisis was to break out at the head of the system, where the bulk of the research work is done and where the professors who will go out to teach in lower-level institutions are trained. The unity of the system derives primarily, then, from the role of the state, the main supplier of research funds and, therefore, the agent of change for the whole system. In other words, the system's unity derives from its role as producer of knowledge. I have already introduced this theme. As we examine the period that witnessed the student revolt, I will comment further on this role of the state in American society, for the student movement has directed most of its action against it, especially as it manifested itself in American imperialism in Vietnam and Latin America.

The American nation-state
The United States is no longer a wide-open economic and cultural field; it is primarily a state that plays a vital role in investments— especially those relating to technological development—and assumes a much more important international role than in the past, when this role was sufficiently limited for isolationism to be strong.

The basic fact is that the United States no longer defines itself by an image of its own creation. Until recently, the Americans liked to define themselves in relation to Europe as the son in relation to the father, the future in relation to the past. The young nation was justified in its own eyes by its ability both to break with the old social order—its injustices, its barriers, its poverty—and to take over the best of its cultural heritage. It killed its father to marry its mother. It rejected authority and hereditary class status and offered to its citizens coming from old Europe its wide-open spaces and the high wages peculiar to a society where labor was scarcer than space or capital. At the same time, it fostered education, morality, and religion. It was, in a way, like Rome, which attracted the intelligence and cultural resources of Greece and gave itself a universalist mission. Occasionally, some American intellectuals rejected the climate of old Europe, for they were very isolated and Europe did not represent for the American nation the image of "the other." This was all the more true since Europe itself saw in America the inspiring and disturbing image of a future it both desired and feared, as René Rémond showed in his study of the image of America in French thought at the beginning of the nineteenth century (Rémond, 1962). The reason why American social scientists like Tocqueville so much is that he justified the natural tendency of the Americans to identify with progress and modernity. The American conscience was not particularly troubled by Latin America either; these inferior cousins exhibited but a worn-out image of old Europe. Their very backwardness was an invitation to consider Latin America as a choice field for expansion, a special preserve where United States business enterprises, with the support of the Marines, could make valuable profits in the name of progress.

This enduring combination of brutal conquest and idealism is not peculiar to the United States; the French proved capable of taking it to the extreme. In carrying out a brutal colonial repression in Algeria, the social democratic government of France claimed it was waging the just struggle of lay universalism and the French Revolution against the backward provincialism of the Moslem world.

The situation changed when this American expansionism and idealism met "the other," that is, a powerful and threatening society based on a radically different social organization and dominant ideology. During the Stalin period, the conflict with the Soviet Union created no crisis of conscience for America. It led, rather, to greater national integration and to the elimination of the critical tendencies born during the Depression and encouraged by the Soviet-American alliance against fascism. But the United States was already becoming a nation-state, obliged to intervene in Berlin and in Korea, only to discover to its amazement in the fall of 1957 that the "barbarians" of the East were the first to conquer space.

An even more unprecedented situation was created by the war in Vietnam, started at a time when a president who was giving new dynamism to the American society revived the great American myth and gave a new face to imperialism, particularly in Latin America. An America more attached than ever to its own self-image found itself waging a war against what was most foreign to it—a nation led and inspired by a Communist party and able to mobilize its people to the fullest extent, despite the destructive action of bombs, chemical warfare, and corruption. This extraordinary national and social resistance provoked an unprecedented crisis in the American conscience. It forced the American nation to see itself as others saw it and to perceive itself as an inhuman aggressor rather than as the bearer of principles born of eighteenth-century enlightenment.

The nation realized that it was the instrument of the state and rediscovered within itself the reality of power—the combined power of the government, the military leaders, and big business and their academic auxiliaries.

It is clearly impossible to isolate the academic crisis from the more general political crisis caused not so much by the attack against Vietnam as by the failure of the aggression. The university can no longer be seen merely as a force for the production of knowledge and education; its links with the forces of social domination and with the state are challenged.

The role of cultural integration

But it cannot be claimed that the entire academic system has become a direct instrument of the technobureaucracy. Only a few big academic centers have established close links with the ruling political, economic, and military apparatus. On most campuses the majority of students are engaged in scientific, technical, or professional work, far removed from any contact with the ruling circles. There is nothing paradoxical in saying that I found on some of the best American campuses a more traditionalist spirit than in many European universities and schools.

Nineteenth-century England—the most modern country of its time—had embarked on industrial capitalism without political disruption, and for that reason had best preserved, especially at the top, the ways of life, the ideas, and the social relations inherited from the previous state of society. Education had played only a minor part in social change. In the same way, the United States, the most modern country of the twentieth century, which shifted from liberal capitalism to a technobureaucratic society without any violent political break, is also a society and a culture where the ways of life, the ideas, and the social relations inherited from the previous period are largely preserved. The European visitor is particularly struck by the sense of continuity in the United States, the many and frequent references to the past, the cults of eponymous heroes and of group values.

I tried to show in the preceding chapter how the strengthening of the social order and of the ruling class, before and after the First World War, had resulted in considerable academic efforts to develop a general education—a "general culture" based on the claim to a cultural heritage. Despite the new role conferred upon the university by scientific and technological progress, its production function did not replace its function of reproducing the social order. On the contrary, the two roles seemed to keep abreast of each other, just as the development of federal research funds kept abreast of the increase in private donations and of the interest of local communities in education. The outstanding progress of sociology in the United States and the for long, almost undisputed triumph of the view that society is a community based on values, a community where norms are created that in turn determine roles and modes of interaction—in other words of a purely idealistic view—testify to the role played by the university in strengthening the social order. Referring in particular to the behavioral sciences, J. Lacan calls them "orthopedic."

Some liberals and radicals on the one hand and some scientists distrustful of this ideological hold on the other did keep their distance from the prevailing ideology and greatly contributed to the intellectual creativeness of the American universities. However, it is no exaggeration to say that social and cultural integration around models inherited from the past has, in a lively and effective way, remained one of the essential characteristics of American university education. In the European universities, by contrast, heritage from the past is transmitted only in an ossified form that meets with nothing but indifference from the students.

As we shall see, education's predominant concern—to preserve liberal values and promote social integration—put the teachers in a difficult situation. Caught between two roles—the production and the reproduction of the social order—they tried to resolve this dilemma by taking refuge in professionalism and in a wishy-washy defensive conception of academic freedom. This dual aspect of the university also explains the complex student reactions and the penetration into the university of problems inherited from an earlier state of the society (especially those created by the near-exclusion from the academic world of those categories described by the deliberately vague term "minorities").

But before dealing with the various aspects of the academic crisis, we must first examine the changes in the university most directly associated with the increasing role of the state and the consequences of these changes on academic organization. We must look as well at the reactions of the professors, who are now an important professional category, acquiring prestige and material advantages, and who work at the heart of a system where research and education remain closely linked.

THE FEDERAL STATE AND THE UNIVERSITIES

The role of the federal state in the academic system is not new. At the beginnings of the republic, George Washington proposed the creation of a federal university (1796) and the Ordinance of 1787 stated: "Religion, morality and knowledge, being necessary to good government and the happiness of mankind, schools and the means of education should forever be encouraged" (Kidd, 1959, pp. 200–205). This text clearly shows that it is the role of the government to promote education and thus to further the ideals of independence.

In the following period, as we have seen, federal intervention was directed to the development of means of education designed to serve social progress. Let us recall the aims of the Morrill Act of 1862: "To keep such branches of learning as related to agriculture and the mechanical arts in such manner as the Legislature of the States may respectively provide in order to promote the liberal and practical education of the industrial classes in the several pursuits and professions in life."

But the federal government went no further than to promote agricultural and technical education by means of various laws. It hardly intervened in the basic organization of the academic system and, in the first decades of this century, the role of a national ministry of education was virtually played by the private foundations.

The New Deal period was marked by more active state intervention, but mainly in the context of a public works policy designed to give work to the unemployed. Administrations such as the Public Works Administration (PWA) and the Works Progress Administration (WPA) launched extensive university building programs, which, by March 1, 1939, resulted in construction totaling $20 million (Rivlin, 1961, pp. 28–40).

Federal Funds But a research policy was already under way with the creation of the National Research Council (Kidd, 1959) during the First World War and then, in 1933, of the Science Advisory Board, which created a Recovery Program of Science Progress. The founding of the National Cancer Institute in 1937 marked the beginning of organized medical research. During the Second World War, discovery of the technological advances made by the German Army led to the establishment of the National Defense Research Committee, headed by Vannevar Bush, and then, in 1941, to the creation of its successor, the Office for Scientific Research and Development, which embraced both the original committee plus another one devoted to medical research. Since important research institutes such as the Radiation Laboratory at MIT were already being established, this office decided from the outset not to create its own laboratories but to promote joint efforts by the federal government and the universities. The National Science Foundation, established in 1950, openly stated that its aim was to inspire research, not to direct it.

Whereas the first change was brought about by World War I, a political and scientific event, the launching of the first sputnik led to the more recent federal policy of massive aid for research and education. Up to 1957, large-scale state intervention had been concentrated on applied research, primarily on the development of the atom bomb, which mobilized theoreticians, experimentalists, and technologists in an unprecedented effort. With the launching of the sputnik, however, the United States came to understand the necessity for an overall educational policy. In November 1957, the post of Special Assistant to the President for Science and Technology was created and was filled by J. R. Killian, a former president of MIT who gave new life to the president's Science Advisory Council. A federal Council for Science and Education was also established. The hearings of the House Committee on Education and Labor, in which scientists like Lee DuBridge, Isidor Rabi, Wernher Von Braun, and Edward Teller played an essential role, led to the National Defense Education Act, signed by President Eisenhower on September 2, 1958. There was at that time a marked increase in federal expenditures for research and education, with the major portion of the increase coming from sources closely linked to the military. The creation of the National Aeronautics

	1952, %	1959, %
Department of Defense	73	36
Atomic Energy Commission	2	13
Department of Health, Education and Welfare	12	27
National Science Foundation	1	13
Department of Agriculture	10	10

TABLE 14
Source of federal funds allocated to universities

SOURCE: Kidd (1959, p. 47).

and Space Administration (NASA) in 1958 further increased the funds from military sources. But financing from other sources was also increasing rapidly. In fact, military expenditures spurred such a broad funding effort that their share of the total actually diminished (see Table 14).

These 1959 figures are misleading, however, for they should be supplemented by the expenditures for the support of research centers, 35 percent of which came from the Department of Defense and 65 percent from the Atomic Energy Commission. In 1960, federal subsidies totaled $1.5 billion, of which one-third was devoted to research centers, one-third to research carried out by the universities themselves, and one-third to scholarships, housings, and other special programs.

Federal funds for research represented 75 percent of the research expenditures of all universities and 15 percent of their total budget (Kerr, 1963). For recent years, the sources of these subsidies can be subdivided into three broad categories (ibid., p. 53):[3]

	Percentage
Military purposes (Department of Defense and Atomic Energy Commission)	40
Scientific purposes (National Science Foundation, NASA, Department of Agriculture)	20
National Institutes of Health	37

[3] In 1962, for example, according to Allan Cartter (1964, p. 58), the sources of federal research funds were as follows: Department of Health, Education and Welfare, $243.4 million; Department of Defense, $197.9 million; National Science Foundation, $59.3 million; Atomic Energy Commission, $52.3 million; Department of Agriculture, $35.6 million; NASA, $18.8 million; and other departments, $5.8 million.

Military expenditures clearly play a significant role. The establishment of a policy of massive aid to education and research is, in particular, directly related to the Soviet challenge and to the scientific and military competition between the two super powers, especially in the fields of atomic energy and the conquest of space.

This financial effort is not restricted, however, to research for military purposes. It also extends to the important fields of medical research and the general improvement of the educational system.

The increase in research funds to medical schools between 1947 and 1967 represents more than half the total increase in the resources of these schools during that 20-year period; federal funds represent 85 percent of this total (Fein & Weber, 1971). The National Institutes of Health bring to this sector a much more important contribution than that received by any other scientific field.

This largely explains the growth of medical school teaching staffs, the number of full-time teachers increasing from 3,577 in 1951 to 22,163 in 1967, and the number of part-time teachers from 11,971 to 44,000. It also explains why the number of those most directly involved in scientific work increased more rapidly than the number of medical students.[4]

In the field of general education, the federal effort antedated the great movement in support of academic research and teaching. It first assumed the form of massive aid to veterans, of which an important part was channeled to the colleges and universities (see Table 15).

TABLE 15 *Veterans utilizing various types of educational benefits (in thousands)*		*Vocational rehabilitation*		*Education and training*	
	Total	*World War II*	*Korean War*	*World War II*	*Korean War*
Institutions of higher education	3,435	152	22	2,200	1,166
Schools below college level	4,364	149	26	3,500	824
Apprentice, on-the-job, on-the-farm	2,656	312	14	2,100	312
TOTAL	10,455	614	62	7,800	2,302

SOURCE: Morse (1960, p. 67).

[4] Ibid. The number of M.D. candidates increased between 1951 and 1967 by only 31 percent, that of interns by 141 percent, of residents by 311 percent and of graduate students in the basic sciences by 223 percent.

The same concern for general aid to education can be observed in the National Defense fellowships, which numbered about 1,500 in 1960–61, with 27 percent going to the humanities, 30 percent to the social sciences, and only 10 percent to engineering.

Aid to students, which is often included in aid to research, goes mainly to graduate students. In 1962, for example, aid to students was distributed as follows:

	Amount
Graduate predoctoral (total)	$132,387,000
Postdoctoral fellowships	28,204,000
Undergraduates	5,046,000
Veterans	75,262,000
War orphans	16,400,000

SOURCE: Cartter (1964, p. 59).

International programs provide for sending Americans abroad and bringing foreigners to the United States.

But the distribution of funds is becoming increasingly diversified. The Higher Educational Facilities Act of December 1963 provided for a three-year expenditure program of $1.2 billion. Of this total, $230 million was intended for the building of classrooms, libraries, and laboratories, and 22 percent of this amount was earmarked for community colleges and technical institutes.

The natural and medical sciences are largely financed by federal funds. The social sciences, on the other hand, get a high proportion of their research funds from private foundations, especially from the Ford Foundation, which, from 1951 to 1957, spent $900 million, including $517 million for education and $70 million for the social sciences.

University budgets have been radically altered by the addition of these federal funds. Total expenditures of the entire academic system for organized research amounted to no more than $18 million in 1930 and $27.3 million in 1940. This total had increased to $225.3 million in 1950; $733.9 million in 1958; and, as we have seen, over $1 billion two years later.

The proportion of expenditures connected with resident instruction dropped from 44 percent in 1930 to 32.5 percent in 1958 (Machlup, 1962, p. 83). In 1964, Cartter listed the following sources of academic funds for 1961–62:

	Percentage
Tuition and fees	20.7
Federal government for research	15.3
Federal government for other purposes	3.6
State governments	22.9
Local governments	2.6
Gifts and grants	6.4
Other educational general income	9.4
Auxiliary enterprises income	17.5
Student-aid income	1.6

SOURCE: Cartter (1964, p. 34).

In some universities, however, the share for research is much greater.[5] At Harvard in 1962, research contracts accounted for about $31 million out of a total income of about $103 million. The case of MIT is even more extreme, research contracts accounting for $113.6 million out of a total budget of $137.3 million.

There is, indeed, a remarkably high concentration of research funds. In 1962, ten institutions received 38 percent of the federal funds (by order of importance: California, MIT, Columbia, Michigan, Harvard, Illinois, Stanford, Chicago, Minnesota, Cornell); 25 universities received 59 percent; and 90 percent were distributed among 100 institutions. Federal funds accounted, then, for more than 50 percent of the total expenditures of MIT, Stanford, Princeton, California Institute of Technology (Cal Tech), and the University of California at San Diego.

Finally, a certain number of laboratories are autonomous organizations, more or less loosely connected with universities. This is the case, in particular, for: Argonne National Laboratory (Chicago), Jet Propulsion Laboratory (Cal Tech), Lincoln Laboratory (MIT), and the Lawrence, Livermore, and Los Alamos Laboratories (California). Some research institutes originally connected with a university later became totally independent, like the Stanford Research Institute; others strengthened their links with the university, as did the Institute for Social Research of the University of Michigan. Every possible combination of university and institute or laboratory can be found. But in every case, financing the research projects of

[5] On the major sources of income of the best private universities, see Bowen (1968).

either the universities or the research institutes entails radical changes in academic administration. In some cases, nonprofit organizations are established, but more often the university itself assumes management responsibility, which strengthens its central administration (Kidd, 1959, pp. 155–171). At the University of California, control is very strict. The president has organized a special staff to examine the projects, which are then submitted to the regents. In other cases, there is less control.

The Management of Research

The main problem in the case of university projects, however, is the method of allocating subsidies. As a rule, the funds are given, not to an institution, but to a professor or a team. Consequently, the university's authority over the activities of many professors is weak, especially in fields where considerable funds are available. In medicine, for example, where the dean's authority is limited to education, the relations of a noted specialist with the National Institutes of Health and the big foundations are more important to him than his relations with the medical school administration. Some teachers become real entrepreneurs. Finally, the remuneration of many professors is directly or indirectly improved by the allocation of research funds.

It is not easy to describe clearly the whole pattern of these changes. Two seemingly conflicting trends emerge: On the one hand, the independence of the professors—one aspect of a general tendency towards professionalization that will be examined below—tends to weaken the university; on the other hand, there is a strengthening of the academic administration. But these tendencies can be reconciled if we observe that the universities, or at least the big scientifically oriented ones, are less and less units commanded by a general conception of education and more and more an administrative management apparatus. In this change, the main loser is the president, at least as he had been created by the period of the great reforms. Kerr's description of this change has become famous (1963). As conceived by Flexner, Hutchins, or Lowell, the president was the man whose vision counterbalanced the anarchistic tendencies of the professors. Now he can only be the coordinator or the manager, rather than the inspirer—the person who is capable, through his mediating action, of combining initiative and balance within the university. But we can also take a more pessimistic view and agree with Lazarsfeld (1962, pp. 751–756) that the decline of the president's role denotes, in fact, a power vacuum and an increased probability of a specifically political crisis within the university. The remarks of Edward Shils point in the same direction and expose "The hole in the center": "Intermediate deliberative and decision-making organs did not develop in the area left by the gradual ebbing of autocratic presidential power and the gradual swelling of departmental and individual power."[6]

The reduction of the president's power also results in a reduction of the power of the trustees, who, although they are the highest authority, lack the means, in most cases, of effectively intervening in the orientation of the university's scientific work (Corson, 1960, pp. 49–58). The great majority of university people undoubtedly look upon such a development as a normal and desirable one, for they reacted unfavorably to Ruml's reminder (Ruml and Morrison, 1959) to the trustees that they should really exercise their responsibilities.

Talcott Parsons has attempted to define university government in terms of concepts borrowed from the political system (Parsons, 1968, 173–197). He describes the students and the alumni as the constituency; the administration and the trustees exercise an executive power limited by the faculty, whose role is intermediate between that of a legislature and a judiciary. Let us assume we can leave aside the role of the students, which is a minimal one in the academic organization, since they do not vote and contribute only a small proportion of the funds. But how can we speak of an organized decision-making system when many significant decisions are made without any need for actual participation by the entire faculty or even by the president? It is almost as if a government department were receiving important funds from a foreign country without the need for any previous consultation with the cabinet.

Lazarsfeld's remarks seem to provide a better analysis of academic reality. It is true that the universities retained their place at the center of the research apparatus and that no complete separation occurred between education and research. But the universities cannot be said to have established a genuine research policy. Some, like Harvard, proved capable at least of laying down certain principles, such as refusing research projects whose results had to remain

---

[6] Edward Shils (1970), quoted in Carnegie Commission (1971*b*, p. 66). This report suggests a series of measures designed to re-create academic institutions and reform the government and judicial systems of the universities and colleges.

secret. But it cannot really be said that any university actually chose to engage in one type of research rather than in another. This absence of power and planning led to many favorable results. On the one hand, it left considerable freedom of initiative to the laboratories, which sought funding for their projects from a variety of sources. On the other hand, the role of the university administration has clearly been reduced to one of management.

Society's problems, along with the funds, are also making their way into the universities, which are becoming less exclusively educational centers and increasingly centers of scientific production. This new situation explains certain aspects of the academic crisis.

PROFESSION-ALIZATION Scientific development and the growth of research funds make it impossible for professors to accept their old definition of agents of transmission of a cultural and social heritage. Their main loyalty is no longer to their educational role or even to their institution, but to their profession. They come to define themselves as pure professionals fulfilling a mission of the government and of social importance, a mission above social and political problems.

The Academic System and the Social Order Despite the very rapid growth of research, especially in the natural sciences and medicine, but in all other disciplines as well, the academic system did not break down.[7] Quite to the contrary, we can endorse Berelson's view that this very growth has both strengthened and unified the system, as well as accentuating its hierarchical structure:

> In an informal way we have what might be called a national system of higher education. At the very top are the best "national" universities. For their graduate schools the in-put consists of the best students from themselves and the best colleges, plus award-winners and their equivalents from other places. The out-put is taken first to staff themselves and the best colleges, and then to staff the rest of the system as far as the system lasts. And so on through the layers of lesser universities and regional universities. In this sense increased production down the line, even if it is of lower average quality, is useful in staffing other institutions still further down the line who cannot afford or attract the products of the best institutions (Berelson, 1960, p. 116).

[7] The most recent, and probably the best, book on the transformation of academic life due to the progress of research activities is Dael Wolfle's *The Home of Science* (1972).

This organizational unity is inseparable from a cultural unity that is consistent with the "instrumental activism" Parsons sees as the central value of American society.

The orientation of cognitive rationality is implicit in the common culture of instrumental activism but it only becomes more or less explicit and is more highly appreciated among the educated classes by whom it is more evidently applied in their occupational pursuits. There is a more or less unconscious sense of affinity with cognitive rationality among most of those who share the instrumentally activist orientation; that sense of affinity becomes more positive and more explicit in the increasingly large proportion of the population which has itself received a higher education (Parsons & Platt, 1968, p. 507).

These two judgments bring out clearly the hierarchical structure of the academic system, which, in turn, has as its primary function the organization of society's hierarchical structure. In the American society, as in any society where technological and scientific knowledge plays an increasingly important role, it is normal that social hierarchy should be based on the possession of knowledge. At the end of the nineteenth century, when a different academic system was getting organized, a different hierarchy-building principle prevailed. The aim then was to shape men capable of plunging into the adventure of progress. The role of education could not be a central one, for the real selection process took place on the market. It was there that people's energy, initiative, and enterprising spirit were put to the test. Today, on the contrary, the academic system is the main agent of social hierarchy. At the head of the society are those whose knowledge is greatest and, who are above all, apt to develop furthest. They constitute a capital that bears interest, for they are constantly producing new knowledge.

Three main strata can therefore be identified: The upper stratum is composed of those whose knowledge is constantly renewed and expanded; the middle stratum is composed of professionals who depend on the knowledge created at higher levels, but are able, through their occupational practice, to maintain and preserve their own level of technical skill; the lower stratum is filled with those whose knowledge wears out and sooner or later becomes "obsolete." The hierarchy of academic institutions—the most advanced universities, the growing number of good universities, especially public ones, and the great mass of junior colleges—reproduces and perpetuates this social stratification. It also ensures the continuity of the social hierarchy, because each level of academic institutions continues to recruit from a different social level.

It is undoubtedly impossible for any contemporary academic system belonging to a class society to completely escape this role. The only question is whether the identification with it is complete. We can readily admit that cognitive rationality is a value peculiar to an industrialized technological society, but to go no further would be to neglect two equally important facts. In the first place, this value does not soar above the society, compelling universal recognition in a disembodied form. It is instead a general orientation for social activity whose implementation is inseparable from the social power. But this power, which is that of the ruling class, is not exerted exclusively in the service of "rationality." Private interests also use it to appropriate the productive forces, including rationality. In their defense of their interests and of their social and ideological domination of the entire society, private interests are in many ways opposed to the progress of cognitive rationality.

Moreover, the efforts of the rulers to promote the participation of all in a process of development controlled by a few encounters the resistance and opposition of those who rely on the other basic orientations of our society: the desire for consumption, enjoyment, and identity that is constantly threatened by the restrictions of production and profit, as well as by the manipulations of demand by the economic and political apparatus.

Independently of these social conflicts, it is hardly possible to believe that any society is guided by a unified value system. The old agrarian societies were indeed inspired by values that can be termed religious; they were no less shaped by the functional requirements of community preservation and by the importance of ascription, internal rules, kinship systems, and so forth. In the same way, a society that is driven to increasing rapid change by technological progress, and that is increasingly dependent upon big decision-making centers, also values consumption, the search for identity, and therefore a conception of education that gives key importance to expression, personality formation, and the peer group.

Professors are not merely professionals or scientists; they are also the people who operate and, to a large extent, manage the academic system. The more they define the aims of the university in terms of their own professional function, the more even that they assert their specific role and their independence, the more willing they are—consciously or unconsciously—to identify, not with all the values of the society, but with those that correspond to its ruling interests. Parsons analyzed this very clearly in acknowledging that cognitive rationality is increasingly valued as one rises in the social hierarchy.

Should we draw the conclusion, as we might easily be tempted to do, that the professors should restore to education its former importance, and reintroduce the spirit of the liberal arts colleges into big research centers that the best universities have become, and into the higher professional schools that the middle-level universities have largely turned into? Not only does such a return to the past seem practically impossible, since the development of new knowledge requires the participation of an increasing number of professionals, but giving to the reproduction of the social order more importance than to its production could only strengthen existing social inequalities and the continuity of the ruling class — as was the case in the period between the two world wars. The changes that have occurred during the past twenty years are irreversible. The alternative is not a scientific university or a "liberal" one, but either a university that identifies totally with the production of a new social hierarchy or a university into which intrudes either violently or through institutional mechanisms, the debate between differing cultural orientations and conflicting social interests.

But before dealing with the recent events that have dramatized this problem, I should give a more detailed description of the development of the new academic system. All I have done so far is establish its motive force — the growth of research owing to federal funds — and discuss the professorial ideology that emerged.

The essential feature, let us emphasize once again, is the unity of the academic system. This unity enabled the academic system to identify largely with the prevailing social order. The powerful professional development of the universities enabled the system to assign itself specific aims, for which it claimed at the same time a general value. The academic system, however, never questioned the ties created by this general value, ties not only between the university and a given culture, but also between the university and a given social organization, social order, and type of ruling class and state power.

Ideology and Rhetoric

I do not mean to say, of course, that the university people have placed themselves voluntarily at the service of the established order. Quite the contrary. To use terms previously employed, we might say that this period witnessed the ebbing of the academic ideology that had been so strong during the preceding period and the rise of an academic rhetoric that stressed professionalism and a certain conception of academic freedom. The scientific and professional aims of most of the universities are an indisputable fact, as evidenced by the magnificent development of American science in every field and the harvest of Nobel Prizes reaped during this period.[8] Fervor for scientific research is a basic reality for the American scientists; and many of them have no other political and social attitude than the search for conditions most favorable to science and the will to devote themselves to work that is both intellectually creative and socially useful. But insofar as we are less interested in the subjectivity of the scientists than in the role of the academic system in the society, we cannot ignore the fact that between scientific motivation and academic rhetoric lies the functioning of the educational system and the social and cultural choices it makes, even if unconsciously.

This is the place for an exact definition of the terms ideology and rhetoric as I use them here. Much confusion arises from the fact that the concept of ideology is used on the one hand to refer to the ideology of the agent and on the other to the ideology of the system. The ideology of the agent is a set of judgments made from the viewpoint of the agent's of his interests and images and is related to the place he occupies in a network of social relations. Any agent's ideology should be defined and analyzed in terms of how it conflicts with the ideology of a social antagonist. The nature of the agent's social relations is displayed through these conflicting ideologies, each of which denies the subjectivity of its adversary, who is viewed as an obstacle to the agent's objectives and values.

On the other hand, when I speak of the system's ideology, I mean that a dominant agent has the ability to impose his viewpoint and his interests on an entire community through its forms of social organization and its culture. For example, the organization of the educational system can be analyzed as a means of preserving and strengthening a particular mode of domination, the power of a ruling class.

We can speak of the ideology of the system in its full sense only if

[8] From 1951 to 1966, the United States received 44 Nobel Prizes for science, as against 18 for Great Britain, 7 each for the U.S.S.R. and Germany, 4 for France, and 8 for all other countries, which shows the overwhelming superiority of American scientific organization.

we accept the Marxist proposition that the ideology of the ruling class is the prevailing ideology. This line of reasoning can be carried further by stating that general principles—the appeal to rationality, to equality, and to progress—serve primarily to convert the ideology of the dominant class into a prevailing ideology, concealing under the mask of universalism the actual interests of the dominant class. Such is the role of lawyers, for instance, and also that of teachers. The more they repeat "liberty, equality, fraternity," the better they serve the class interests of the bourgeoisie, taking power from the hands of the aristocracy under the cover of these supposedly universal and disinterested principles.

I have introduced the concept of rhetoric because the view outlined above is, in my opinion, an exaggerated one. It is true that culture is, in part, the ideology of the dominant class; this idea can be discarded only if we discard the very notion of a dominant class. For what would it dominate if it could not convert its own interests and ideology into generally recognized rules of social organization and into cultural forms? What I have called the model of knowledge and the cultural model, however, are not products of the dominant ideology; they are societal activities and images, appropriated by the dominant class, but having, nevertheless, a real and autonomous existence. A given type of knowledge and of human creativeness are peculiar to a society, not to a class. They are stakes in the contests between the classes, not instruments for the action of a particular class.

In addition, the dominant class itself restricts its integrating role. Since, while trying to dominate the entire society it is also faced by the opposition and revolt of the dominated class, it rejects the antagonistic forces and divides society, creating, for example, one school for the people and another for the bourgeoisie, or eliminating those educational demands that do not conform to its interests. To attribute exclusive importance to the ideology of the system means to neglect the repressive action of the ruling classes.

Lastly, class antagonism is not expressed through absolute domination alone. Partly because the dominated classes might have political potential, and partly because in an actual society, ruling classes—or fractions of ruling classes—with diverging interests might coexist, breaking down the unity of the system's ideology.

For all these reasons, social and cultural forms of organization have no intrinsic unity. Analysis leads us to distinguish (1) cultural and social themes peculiar to a given type of society, which I have called an historical action system, (2) an ideology of the system that characterizes the hold of the ruling class, and (3) other ideological themes indicating the influence of other social groups.

It is this diversity that confers autonomy on the rationalization efforts of those who attempt to define the unity of a given social or cultural system. It is these efforts that I have called the rhetoric of a system.

The significant point is that this rhetoric, which appears as an attempt at ideological unification, always has several meanings. Because it develops within the context of class relations, it is indeed a cover for domination. But, at the same time, it resists this domination, insofar as, on the one hand, it unifies themes from various origins and not only those imposed by the ruling class and, on the other, it is based on a cultural model and a whole historical action system that is more general than the action of the ruling class, since the rhetoric is both the field and the stake of this action.

Teachers belong to a class society and therefore serve the prevailing social order, participating in its reproduction. At the same time, they support their actions by invoking science on the one hand, and their professional autonomy on the other, a double claim that can easily combine with the action of forces opposed to the ruling class.

The professional rhetoric of university people has all these meanings at once. And in a wide-open situation, like that of the academic crisis of the sixties, they intermingle so constantly that the professors' position seems both conservative and liberal at the same time. As a result, they are very active but have a low political potential. Professional and corporative defense, known as "academic freedom" in academic rhetoric, means both resistance to the pressures of the prevailing order and resistance to the radicals' questioning of the links between the university and the ruling class. It is the defense of science against the intrusion of ideology, but at the same time it is a naïve or seemingly naïve identification of science with a particular social order and corporate interests.

These ambiguities are typical of all scholars. The scholar of the Middle Ages was at the service of the kings and the lords, but he also opposed the demands of the sacred to the temporal power and defended the material and moral interests of the ecclesiastical body. The professionalization of the academic world led to the parallel development of its liberal rhetoric. We must begin by a critique of its illusions. The academic system is not the pure servant of what is sacred today, namely rationality. It functions in accordance with the interests of the technocratic power, for the universities are themselves apparatuses for the production and the accumulation of knowledge. But the liberal rhetoric both serves and opposes the established order, or rather it has an opposition or defense potential within an established order that it is unable or unwilling to put in question.

Before examining the ambiguous social behavior and images of the teachers, we must first define the unity of the academic system, a unity that is not to be found in professorial rhetoric but in the very functioning of the academic system, and particularly in the role played by research. This study will be complemented by the analysis, in the next chapter, of the teachers' role during the academic crisis.

The Graduate Schools and the Ph.D. One fact sums up the change in the academic system: the development of the graduate schools. This development is a recent one. In 1900 there were no more than 5,831 students in the graduate schools. By 1940 their number had already reached 106,119. With the development of research, the proportion of graduate students in the total student population increased more and more rapidly. According to serious forecasts, the number of graduate students should reach 2.5 million in 1980, that is, the size of the total student population of universities and colleges in 1952 (Mayhew, 1970). Although other estimations are more cautious, the progression is impressive.

According to Mayhew, the number of Ph.D.'s awarded, which was 4,000 in 1958, 9,800 in 1960, and 26,100 in 1969, will reach between 50,000 and 77,000 in 1980.

This progression is due much less to the growth in the graduate student population of the bigger universities than to the rapid increase in the number of institutions organizing doctoral programs. The development of graduate studies is therefore not concentrated in the most advanced sectors of scientific research. On the contrary, Mayhew observed that most of the new programs are being created in the fields of modern languages and humanities (although, in absolute numbers, the physical and social sciences are still ahead). The most rapid increase of all, however, is registered in training for the various professions, as shown in Table 16.

TABLE 16   *Distribution of doctoral degrees, by field, by percentage*

	1911–1920	*1921–1930*	*1931–1940*	*1941–1950*	*1951–1958*
Professions (education)	9 (6)	16 (13)	18 (11)	23 (13)	34 (17)
Physical sciences	30	29	29	28	24
Biological sciences	14	15	17	15	12
Social sciences	22	22	19	17	19
Humanities	25	18	17	17	11

SOURCE: Berelson (1960, p. 37).

Certain regions of the country, especially the West-Central and the North-Central, are traditionally oriented towards the professions: agriculture, engineering, business, education, etc.

The value of graduate studies, particularly of the Ph.D. programs, is quite variable, but the predominant tendency is toward work of a high scientific or at least technical level. As a result, the Ph.D. has become more and more the normal conclusion for these studies. The M.A., which is no longer even a requirement in one-third of the universities for the preparation of the doctorate, is becoming increasingly a diploma useful for the recruitment of teachers (half the M.A.'s are in education), and is prepared in about 600 institutions.

The increasing favor in which the Ph.D. is held can be explained by the expansion of the scientific disciplines, but even more by two quite distinct tendencies. On the one hand are the demands of the teaching profession, which increasingly regards the Ph.D. as the normal gateway to the profession. This demand is encouraged by the presidents, anxious to raise the level of their respective colleges. Since, as we have already seen, the proportion of teachers with a Ph.D. is increasing rapidly in the junior colleges, it is clear that the unity of the academic system is being built and the influence of the big universities is spreading.

On the other hand, Berelson has shown that, contrary to a widespread opinion, the proportion of Ph.D.'s employed in the universities has been constantly decreasing. It was between 70 and 80 percent in 1900, between 70 and 75 percent at the end of the 1920s, 65 percent in the 1930s, and 60 percent in 1958. In 1958, Ph.D. holders were distributed as follows among the three main categories of employers (Berelson, 1960, p. 37).

	Colleges or universities, %	Government, %	Industry, %
Physical sciences	41	9	47
Biological sciences	61	19	12
Social sciences	67	15	4
Humanities	82	1	1
Professional field	59	8	13

In the scientific fields, the Ph.D.'s, when they remain in the university, rarely go into undergraduate teaching. Only in the humanities do more than half the Ph.D.'s teach in colleges. A series of private and public research and development centers are being established that employ the majority of the science Ph.D.'s. This trend is more marked in the United States than in Western Europe, owing to the fact that the American research and development effort is not only much greater, but is also largely devoted to the application of research, as is shown in Table 17.

TABLE 17 *Comparison of expenses in R and D*

	Dollars per capita	Percentage of GNP	Basic research	Applied research	Development
U.S., 1963–64	110.5	3.4	12.4	22.1	65.5
France, 1963	27.1	1.6	17.3	33.9	48.8
U.K., 1964–65	39.8	2.3	12.5	26.1	61.4
Netherlands, 1964	27.2	1.9	27.1	36.4	36.5

SOURCE: Ben-David (1968, pp. 49–50).

The academic system functions indeed as a hierarchical one. Rather than operating as a whole set of functions ranging from research to general education, it is driven by the world of research and development, which offers the main inducements. As a result, the colleges receive the more mediocre products of a training that is not oriented towards education. This situation can be avoided only where research plays a weaker role or requires more limited means, as is the case for the humanities, which have few outlets apart from teaching.

This impression is confirmed by a more detailed examination of the production of Ph.D.'s.

It is true, as it has been pointed out, that the role of the best universities in this production has decreased considerably. We are reminded by Berelson that, until the mid-1920s, Columbia, Chicago, Harvard, Johns Hopkins, and Yale delivered half the doctorates, and that in the 1930s, Columbia, Chicago, Harvard, Wisconsin, and Cornell were still awarding 30 percent of them.

On the contrary, in the 1950s, the five largest producers — Columbia, Wisconsin, California, Harvard, and Illinois — delivered well below one-fourth of the Ph.D.'s. However, by lengthening this list we find that, for the entire period 1953–1962, 12 Universities account for 40 percent of the number of Ph.D.'s. But above all, the spreading of the doctorate means that the production of Ph.D.'s becomes a less and less reliable index of the high quality of an institution.

The capacity for scientific production does not seem to have become more widespread. Kerr points out that the East Coast group, from Boston to Washington, possesses 46 percent of the Nobel Prizes and 40 percent of the members of the National Academy of Sciences, California 36 percent and 20 percent respectively, and the region of Chicago and the Great Lakes 10 percent and 14 percent.

New centers may make their appearance, especially in Texas and Louisiana. But the needs of science tend to require huge scientific institutions, so Harvard and MIT, Berkeley and Stanford, Princeton and Pennsylvania, Chicago and the Big Ten of the Middle West, have to join forces to carry out certain scientific projects (Kerr, 1963). Of course these centers exert considerable influence on the rest of the country, for their doctorates have the highest reputation. In the case of sociology, it was first the University of Chicago whose national influence was the greatest; later, Harvard and Columbia took over Chicago's leadership.

The big universities seem least sensitive to the problems faced by the colleges. In fact, there is much truth in the bitter conclusion of Jencks and Riesman: "The graduate schools have an essentially imperial relationship with many of the institutions and subcultures on their borders, particularly the undergraduate colleges. Their apparent success depends in many cases on exploiting these underdeveloped territories" (Jencks & Riesman, 1968, p. 515).

Professors issuing from the big universities try to maintain contact with their alma maters when working at middle-level universities or colleges. Riesman clearly showed this to be the case for Oakland College (Riesman et al., 1970).

This situation is not too different from that of France, which has a completely centralized academic system whose best products seek employment in research. When forced to accept purely teaching duties, however, they attempt to transpose to the last years of the lycées — roughly the equivalent of undergraduate colleges — the spirit and forms of university teaching they themselves received, displaying only indifference and contempt for pedagogy or for any knowledge of the social environment in which they teach.

The domination exerted by the research universities is not limited to the American middle-level universities and colleges, but extends to foreign countries as well. While the best American universities have given numerous research workers from relatively advanced countries, especially those of Europe, the priceless opportunity to study in first-rank research organizations, thus allowing them to benefit from the work accomplished in the United States, American scientific production has been reinforced by the contributions of foreign elements. The foreign contribution may be minor from the standpoint of the United States, at least after the wave of intellectual immigration caused by Nazi domination and the consequences of World War II, but it is quite significant from the standpoint of the countries of origin. Latin America and Asia have made a contribution to the activity of the American research centers that is far from negligible in their own eyes, since they have borne the training costs of many professionals who, after completing their higher education in the United States, remained there as research workers. This brain-drain, from which some European nations have also benefited, is evidence of the domination exerted by the powerful scientific and technological centers. American universities, as well as European ones that have benefited from this attribute of power, have shown little concern for this issue.

The recent change of circumstances has brought to light the consequences of the supremacy of the Ph.D., a supremacy that has severely unbalanced academic activity.

Economic stagnation, together with reduced appropriations for agencies like NASA and fewer research grants for universities, caused unemployment among science Ph.D.'s in 1970–71. But many observers, notably Allan M. Cartter (1971), believe that the only effect of these unfavorable circumstances was to bring to a head a few years early a crisis whose causes are more permanent.

Over a long period, the demand for Ph.D.'s will probably be on the decrease, after an initial period of rapid growth in the university population. As a result, the country will experience a considerable overproduction of the Ph.D.'s.

This situation partly explains the proposed reforms in university degrees mentioned in the final chapter of this book. It also shows to what extent academic activity has been driven toward a type of production that does not entirely correspond to the expected needs of the labor market. Clearly, this proves that higher education has been subordinated to an image of society that big organizations have created at the expense of other social functions, functions enjoying less prestige because they are related only to the desire for education or the improvement of living conditions.

The Accumulation of Resources

The graduate student population is obviously quite different from the undergraduate one. In fact, it is for the most part closer to the faculty than to the student population proper.

True, the graduate school has no autonomous organization at the faculty level. At the beginning of their graduate studies, the students take some of the same courses as the seniors or the juniors, and sometimes, as at Yale or Cincinnati, even nonspecialized graduate programs are organized.

But the relative decline of the master's degree and the increasing importance of the Ph.D. have led to a rapid rise in the number of the most advanced students. Although the average time interval between the B.A. and the Ph.D. has not lengthened for the past 40 years (Berelson, 1960, pp. 156–185), the large increase in the number of doctoral students has dramatically raised the proportion of older students attending the universities. The average age for the doctorate is 29 in the physical sciences, 30 in the biological sciences, 33 in the social sciences, and 35 in the humanities.

The students are frequently married and must have their own means of support, since they are much less likely to receive help from their family at that age. Therefore the graduate students, and especially those well along in their doctoral program, practically constitute a wage-earning group.

Some of them, of course, receive graduate fellowships, especially from the National Science Foundation, the Public Health Service, the National Defense Education Act, and the Woodrow Wilson Program. The universities also award their own scholarships, almost equivalent in number but not in amount.

Some graduate students are employed as teaching assistants and do a large part of the lower-division teaching in their colleges; others take teaching jobs in community colleges, where they get better salaries. Still others, especially in the scientific fields, are employed as research assistants.

A study by the National Opinion Research Center showed that nearly three-fourths of the students receive some help, the scholarships and the teaching or research jobs being supplemented by loans. These various types of help extend over almost the entire duration of their studies for students in science and engineering, but only over part of it for those in the social sciences, humanities, or education.

Studies on the social origin of students have already shown that students' backgrounds exert an influence not only on their entrance to college, but upon their entire academic career.

This conclusion, however, should be completed and probably revised so far as the social background of research students is concerned. Thanks to the size of the available aid, the scientific world does not have to resort to further selection within the social selection that has already, to a large extent, taken place. Berelson found that among students completing their doctorates 20 percent were sons or daughters of skilled and unskilled workers, and only 27 percent were from professional or executive families. In 32 percent of the cases the fathers had not completed high school. The social level of the recruits is obviously higher in law and medicine. This observation might be carried further. The big universities, Harvard for example, are more anxious today to recruit "talents" throughout the country than to provide for the education of children of the upper bourgeoisie. This does not mean that social selection no longer enters into play, but rather that a different trend also exists. The university is becoming a center for producing high-level professionals and technicians rather than for transmitting upper-class values and status. The Soviet Union has carried much further the early recognition of talented students, although that does not prevent the universities there from being at the same time centers for the transmission of social inequalities. In the United States this second function is the more important one, and the search for and training of talented students is less methodical. However, owing to the average length of graduate studies—six years in the physical sciences, eight in the social sciences, ten in the humanities and the professional fields—a special group of workers is created that sometimes remains within the university and sometimes participates in outside research and development work.

These student research workers do not constitute a homogeneous category. They might, in fact, come from the upper social categories and be preparing to enter a professional elite; they are thus the "cadets" of a new aristocracy. But those students who stand the best chance of remaining in the university are both relatively cut off from their social background and only marginally employed by the academic system. They are often conscious of being exploited and, inasmuch as their influence in the professorial world is limited, they turn to the students who are close to them and with whom they have numerous personal and professional contacts. Their potential for autonomous action is low, but when a university crisis occurs, their role is important, for while often participating in the student movement, they strive at the same time to defend their own professional interests. This category, which is the one most completely determined by its academic status as well as the most dependent, is also most directly affected by events occurring in the academic system, by the tensions born from the subordination of teaching to research.

Often, the doctoral students express more immediate demands during the crisis, complaining of the "ritualism" of the theses and of the uninteresting nature of their usually limited work, which to them seems to be more useful to the professor, who uses its results in a broader context, than for their own intellectual training. The validity and the extent of these criticisms are not easy to evaluate. I am personally inclined to consider them as signs of the students' dissatisfaction with their status in the academic system, rather than an expression of really poor working conditions with professors. But it is true that many professors harshly judge the quality and the scientific interest of the theses. Here again, this issue is not so much the quality of the scientific work "at the top" as the hold of a certain model of activity that deteriorates to the extent that it oversteps the limits of its normal field—that is, to the extent that the Ph.D. is forced upon a great number of students (and, we might add, a certain number of professors) whose involvement in research is a subjection rather than a genuine preference.

All these remarks contribute to a more accurate definition of the unity of the academic system and academic world. This unity is neither that of a value system nor that of a political system whose members all participate in the decision making. The academic system is neither a community nor a microsociety. It is a production apparatus that, although quite different from a business organization, while fulfilling its own specific function, depends too on the general organization of society and acts also in terms of its own interests and strives to accumulate power.

Fein and Weber, analyzing the medical schools, whose quality is often particularly outstanding, wrote (1971, p. 43): "Medicine's success in expanding knowledge, combined with its relative failure to develop institutions to provide health services in an organized and efficient manner, has led to the major problems facing the medical sector."

Would it be possible to generalize this courageous comment? Huge human and material resources are accumulated in the academic system and are put at the disposal of the cultural model of the society—that is, of scientific and technological development. For lack of a genuine internal political system, however, these resources are utilized in terms of the demands formulated at the top of the society, in the power centers. The development of medical research is magnificent, while the state of health of a large part of the population remains mediocre; the campuses are impressive, but the educational demands of blacks and other minorities for education are not given serious consideration; youth is provided with considerable educational means, but how much attention is given to their own image of their education? Finally, technological progress goes forward, but where and how are priorities established, and who can question the "natural" link between the academic centers and the centers of economic, political, and military power?

Let us try to avoid caricaturizing. It is not true that federal funds have frequently entailed intolerable coercion. It is easy to point to campus research centers or projects directly linked to the state's political and military plans, but military sources such as the Office of Naval Research have also given support for quite disinterested research that has contributed to progress in a number of scientific fields. Today, as at the time of Veblen, it would be naïve to speak of a conspiracy and to question the intentions of the overwhelming majority of scientists and university people.

It is probably in the social sciences that the search for knowledge has been most conspicuously subordinated to political objectives, perhaps because they are so much "softer" than the natural sciences. Some social scientists have even defended the necessity for this subordination: "The social sciences can be described as the new humanities of the twentieth century. They have the same relationship to the training of mandarins of the twentieth century that the humanities have always had to the training of the mandarins in the past."[9] But most social scientists would certainly not agree to be considered as one of the prince's advisers. The participation of university people in the framing of policy is a fact. However, when Operation Camelot was launched by the Department of Defense, calling on social scientists to participate in real counter-espionage activity against revolutionary movements, particularly in Latin America, only second-rate figures got involved and many big names in sociology denounced the project.

It is not surprising that the academic world's participation in military research has been one of the issues most consistently raised by the student movement; but it would be a mistake to think that such participation is the most significant aspect of the link between the academic system and the dominant social order.

The fact remains, however, that the links between the university and the society cannot be adequately described in terms of an adherence to the common values of the entire society. The significant point is not that some university people have become new mandarins, the intellectual agents of a particular policy, but that the university lacks political potential. Most university people cannot be classified among the most conservative or reactionary public opinion categories. Their liberalism has manifested itself mainly in favor of the university's autonomy and closure, and such closure is a much more effective means of preventing the expression of demands from below than of sifting out offers from above.

The academic system has no homogeneity. A great distance exists between the professors—especially those concerned with research if not with influence and power—the student youth, and the intermediate and marginal group of the TAs. Nor is there any unity between colleges and universities of different levels.

But the unity of the system is determined by its role of production of the social order. This unity is much more real than was possible at the end of the nineteenth century, when scientific

---

[9] Ithiel de Sola Pool, "The Necessity for Social Scientists Doing Research for Governments," *Background,* August 1966; quoted by M. Windmiller, in Roszak (1968).

knowledge still played only a marginal role. It is also much greater than it was between the two world wars, a period when the "aristo-cratic reaction" of the big colleges was growing.

The Career: Research and Teaching Professors are specialists who fulfill a social demand and help strengthen it by the very success of their work. The more specific the demand they meet, and the more individual autonomy they en-joy in fulfilling it, the more likely is the intrusion among them of the prevailing ideology. This has often been the case in the profes-sional schools, where, for example, the law professor identifies with the lawyers and judges, and the business administration pro-fessor readily embraces the interests and ideology of big business.

But the university professor is a two-faced Janus. As an expert, he faces the outside world; as a research worker he faces the inside of the university. Sociologically speaking, a field of education does not become professionalized simply by reaching a high scientific and technical level. The professors must also have set up an asso-ciation competent to determine appropriate behavior—in particular, the conditions of admission into the group—as well as to sanction infringements of the group's binding rules and to act in the defense of the group's interests. This autonomy of organization, decision, and judgment distinguishes professionals from technicians, what-ever their level. It could be added, not without reservations, that this professional autonomy is inseparable from the independence of the individual with respect to the profession, so far as conditions of work, employment, and remuneration are concerned. A profes-sor is a professional insofar as neither the university administra-tion nor the American Association of University Professors can determine for him the content of his teaching. Strictly speaking, the organization does not engage in collective bargaining on behalf of its members, although it does work to obtain and defend the best possible working conditions. In this sense, every profession can be termed a liberal profession, even when its members' main source of income is a salary. Moreover, a large number of profes-sors do draw a sizable income, in addition to their salaries, from counseling, publications, invitations to other universities in Amer-ica or abroad, and so forth.

As we have seen, the American academic world long ago devel-oped some form of group life. It began with the establishment of the learned societies, of which the first important one was the American Chemical Society, founded in 1876. It was followed in

1883 by the Modern Language Association of America and, in 1884, by the American Historical Association. The social sciences were the last to organize (the American Anthropological Association in 1902, the American Political Science Association in 1903, and last, the American Sociological Association in 1905). Simultaneously, scientific journals were founded, beginning in 1878 with the *American Journal of Mathematics.* Organization of the professional groups was at first accomplished indirectly through the establishment of the Association of American Universities in 1900; then, as mentioned earlier, the American Association of University Professors made its appearance in 1915. At the same time, starting at the University of Chicago the professors began to win the right to choose their department chairmen from among their own numbers. The generalization of the Ph.D. strengthened, de facto if not de jure, the faculty control over the recruitment of professors.

Very soon the profession's supervision over careers was organized within the departments. Committees proliferated, not only to solve problems effectively and rapidly but also to assert the autonomy of the profession with respect to the administration. These procedural excesses provoked ironical comment from Caplow and McGee (1965, p. 97): "The average salary of an assistant professor is approximately that of a bakery truck driver, and his occupancy of a job is likely to be less permanent. Yet it may require a large part of the time of twenty highly skilled men for a full year to hire him." Though the role of the trustees and the president is in principle a determinant one, in the majority of cases decisions in this domain are actually made by the chairman and the senior members of the department after wide consultation within and outside of the department.

Inside the department, a fairly clear division is made between administrative problems left to the chairman and professional problems dealt with by a group. Demerath and his associates (1967, p. 197) remark humorously: "The more important the area is thought to be to department success, the fewer are the chairmen in the top power-position." The higher the scientific level of the university, the less aristocratic is the behavior of the chairmen. Caplow and McGee (op. cit., pp. 168–169) have drawn a gallery of typical portraits: the Robber Baron, autocratic boss; the Lord of the Mountain Fief, elder statesman; the Yeoman Farmer, conscientious worker with limited views; the Gentleman Adventurer, a colorful figure who lends luster to a department that lacked it; the King's Man, strong ally of the administration; and the Boy Ruler, young professor to whom the seniors leave their administrative responsibilities. But these amusing characterizations may well apply to a situation that is changing rapidly. The chairman is not the one who administers and utilizes research funds; moreover, the senior professors, at least, are not so willing as they were 20 years ago to leave professional decisions in the hands of the chairman alone. Parsons has shown that the power of the chairman is weakest in the best universities.

Professional supervision is exercised not only upon the teacher's entrance into the university but throughout his career, although the most vital decisions in this connection are made by the administration. The professors intervene directly in the decision to dismiss a colleague, often expressed through the tacit rule of "up or out," which applies to instructors and assistant professors without tenure. This brings out the prejudices exhibited by some faculties, which, for example, recruit exclusively white Protestant males.

Professionalization is also expressed in a more diffused, though extremely significant, way through the existence of a professional group whose opinion usually counts more than that of colleagues from the same university but who belong to other disciplines. Although conventions may not be "slave markets," as they are so readily dubbed, they are one medium — scientific journals being another — through which the professors' reputations and careers are made.

In this regard, there is no marked difference between the American situation and that of the better European universities. At the most, it might be said that the American academic world probably has a stronger taste for ceremonies, awards, presidential speeches, and other paraphernalia of professional life than its counterparts in most European countries.

A professor's career depends not so much on the quality of his teaching as on his scientific production — "publish or perish" — and also on the place he occupies in the academic system. A Ph.D. from a high-ranking university, participation in a professional association, and friendships in the right places — all are important elements for a career.

But these rather standard remarks are of interest only to show that the great majority of university people experience their careers as being purely professional. Only a small number of them try to obtain administrative positions. Recent developments, in fact, have led university people to define themselves increasingly in terms of their scientific role; neither teaching nor administrative problems are major preoccupations. These are the conclusions suggested by the results of a survey by Parsons and Platt (1968, pp. 497–523) (see Table 18).

TABLE 18
Average actual and ideal distribution of time among academic role-components by degree of institutional differentiation

Activity	Degree of institutional differentiation, %		
	High	*Medium*	*Low*
Undergraduate teaching			
Actual	29	46	64
Ideal	25	34	43
Postgraduate teaching			
Actual	18	13	
Ideal	22	23	19
Research			
Actual	32	22	15
Ideal	43	35	28
Administration			
Actual	21	19	21
Ideal	10	8	10

NOTE: A high degree of differentiation denotes a high scientific level.
SOURCE: Parsons and Platt (1968, p. 519).

The research orientation is predominant in the best universities and especially in the most scientific fields, and professors would like it to be developed still further. When asked about their conception of the doctoral program, professors in all disciplines acknowledged that it is oriented mainly toward research. As Table 19 shows, only in the humanities did a significant proportion of professors express the desire that it be oriented more toward teaching.

In the middle-level and low-level colleges, the concern for teaching is more general, but the teachers do prefer its role to be secondary. The teachers usually realize very well that their status and material rewards depend not only on their personal scientific activity, but on the scientific role of the academic profession. The increase in the student population does not account for the rise in wages, for they remained low during most of the period when this increase was taking place. On the contrary, it is the recognized importance of science and the desire of the universities to attract

TABLE 19 *Preference for teaching or for research*

	The program is now			The program should be		
	More for research, %	More for teaching, %	About equivalent, %	More for research, %	More for teaching, %	About equivalent, %
Physical sciences	79	6	12	60	5	28
Biological sciences	74	6	18	48	4	45
Social sciences	63	15	18	37	16	43
All professional fields	58	21	17	32	19	42
Humanities				25	32	39

SOURCE: Berelson (1960, p. 47).

or hold the best Ph.D.'s that caused this rise, which over the past 15 years has brought about such a change in the living standards of the professors.

June O'Neill (1971) has proven, however, there has been no improvement in productivity during those 15 years. In fact, the cost of the credit hour has not changed since 1930. Since the professors' salaries have increased more than the overall price level, this stability implies that the teaching is dispensed to a greater number of students, or that the average qualification of teachers is lower, at least so far as teaching assignments are concerned. This is indeed the case. Trow (1970a, pp. 295–308) points out that in Berkeley the undergraduate departments are very poorly staffed in comparison with Harvard, Columbia, or the English universities. TAs teach 30 percent of the undergraduate courses and 41 percent in the lower-division classes. Two-thirds of the courses attended by fewer than 30 students are given by TAs; at that level, full professors usually address huge audiences. Basic teaching is therefore deteriorating in the big universities; at least in those not protected by the elitist traditions of the Ivy League, that is, those whose established function (at the college level) is not the recruitment of the social elite. In the best liberal arts colleges, which are also the most expensive ones, concern for education predominates; there the professors are the tutors of the social elite, just as in centuries past so many intellectuals were the tutors of the princes. Where they have lost this role, as in the mass universities, the links with the elite are established and preserved through research rather than through teaching. Once again, this does not mean that research in itself is at the service of the ruling class. Such an assumption is ridiculous, of course, but it is nonetheless refuted too complacently and with too good a conscience.

It is not scientific knowledge that is in question. It is both the orientation of that knowledge toward objectives not always determined by the needs of knowledge itself, and the nature of the relationships established within the university between research and teaching. It is not scientific activity that is in question. It is the subordination of teaching to what is called research, research that is not determined exclusively by scientific creation, but equally by professionalism. His concern for the career, and therefore for money and influence, weighs the more, the further one goes from basic research in which the specific requirements of knowledge are most compelling. Professionalism is easy to understand. The scientists are the clerics of the new society, just as educators and theologians were in earlier societies. Whatever the type of relationship established between the university and the society, a relationship necessarily exists. In the Soviet Union, as well as in the United States, this relationship encourages an ease of exchange that tends increasingly to the formation of an international professional group that sometimes, as in the case of the Pugwash movement, strives to exert a political influence in favor of "peaceful co-existence" based on strengthening the professional community.

To sum up, the dominant feature of the academic system is not a professionalism defined by values and an autonomous organization, but rather the complementariness between the strengthening of the university's own power and a scientific development linking more and more closely the big universities to social power. Professionalism, rather than being a fundamental principle, is the unifying factor between these two tendencies, linked to each other and capable of reaching a state of mutual tension. They are linked because the big universities, like all big organizations that conform closely to a cultural model, also use the cultural model to strengthen their power. (It is always *ad majorem Dei gloriam* that churches are strengthened, and in the name of progress and democracy that Communist parties establish their absolute power.) The two tendencies are also in a state of tension because scientific and technological progress depends less on the work of the academic system as a whole than on that of its upper part and of the outside centers of scientific and technological research: the world of the Ph.D.

does not coincide with the academic world. This tension is felt especially in the science departments, where the research assistants tend to be the best graduate students and the less able students become teaching assistants. The best universities have successfully resisted the dismemberment this tension has created. For example, Cal Tech, and especially its biology department, has strictly adhered to the principle that a Ph.D. must be the product of personal research work and not the by-product of a research contract. Most professors and administrators believe that the growing number of research projects and the constraints they entail have in no way lowered the level of graduate training, but in fact have done quite the opposite.

The capacity of the big academic institutions to organize extensive research work is greatly reinforced by the extent of their own financial means. This is particularly true of a small number of elite institutions, for half the total endowment for all colleges and universities in the United States belongs to 24 institutions, and three-fourths to less than 100. In 1962–63, the market value of the endowment assets of the richest institutions were as follows: Harvard, $765,564,821; Texas, $425,000,000; Yale, $392,403,-992; Princeton, $257,373,000; Chicago, $253,418,199; MIT, $228,876,000; Rochester, $210,000,000; Northwestern, $187,-800,000; California, $179,895,474; Cornell, $172,062,588; Columbia, $158,039,525; and Stanford, $140,247,000. These institutions are also often—but not always—among those where the tuition is highest. Consequently, they are those that both depend the most on outside contributions for their scientific work and depend on them the least for their operation.

Professionalization is therefore not separable from the defense of the academic institution.

In countries where the integration of the academic system has been weaker, professionalization has been easier, but has found expression in two different ways: on the one hand, a greater indifference to academic problems; on the other, a greater freedom of judgment with respect to the social power to which the university is linked. In this connection, the French case again is interesting because it is so different from the American. The French professor's usual indifference to the functioning of the university shocks his American colleague. He is a specialist and devotes as little time to personal contacts with the students as to the administration of his university and his department. He prefers to see himself as a member of the intelligentsia or of a professional circle rather than as an employee of the state and the educational system; he likes to be, as the philosopher Alain put it, the intellectual against the power. Not, in the great majority of cases, in the name of a revolutionary or merely critical vision, but in the name of his distrust of every form of administration. This picture brings out more clearly the nature of American professionalism, which is inseparable from attachment to an institution. This helps explain the attitudes and behavior patterns of American university people in the face of problems connected with the relationship between the university and the society.

Academic Freedom The silent generation was the golden age for academic rhetoric. Abundant resources that were sufficiently diversified to give everyone a chance to find the financing best suited to his needs; striking scientific progress; growing prestige of the universities; improvement of the teachers' material conditions and an increase in their independence from the administration; good graduate students trained in greater numbers every year; and finally, the partial transfer of undergraduate teaching duties to the younger, nontenured teachers. The Kennedy administration listened to the advice of Harvard professors, and student agitation was limited to a few panty raids. McGeorge Bundy—whose brilliant career at Harvard, in the Kennedy administration, and finally at the Ford Foundation, appears as the perfect success story of that period— best eulogized the virtues of the dying epoch, whose key words were "learning, freedom, excellence, community, and humanity" (1970, p. 565). At Harvard in the 1950s knowledge was king. Real power belonged to the professors, and only secondarily to the administration, which collected ample funds and attached the greatest importance to the opinions of the professors. The university was politically independent. It had its own specific values—primarily, excellence in the pursuit of knowledge—and these values, as Huntington (1969) pointed out, were shared by professors and students. It is the great theme of the university community of scholars:

In the ideal sense of its purpose, a university is a community of scholars. It is a community of cooperatively disposed and friendly individuals sharing common ideals and aspirations which unite them in a good cause transcending the boundaries of their separate specialties and capacities. A University is made up of scholars with a devotion to truth as each under-

stands it, ever concerned with broadening the boundaries of man's knowledge with others for their material and spiritual well-being, ever loyal in
the service of scholarship, and ever free from any form of tyranny over
mind or body (Millett, 1952, p. 28).

This quasi-religious discourse, coming from a scholar extolling
the greatness of scholars, puts the university not just at the apex
of society, but above society. University people are mediators between values and society, high priests of a culture based on the
universalism of knowledge.

Like Julien Benda, university people were wary of the "treason
of the intellectuals" of anything that might cause the disorder and
the darkness of interests, feelings, and pressures to intrude into
the crystal realm of knowledge.

Hence the distrust towards an administration involved in worldly
affairs. A survey carried out in the College of Arts and Sciences
of a Midwestern university shows the ambiguity of the professors'
attitudes in this domain. While professors want to have a voice
on all matters they consider important, both academic affairs and
personnel matters, they have no desire to devote their time to management. They are quick to accuse the administration of authoritarian methods, and they resent not having been consulted, even
though they were. Hence the importance of the department, professional milieu par excellence. The main thing in solving any
problem is to rely on the most scientific criteria possible (Dykes,
p. 968). All the students making the best scores on the scholastic
aptitude tests must be admitted. At the most, some regret that the
results of the blacks, for example, are so bad that more of them
cannot, in all fairness, be admitted! Let us refer once again to the
judgment of Lazarsfeld, who views this situation more realistically
(1962, p. 7641):

Academic freedom is more and more interpreted in such a way as to keep
the administration out of truly academic affairs, and the faculty, in turn,
has come to consider administration beneath its dignity. But educational
innovations are, by definition, intellectual as well as administrative tasks.
And, so, they have fallen into a no-man's land: the president and his staff
wait for the faculty to take the initiative; the professors on their side consider that such matters would take time away from their true scholarly pursuits. As a result, many of our universities have a dangerously low level
of institutional development.

When trouble broke out, the professors, in many cases, tried to shift the problems onto the administration, following the norm of issue avoidance, as David C. Knapp of Cornell expressed it.

Thus, devotion to scientific knowledge and a lofty conception of its importance and grandeur were converted into a rhetoric far removed from an accurate picture of reality. This rhetoric declared the independence of the university, but at the same time welcomed the influx of resources and raised no questions concerning the social role of education. In even simpler terms, it was far removed from the experience of those who, like Lazarsfeld himself, had to struggle hard to organize research, and sometimes even to get it admitted into the university.

Gross's survey (see Table 20) shows clearly the image that professors (of nondenominational institutions) have of the academic institution. Everything related to the excellence and independence of the university ranks high on the list of their concerns. Conversely, problems related to the education of students rank lowest, and the issue of student participation in university government neither *is* nor *should be* important.

Their view, therefore, is an inward-looking one. These results depend, of course, on the formulation of the questions, which, in this case, are phrased to prevent any deeper analysis of professorial attitudes, and to make the university appear as a sovereign source of decisions. But the professors do reveal a strong desire to free the university both from external limitations and from the internal limitations represented by the students.

This blindness concerning the functioning of the university reappears when we deal with a more general aspect of academic freedom—that is, the relationship not just between the professors and the academic administration, but between the university and society. Which does not mean that the professors' attitude is, in principle, a conformist one. They readily admit that they should deal with controversial social issues and express personal conclusions that challenge traditional values. These attitudes are the more widespread as the college is more independent, the teachers are more closely linked to their professional milieu, and the problems dealt with are closer to the respondent's specialty (Maccoby, 1960, pp. 884–893).

But Maccoby also observes the limits of this independence: neutrality must be preserved. Therefore, a professor should be able to

TABLE 20
Goals of
academic
institutions as
ranked by
faculty members

Goals	Is	Should be
Academic freedom	1	1
University prestige	2	11
Top quality	3	7
Ensure confidence	4	26
Keep up-to-date	5	6
Train scholarship	6	2
Pure research	7	16
Student character	38	12
Education to utmost	39	37
Accept good students only	40	39
Student political rights	41	42
Development faculty loyalty	42	29
Keep harmony	43	41
Undergraduate instruction	44	44
Student university government	45	46
Preserve character	46	47
Student taste	47	45

NOTE: 3 = maintain top quality in those programs we feel to be especially important; 4 = ensure the continued confidence and support of those who contribute
substantially to the finances and material resources of the university; 44 = emphasize undergraduate instruction even at the expense of the graduate program; 46 =
keep the place from becoming somewhat different from what it is now; 47 = make a
good consumer of the student.
SOURCE: Gross and Grambsch (1968, p. 164).

show greater open-mindedness to the extent that he can rely on his
knowledge. This is all the easier when an independent institution
protects him against external pressures. Thus, he is more inclined
to defend his freedom of thought in a junior college with an autonomous board than in one more directly incorporated into the public
school system.

These issues become most acute, of course, in the social sciences,
and so give particular importance to the research carried out by
Lazarsfeld and Thielens (1958).

Their study brings out, first of all, the significance of the academic environment and its internal norms.

It is not enough to contrast the reactions of liberal and conservative individuals to the pressure of McCarthyism. Individual attitudes also depend on the college, as evidenced by the significant
differences among colleges as to their degree of "permissiveness":

Institution	Percentage
Private	
Large	57
Small	53
Public	
Very large	55
Large	44
Small	23
Teachers colleges	27
Protestant colleges	32
Catholic	
Large	12
Small	3

SOURCE: Lazarsfeld & Thielens (1958, p. 128).

The more secularized the college, the more tolerant it is. By the same token, the professors who feel best protected in any given college are those who are most integrated into the college's academic world: the older ones, especially the most productive among them, are the least fearful; it is also they who are most likely to belong to the American Association of University Professors.

Permissiveness is a sign of a greater inclination to dissent. The most permissive faculty read more liberal magazines and are more often members of controversial organizations. And, especially, "The more permissive a social scientist, the more likely he is to approve classroom discussions and the more frequent is his belief that he should try to prepare students for participation in future social improvements" (ibid., p. 138).

But in the observed situation, the comparison is not merely one between liberals and conservatives, as if we were dealing with general attitudes. The academic world was subjected to definite attacks: the requirement of a loyalty oath that caused a deep crisis in California, for example, and numerous personal attacks. The 2,451 professors questioned reported 684 incidents, of which 130 resulted in dismissal or forced resignation for political reasons. The accusation of communism was vague enough to cover a wide range of opinions and behavior patterns regarded as un-American.

Academic liberalism was therefore faced with a serious crisis. Nice, heartfelt speeches about the material and moral contributions of knowledge to the community were in stark contrast to the condemnation of the "reds" by a section of public opinion and its representatives, particularly at a time when international tension led everywhere to a hardening of what is called "fundamentalism" in the Catholic Church.

In this crisis, how much power of resistance did the permissiveness of the academic world have; how did it experience its conflicting loyalties? It is in this connection that the results of the study are the most interesting: "In matters of academic freedom, however, the teacher seems inclined to be courageous in public and cautious in private. This is so because he really deals with two publics. What at times appears dangerous to the large community is proper in the eyes of one's peers, and they are the ones who matter more" (ibid., p. 105). This is an acceptable explanation. The support of the academic world did enable the professors to act with greater courage in the outside world than they would have if they had been alone or, say, employed as executives in a business organization.

But what is even more striking is that precautions had to be taken within the university. Professors avoided controversial subjects, refrained from taking initiatives, sought cover behind the administration, distrusted the students, felt spied upon. Relations with their colleagues were affected, although two-thirds felt they would be supported by them if they were under attack. Some even had guilt feelings in the university context, aware as they were of not always acting in accordance with their principles.

The academic world resisted the attack and wanted to preserve its independence, but it was not inclined to give the impression of approving opinions and behavior condemned by a very active element of the public. Permissiveness—the word is well chosen: leave me alone. So, there was no counterattack. The huge and powerful academic system did not protest, and, while some of its members fought to save their professional lives and defend their opinions, no support movement was organized.

I would like to recount here my personal experience at Harvard in 1952. When I raised political issues with the young teachers whose life I shared at Eliot House—and whose permissiveness was a product of their professional milieu, reinforced by an aristocratic contempt for the wave of right-wing populism then sweeping the country—I encountered only embarrassment and silence. Perhaps this was wisdom on their part and they felt it was best simply to let the storm blow over. But it cannot be said that the American academic world exhibited much intellectual courage at that time.

Academic freedom had only a negative content. It was a far cry from the intelligentsia's struggle for freedom in many less cohesive societies, and from the struggle revived with such vigor in the United States fifteen years later.

The community of scholars had no desire to come into conflict with the national community with which its ties were so strong. Its political philosophy was as weak as that of King Prusias: "Oh, don't get me into trouble with the Republic!" Even the social sciences, so long imbued with the spirit of reform, and whose inspirers had often been strongly marked by the Depression, were more inclined to accept society as it was—to observe the functioning of its rules, its roles, and its values—than to examine the darker side, the repression, the silence, the conflicts inherent in every social order.

The influence of the opinion trends that had developed during the Depression and World War II was on the wane. In part this decline can be attributed to specific features of the American society, but in large part it was also caused by the increasingly visible characteristics of the Stalin regime. The renewal of radical ideas took place on the fringes of the academic world, not at its center, for this world was certainly no haven for intellectual pursuits that opposed the dominant ideology. The difference in this respect between the American universities and those of Britain, Germany, and France is clear proof of the hold that cultural and political integration exerts in the United States over an academic system that prides itself above all on its academic freedom.

It is true that the academic system was not shaken permanently by this crisis; the following years witnessed both a tremendous scientific expansion and a relaxation of the internal political tensions. But it was a turning point. Until then the great debate in the colleges and universities was between education and utilitarianism and between programs designed to produce a certain kind of man— the gentleman, the well-rounded student, or the heir to the Western cultural tradition—and scientific research activity, either after the German example, or of a more applied nature to answer the needs of a society proud of its resources, its work, and the future opening up before it.

At the beginning of the second half of the twentieth century, the liberal arts colleges had lost much of their importance; the college was subordinated to the university. Scientific research, carried out in highly professional surroundings, was increasingly accepted as the specific function of the academic system. At the same time, the main academic institutions were linked more closely not to the many demands relating to progress in areas of general concern, but to the interests and policies of the state and to the huge apparatus on which its power is based. This social and political role of the university was being challenged, no longer by an aristocratic conception of education, but rather by the pressure of social forces excluded from the dominant social order or by the critique of the power structure. A complete reversal! The education theme was once aristocratic, while the technical-professional theme was the "democratic" one; now it was just the opposite. The highest type of scientific activity linked the university to the social and political elite, while the education theme became a grass-roots demand, the demand for an opening of the university to social issues. This also means that the education theme, which once emanated from within the university and was an ideological construct invented by presidents, deans, and educators, now became the instrument of pressure of outside forces. Conversely, the theme of research and technology, once linked to the desire to put the academic system at the service of the social demand, now increasingly became the expression of an academic rhetoric, of a professionalism no less indifferent to the university's role in society than the old educational ideologies had been in their time, and, like them, showing no concern for their elitist implications.

We can easily understand the nostalgia with which some great figures of the academic system evoke the fifties (rarely mentioning McCarthyism in this connection). In wealthy institutions like Harvard, which, thanks to the efforts of Presidents Conant and Pusey, were able to attract both research grants and private donations, the old and the new situation seemed to combine harmoniously. Indeed, the transition from the old to the new ruling elites was carried out without difficulty in these elite institutions, as it was at the same time in the French Grandes Ecoles, where the sons of the liberal upper-class capitalist bourgeoisie learned to become technocrats.

But this continuity of the ruling classes did not prevent other forces from acting. And we could just as well—or rather just as badly—sum up this period by saying that while the old ideology of progress was weakening, the academic system's inability to answer the latent demands of an urban and multiethnic society was also increasing.

In this respect, the American university is no different from others. It may be better organized and richer in means and institutions, but it is just as pleased with its own rhetoric and as indifferent to any serious examination of its social and cultural role. The absence of a critical university leads naturally to the critique of the university.

5. *Protest*

Since 1964, the powerful American academic system has been
shaken by a series of revolts; Berkeley was the first campus to
experience a crisis of major importance. In 1968, the incidents at
Columbia and the actions of SDS marked a new summit in a crisis
that by the spring of 1970 appeared to have become widespread.
These movements, often extremely violent, took public opinion by
surprise. This was accentuated by the fact that although the action
of revolutionary groups was often decisive, it was not in general
a question of isolated acts of violence, but of a broad movement,
supported by a large number, often by a large majority, of the students and by an appreciable proportion of the academic staff.

During this period, academic unrest was not confined to the
United States. Japan, West Germany, France, and Italy also experienced serious disorders, and in a totally different political context, student movements also played an important political role
in Poland, Czechoslovakia, and Yugoslavia. What is surprising,
however, is that the United States was among the most seriously
affected countries. The academic situations in America and, for
example, in France are hardly comparable. In France the number
of students tripled in 10 years. The outdated French system of
organization, with its bureaucratic central control, just managed
to cope with this extremely rapid expansion, but was incapable of
adapting teaching to new demands, or of creating efficient decision-
making machinery, or even of providing acceptable working conditions for a large number of students. I have shown clearly enough
in the preceding chapters that in the United States the academic
system, which had been expanding on a large scale for quite some
time, had no material difficulties. Offering excellent conditions
for work and study, receiving very considerable financial support
under a relatively efficient management, it had, on many occasions,

173

shown its capacity to produce new initiatives and to deal with new problems. The French students had long belonged only nominally to the university, which dispensed its teaching without either the teachers or the administration making any effort to give the students a sense of belonging. On the contrary, in the United States, the college or university student feels that he belongs in his surroundings and is a member of his institution; he is proud of his campus, where his work and leisure are organized in a pleasant and efficient manner. These remarks are obviously superficial and an attempt has already been made to correct them. Nevertheless, the American academic system was in no way in difficulties in 1964, but was, on the contrary, developing fairly steadily.

The first question that must therefore be asked is: "Was there an academic crisis in the United States?"—for it is not obvious that the answer is in the affirmative. There are two ways, partially linked one with the other, of answering in the negative.

On the one hand, it is clear that an attitude of revolt existed within a sector of the student population. As we noted in Chapter 2, Clark and Trow (1966) distinguished four main types of student culture: the collegiate culture, which, of the four, most strongly emphasizes the earlier traditions of the colleges, insisting on the importance of such extracurricular activities as sports, and supported by the fraternities and sororities; the academic culture, embraced by the serious students who belong to the community of scholars and who aim constantly at perfection; the professional culture, which stresses the learning of a job or a profession and is widespread among the lower middle-class students for whom the college or university is the way to social mobility; and finally, the nonconformist culture, which covers all those who are outside the boundaries of the norms and values of the institution, whether they be bohemians or political activists. These nonconformists are usually good students who come from families with above-average incomes. They are therefore an elite group whose nonconformism is carried to the lengths of opposition and can even become a revolt —for these students are not motivated by a desire for upward social mobility; rather the university serves to maintain them at the same level as their parents and should prevent them from dropping below it. According to this interpretation, there is a student problem or a teen-ager problem rather than a crisis in the academic world; student unrest has developed in the universities only because the universities provide a liberal atmosphere in which deviant behavior is more rarely and less severely censured than in other organizations, like firms and offices. This analysis can be extended to describe what André Malraux has called a crisis of civilization—a crisis whose depth and extent is such that it would be useless to look for the cause in the specific and limited problems of the universities.

On the other hand, it can easily be recalled that the important academic crises have often been directly linked to social and national problems outside the university. Can one for an instant imagine understanding what is going on in Columbia or in San Francisco without taking the black movement into account? Can the general crisis of May 1970 be defined other than as a reaction to the invasion of Cambodia?

Are not the various forms of opposition to the war in Vietnam the only element of continuity of the movement between 1965 and 1970? It is even maintained by some that the importance given to the happenings in the academic world was to a large extent determined by the action of the mass media, aimed, if not at diverting attention from, at least at counteracting awareness of, the war in Vietnam and of the fearful dangers that it entailed for world peace. To speak of a student movement is to isolate one category of actors and problems; consequently, one is deliberately adopting a classical, liberal standpoint; demands appear that the system proves incapable of fulfilling satisfactorily and inventively; the academic system must therefore be reformed. The reformist argument is obviously much less dangerous for American society than the denunciation of the war, its causes, its course, and its consequences; this revelation would expose the power structure in the United States and cast much more doubt on the nature and the legitimacy of the institutions of power than it would on their adaptation to the demands of one category, namely the students—a category that is, moreover, neither the worst off nor the best organized. In the same way, one can be against the use of the term "student movement" in Japan or in France, on the grounds that it seems to be too restrictive a term to designate the protagonists of a movement that should be defined not so much by its protagonists as by its raison d'être, which is the struggle against one form of social domination. More broadly still, the history of many countries bears witness to the leading role of the intelligentsia in the struggle against the established ruling powers, and in particular against the state. In the nationalist movements of nineteenth-century Europe, there were always students in the forefront of the fight against the oppressing state, be it national or foreign; the same applies to the counterparts of these movements in Latin America, Asia, or Africa today. The intelligentsia in the United States is concentrated in the universities; it is therefore there, and for the reasons already outlined, that the intelligentsia has developed its criticism of the university as an instrument of the political forces in power. But the justification and the strength of the confrontation can only be understood with reference to the intelligentsia's real adversary, that is to say, in the American context, to the economic, political, and military ruling forces, for these forces involved the country in the war, as is clearly shown by the secret documents recently obtained and published by the leading newspapers. Cultural crisis on the one hand, political conflict on the other—these two interpretations both agree in granting limited importance to specifically academic problems.

They are entirely correct in insisting that the protest movement went far beyond discontent with conditions of work and administration in the universities; in any event these conditions cannot appear bad when compared with European standards. The vast majority of students themselves said in 1969, and even in 1970, that they were satisfied with their working conditions. But such expressions of satisfaction could lead to serious misunderstandings if they were used to reduce the problems of the academic system to problems of internal administration. I have too often insisted here on the close relationship of the universities and colleges to society at large and on the varying importance of their triple role as producers of social order, as reproducers of the social and cultural heritage, and as adjusters to changes in social organization, not to realize that one cannot simply dissociate internal from external problems. My critical analysis of the "professional" rhetoric current in academic circles and of the narrow conception of academic freedom[1] has, I hope, shown that the isolation of the university's internal problems can only be a defense mechanism of the professorial group, which is thus afforded immense help from the authorities without having to question the implications of that support. On the contrary, the close relationship between academic and social and political problems in general is more obvious in the United

---

[1] President Robert Sproul of the University of California defined it in its most restricted sense when he said: "Essentially the freedom of the University is the freedom of the competent person in the classroom." Quoted in Otten (1970, p. 113).

States than in many other countries. As indicated in Table 21, the
data collected by the research workers of the American Council
on Education demonstrate this clearly.

TABLE 21 *Issues in 1968–69*	In institutions where violent troubles occurred, %	In institutions where nonviolent troubles occurred, %
War	49	51.2
Services to students (housing, medical and food, fees, teaching)	44.1	50.9
Minority groups students	69.1	51.7
Student power	77.9	74.7

SOURCE: Bayer and Astin (1969, p. 345).

For the year 1969–70, another more detailed classification is presented that does not include the two-year institutions (see Table
22), but this should not make an appreciable difference in the results.

TABLE 22 *Summary of protests in four-year institutions only*	Kinds of protest	Percentage
	All protests	80.2
	Protests directed against the institution	
	Total	45.4
	War related	16.3
	Racial issues	24.2
	Facilities and student life	33.4
	Student power	4.9
	Protests not directed against the institution	
	Total	78.0
	Earth day	43.9
	October moratorium	35.4
	November moratorium	26.4
	December moratorium	8.0
	Cambodia invasion	22.3
	Kent State killings	30.1

NOTE: The percentages indicate the proportion of institutions in which incidents
occurred in the year 1969–70. The main source used was the student newspapers
of some 200 institutions.

SOURCE: Astin (1970a, p. 7).

Whatever the importance of such general political actions as the moratoriums in the autumn of 1969 or the movement connected with the invasion of Cambodia and reinforced by the killings at Jackson State and Kent State, the protest movement has never been distinct from a movement directed against the universities themselves. If we go back to a previous period, to the time of the Free Speech Movement at Berkeley between 1964 and 1966, the connection between the movement against the university and the campaign against racial segregation, racial discrimination, and the Vietnam war, which was then in its infancy, is even more obvious.

The protest movement is not really directed against the universities but against the academic system. This is demonstrated in the first place by the widespread character of the incidents illustrated by the above figures. In all, in 1968–69, incidents took place in 70.5 percent of the private universities, 43 percent of the public universities, 42.6 percent of four-year nonsectarian colleges, 17.8 percent of four-year Protestant colleges, 10.4 percent of two-year public colleges, and 8.5 percent of four-year Catholic colleges. No incidents were reported in the two-year private colleges, which, as I have said, are of limited and declining importance.

Finally, it should be added that in 29.6 percent of the cases in which nonviolent incidents occurred, and even in 17.7 percent of the cases in which the incidents were violent, there was a formal statement issued by faculty in support of protestors (Bayer & Astin, 1969). The movement is therefore very widespread, although the main centers of activity are at the heart of the academic system. The names that have attracted the most attention on different occasions are Berkeley, Columbia, Harvard, Yale, and Princeton. The incidents do not break out on the fringe of the system but in those national institutions that are the most independent of pressure from the local community, that are the best endowed in federal research funds, and where the faculty are the most liberal and most supportive of academic ethics.

The very nature of American academic institutions means that student unrest has taken even deeper root there than in other countries. It is true that in Germany, and in Berlin in particular, the universities were extensively criticized, and in Japan extremely violent incidents occurred within the universities. But in France problems of a strictly academic order were of very slight interest to the most active members of the movement of May. In no case, however, was a political process of clash and negotiation within the universities continued as unremittingly as in the United States; this is directly linked to the greater decision-making capacity of the American university presidents and to the importance of the campus as a collectivity.

In fact, not only has the student movement been determined by the nature of the American academic system, but the movement has even done a lot to expose the underlying unity of this system. Even though good observers like Berelson and Riesman had recognized the existence of this unity, I do not think we could today present it as we have done had it not been for the existence of the student movement. Its existence makes it now impossible to give a purely internal view of this system, to define it in terms of its values and norms. We are forced to understand that its unity is based on its dominant role of producing the social order and on the subordination of all other functions to that role.

This is also why the incidents in America should be placed in an international context, wider, to be sure, than a national context, but still limited. At the time of the disorders in the United States, equally important incidents took place in other parts of the world, in particular in such Latin American cities as Mexico City, São Paulo, Buenos Aires and Cordoba, Bogota, and Lima. But one should not conclude that all incidents in universities belong to the same category.

In countries where the politically active population only represents a small part of the total population, and more precisely in the cases where there is a struggle for power between the ruling oligarchy and an urban middle class, supported to a certain extent by the masses, the students represent the vanguard of this middle class. The academic autonomy progressively won in Latin America since the Cordoba movement in 1918 is the symbol of this rise of the middle class. The students therefore have the dual role of defender of the political and cultural interests of their own social class, and at the same time of mobilizers of those known, somewhat confusedly, as the marginals. Consequently, the problems connected with actual academic activity are limited, since the university is above all a political world whose autonomy in relation to the general political system can be considerable. We have only to recall, for example, that Havana University at the time of Fidel Castro's youth had numerous internal clashes and a very great liberty of political expression, even though Batista ruled as dictator.

The direction taken by the student movement is determined to a greater or lesser extent, depending on the situation, by its association with a political force supported by the middle classes or by its role as mobilizer of the masses. But the main point is that it is always more important to speak of the students than of the university.

In my opinion, the new element in the most industrially developed countries is the importance of the problems of the university, that is to say, the problems linked with the role of knowledge in the functioning of society, with the formation of the social hierarchy, and with the power structure. This is why, in these countries, the students act, not in relation to other social groups, but autonomously. They do not consider themselves as an independent social class, and they are not misguided enough to think that they can have a decisive influence on the orientations of society. But they know they live in a society where knowledge is an essential element of technical and economic progress, and they become aware of the fact that class and power structure determine the use made of this progress in their society.

The criticism by radical teachers and students of all manifestations of the universities' dependence on political and military forces in power is therefore of great significance. The butts of their attacks are in fact few, and it is easy, for example, to rebut their call for an end to all classified research on the campus by replying that to do so would not bring about a fundamental change in the research capacities of the universities. But such a reply would miss the point. What this example of concrete, and at the same time symbolic, dependence illustrates is a questioning of the general relationship between the university and society, the parallelism between the academic order and the social order, and the rhetoric of value-free professionalism.

When the academic system is the principal means of forming the social hierarchy, it is natural that the formation of this hierarchy, and the whole system that it serves, should be questioned in the universities.

The student movement is not a movement of professional defense, for the same reason that professorial rhetoric is artificial, namely, because the academic world cannot be defined entirely by its relationship to a cultural model and to technical norms, but has some of the characteristics of a type of domination. The latter determines the way in which:

1   Resources are accumulated within the major corporations.

2   Requirements of the population are defined by their capacity to consume goods and services produced by these corporations.

3   Social level is acquired by means of an education system that is both socially and intellectually selective.

The objection often made to this interpretation of student movements in the industrially advanced countries is that their main strength is not to be found in the most highly scientific and technical departments, and that sociologists, political scientists, or architects are usually more radical than physicists or chemists. This certain and widespread fact in no way constitutes an objection. It can only be used against a rather different interpretation, according to which the new professionals and technicians are themselves the bearers of a new movement of protest. Their position would in effect be comparable to that of the skilled workers in the nineteenth-century industrial economy, workers who were the moving force of trade-unionist and socialist movements. This idea has been put forward by certain members of SDS, who borrowed it from the French ideologists of the new working class—André Gorz and Serge Mallet in particular. It bears an element of truth but cannot account for the general meaning of the student movement. Moreover, if we are to refer to the nineteenth century, the skilled workers, who may have been the militant workers, to use Lenin's term, were also the labor aristocracy, with working conditions and an income considerably better than those of the unskilled workers. They were more often to be found swelling the ranks of the social democrats than those of the revolutionary movements.

Because knowledge is a productive force controlled by large corporations and because the educational standard, to a large extent, defines a person's position in the social hierarchy, those who are training to hold executive functions in large organizations are naturally close to the ruling class; they sometimes become assimilated into the ruling class, but more often they form the bureaucracy attached to it. On the other hand, students in natural sciences envisaging a research career in the university itself tend to concentrate solely on their career and to feel above, or on the fringe of, social conflicts.

On the contrary, those who are more directly and professionally interested in the working of society, who will be less often employed in large firms and are more aware of the ideological role of the university, are more inclined to adopt a critical attitude. The theories on the new working class have led to excesses. Let us not go to the other extreme. The most active in the protest movement are not the humanities students, who are more confined to the academic world. Social science students, and teachers too, are increasingly aware that they play a part in the consolidation of the social order and that they belong to a scientific and technical culture. They are more precisely on the fringe, just as many skilled workers, who with the assurance of their professional training, were able to take advantage of favorable conditions on the labor market, and were, at the same time, in the factory and independent of it. The greatest awareness of social conflicts is therefore to be found among those who are part of the scientific and technical cultural model but who are the most independent of the large-scale corporations. Because of their position, they are more capable of questioning the university's identification of its scientific and professional vocation with its ideological role as a consolidator of, and integrator to, the social order. Those who want to replace technical civilization by an educational ideal can scarcely go beyond a position of militant liberalism, like that of the best of the liberal arts colleges. This is far removed from the position of the radical students, who do not fight in the name of an ideal of man, but in the name of criticism of authority. Neither technicians nor humanists, they have a political approach to the problems of the university and its ties with society.

Their activities are organized primarily in the best universities because that is where the cultural model is adhered to most closely; also, the autonomy of the academic world makes the closeness between this cultural model and its social application more evident there. In the smaller colleges and universities, which are more directly oriented toward preparing students for technical jobs, the cultural model only appears in a diluted form, and the intellectual autonomy of the academic world is also weaker.

I do not claim that this analysis explains the reasons for the content and the forms of protest movements that have developed in the universities. In fact, as we shall see in a moment, it provides only one element of this explanation.

But it is essential to assert at the outset that academic problems play a central role in this movement. It is tempting, as we have seen, to emphasize only the reasons for revolt or for the sensitivity of the students. This sensitivity is all the more developed for having been shaped in an environment in which dissent and even collective demonstrations are more tolerated than elsewhere. It seems that the students express the dissatisfaction of a society forced to admit that its practices are increasingly remote from its values. The Supreme Court's decisions against segregation have met with considerable social resistance, and the war in Vietnam, hideous in its own right, and a danger to world peace, has demonstrated the emptiness of official America's declarations of anticolonialism and progressivism. I am simply maintaining here that the role of the university in society was one of the main issues in the student protest movement and that this fact is linked, not to the personal problems of the students, but to this role itself. When the university is, as it was in various forms up to the present generation, an instance either of reproduction of the social and cultural heritage, or of consolidation of a ruling elite, defined by birth or by money, the revolt is against the dependent situation of the students. This has been a topic in recent years, but no more so than it was a century ago, for the fight against the colleges acting *in loco parentis* has a long history in the United States and has often caused severe and protracted crises. What is new is precisely that instead of the traditional juxtaposition of claims for personal independence and awareness of general social problems (like those of slavery, of the war, of poverty, or of working-class exploitation), there appears a unifying principle in the name of which academic problems become key problems. After World War I, the students conducted pacifist campaigns, but during the Vietnam war they questioned the connection between the university and the politico-military establishment. Before the Civil War, campaigns were conducted against slavery, but today it is the segregative character of the universities and the colleges in the North that has been attacked by the movement for Negro rights, and it is the role of Columbia or Harvard in the urban community that has provoked violent revolt.

When the university had a predominantly ideological role, student protest was essentially situated in the ideological sphere. Today, it is the situation of the university within the technocratic power structure and within imperialism in general that is being challenged.

The protests and beneficence of the liberal elite mix with these radical criticisms; they are not identical with them. The teachers were to become well aware of this. The majority supported the Free Speech Movement at Berkeley in 1964, but those who took their stand the most willingly within the university, sheltered by its professional norms and refusing to consider their true dependence, sidestepped the radical criticism that was also directed at them and which, in the heat of battle, made light, for its part, of the specifically professional problems of the production of knowledge.

Although the radicals formed a small minority, their action was decisive. The student movement became a revolt against the established order and not simply a revolt against the despotic and outdated aspects of the functioning of the colleges or a liberal protest in defense of the universal values of humanism and pacificism.

What is disturbing is that the vast majority of American academics confined their commentaries on events in which they were so directly involved to a study of student psychology and education, avoiding all analysis of the universities themselves. They took it for granted that teachers serve no other master than cognitive rationality. (When the church is attacked, its immediate reaction is to talk of sacrilege and barbarity.) All discussion was centered on the values and norms of society, and any reference to established power, class, and social conflicts was avoided. That is why the young radicals could only protest against the established order in those places where the system was most obviously caught up in its own contradictions, not contradictions between ethical values and practice but between the established power and the masses, between white suburbia and black ghettos, between the Washington government and the combatants of the People's Army in Vietnam.

The obvious weakness of the student movement lay in the fact that those who constituted it belonged to a privileged section of the community. Their criticism of the established order and the role of the universities within the power structure implied going beyond their own situation and their own particular experience. In themselves they did not constitute a social movement: they were merely one of its limbs. Our comparison with the labor movement is again valid. The working-class elite, in which the militant workers had their origins, was also relatively privileged. In a market economy and a society where the educational level was low, their qualifications and education put them in a much more favorable situation than the unskilled workers. It was this association of the skilled and the unskilled—sometimes in a fusion but more often in a complementary relationship—that gave the latter its militant strength.

The Berkeley and Columbia students are not so much the descendants of the Wobblies as of the worker-intellectuals, or the intellectual-workers, of the Paris Commune. That is why it is wrong to seek the significance of the movement uniquely in the political aware-ness of the students. A social movement is not reflection or aware-ness, but a number of actions that have a significance only with ref-erence to the social conflict they express and of which they are a part. Similarly, the role of academic institutions cannot be made to fit the conceptions of them held by the administration and the pro-fessors, arrayed in their trappings of humanist or professional rhetoric, it can only be understood if we take into account what is excluded from, or manipulated by, the university.

It has therefore been my intention not merely to underline the key importance of certain elements of the protest movement but to re-call as well the necessity to proceed from an understanding of the conflict to a study of the people involved, and not vice versa.

The Four Levels of the Academic Crisis

It is now necessary to complete these first observations: no social movement can be merely reduced to one principle of conflict. To do so would be to link it to an ideology that can only partly explain collective behavior. The working-class movement is not simply a struggle against capitalism; it is also the claim for better working and labor conditions and an effort to give the workers, by means of the unions, a greater say in the decisions concerning them. The relation between these various levels of collective behavior varies. Sometimes wage claims do not give rise to higher levels of action, and we have no more than business unionism; sometimes the con-trary is true, and more everyday practices lead to a questioning of social domination. In such cases, the role played by theoreticians in the formation of the labor movement is more important. But a real social movement, capable of producing a new social policy, can only exist where there are links between these various levels of action. In our analysis of the student movement, then, we must distinguish a number of levels that define at the same time partic-ular types of behavior and elements, which, by interaction, consti-tute the social movement itself (see Touraine, 1970 and 1971*a*).

1   In the first place, the students belong to an academic organization. To oversimplify, one could say that they experience a certain degree of satisfaction insofar as their expectations correspond to their experiences. They may feel a dichotomy between, for example, the cultural content proposed to them by the educational system and the norms by which this system judges the apprenticeship to learning. In many countries, students have been wondering whether

learning is not simply a means to an end, the examination, whereas examinations are supposed to be no more than a means of checking intellectual attainment. Hence the hostility to examinations, which, at their most elementary level, appear to be an element of academic bureaucracy.

Satisfaction is therefore always expressed relatively. The student, who judges his own academic attainment in relation to that of others, compares one teacher, or one college, with another. The individual or the group is therefore referred to a whole and stands in a ranking relationship to the other parts of this whole. Moreover, the system comprises relations of authority that are judged according to both expectations and observed norms.

The students always have a more or less informal organization that can either reinforce the rules of the organization or oppose them to the point of provoking a crisis and sanctions. The confusion of norms, the lack of coherence between the position of various individuals and groups, and the dichotomy between expectations and experience can cause disorganization, withdrawal, or disruptive behavior. Merton's well-known analysis of the types of anomie (1957) as a response to the conflict between means and ends in a social system is a good analytical tool for these problems. But there is no place at this level for the idea of a social movement, a movement that disputes the social order in the name of a conflict of interests and envisions replacing it by another order, considered better.

The problems facing a university are not specific and the working of a university can be studied in the same way as that of any other organization.

2   This is no longer completely true when we pass to the second level of analysis and consider the decision-making system of the university. The characteristic of organizations that are directly linked to the cultural model of a society, or simply to activities referring directly to values—organizations, therefore, with a high degree of professionalization—is their incapacity to be wholly political institutions. A university where the mathematics syllabus would be fixed by majority vote is unthinkable, whereas a great many of the problems of running a university can be settled by democratic means. On the other hand, the university is rarely sole mistress of its resources and regulations. Even in the United States, where the economy is much less centralized, some of Hutchins' reforms came up against insurmountable difficulties.

Academic government is therefore an attempt to find the necessarily unstable balance between internal professional necessities and both external and internal influences. The students have generally had very little say in decisions; one of the issues of varying importance in the university incidents has been the demand to participate in academic government. This subject is of even greater importance to the teachers, who demand the autonomy of the university in cases where it is subject to administrative control or who protest against what they consider to be the arbitrary decisions of academic government.

Demands of this sort can lead to a serious crisis, but they are confined to the institution, even if, for the revolutionaries, they are only a means, or a tool, that serves to destroy the institution. This kind of political pressure is not simply focused on organizational demands. It questions the validity not only of the game, but also of the rules. This type of pressure is of considerable importance in the university, particularly in cases where the university tends to assure not so much the reproduction, as the production of social order. Organizational demands, on the other hand, are likely to be more apparent in a university whose main function is to transmit a social and cultural heritage and to correspond to an ideal conception of education and to certain values. It is in an "instrumental" university that political pressures come into their own. If such a university has to satisfy market demands and, by using vocational training plans, adapt the demand for education to the number of available technical and professional openings, academic government becomes a vital problem. An illustration of this problem is the experience of Clark Kerr, who, as president of the University of California, could not forget his background as an arbitrator in labor disputes when he was elaborating his concept of the multiversity and a completely instrumental view of the university.

3   On a higher level than the organizational and political problems—those concerning authority and influence—are those concerning power, that is, the capacity of imposing order on a collectivity. Since the university is not a society but an element of society, disputes concerning the choice of ultimate ends cannot remain confined within the university; they necessarily raise problems in the relationship between the university and society. This critical attitude or antagonistic behavior has two complementary aspects, the fusion of which constitutes a social movement. In practice they can be, and often are, dissociated, resulting in a social movement that

is far from being integrated and organized. In effect, a ruling class, or the implements of power attached to it, is not only a social force. It monopolizes the cultural model of a society, as ecclesiastical power monopolizes the divine, or as technocratic centers monopolize the technique and means of economic development. The result is that those who do not possess power, and whom we can call the masses, are always fighting, as we have already pointed out, on two fronts. On the one they are involved in a defensive action against the ruling power, on the other in an offensive against these ruling classes, appealing to the cultural model that has been stolen and threatened by these classes. This explains how the workers defended their jobs and wages against the hold of the market and the capitalist entrepreneur, while at the same time terming socialism their desire for collective control of the cultural model of progress.

In the case of the university, the defensive action is the call to liberty, to free speech, to the rights of the individual, as against the hold exerted by the university machine in the service of the techno-bureaucracy, or the mixed forms of technocracy and capitalism that are predominant in the West. In the United States, the most extreme form of this defensive reaction is the desire of ethnic groups to defend or rebuild their cultures, which have been largely crushed by the prevailing social and cultural interests. These liberation movements, like the workers' movements of the preceding period, or the nationalist movements in the conquered continents, appeal firstly to a social and cultural specificity, all the more fervently as the pressure to integrate increases or the policy of assimilation is forced upon them. It is certainly not by accident that this refusal was most eloquently expressed by Frantz Fanon, a Negro who was brought up in a colony that was subject to a policy of assimilation and who joined the struggle in Algeria at the time when the colonialists' slogan was "integration." Similarly, the black power movement has its main strength in the North of the United States, where the double threat of assimilation and racial segregation reproduced a new type of colonial situation. Other ethnic groups, and later even women, formed similar movements of break with, withdrawal from, and attack against the prevailing social and cultural order. This defensive action in the American universities could scarcely come uniquely from within, for the most active of the leading revolutionary groups are also those who accorded highest priority to the black liberation movement.

On the other hand, the offensive relies on participation in the cultural model to overthrow the power of the ruling class. This action gains momentum in proportion as the actions of the ruling class appear increasingly dissociated from the cultural model and increasingly preoccupied with the repressive maintenance of order (by means of the state and ideology) rather than with the development, in a contemporary society, of the forces of production. Protest movements of this sort were forceful in France or in Japan and also in the United States, especially when the American government seemed to be more squarely faced, in Vietnam, with the choice between defeat or the spread of the war. As in the previous case, these are problems and actions that concern the university but go beyond it. They can even assume sufficient autonomy for the criticism of the state to be at least as linked to the second level of collective action (which we have termed political pressure) as to a social movement.

But this offensive action is also directed against academic power in order both to oppose it and to reveal the vacuity of its utterances and its autonomy. In many countries (Japan, France, Italy, the United States), the tactic of "confrontation" is employed to show all the students that academic autonomy is a mere facade and that the true protagonists are the revolutionary movement on the one hand and the forces of repression on the other. Police intervention usually has the effect, in the first instance at least, of creating solidarity among the students.

In every case, the main problem facing a social movement formed in the university is that it must be partly within it, partly outside of it.

If the movement has, as its aim, academic reform, it is restricted to organizational demands and "political" pressure. If it is wholly determined by forces and aims external to the university, it splits, for there is no reason, at least in a world in which generalized participation in public life exists, for the academic world to be the center of conflicts and actions that concern society as a whole.

Above all, the limits of the "producer" role of the university must be recognized. If the university was in itself a production center, this problem would not exist. Instead, it is simultaneously the research center of a technologically advanced society and the ideological instrument through which the society is controlled by economic, political, and military institutions whose power is obviously not situated in the universities. The universities, to a certain extent, play the role that was played by the ordinary priesthood in the Catholic church when the church was a central element in the system of social control. This explains why there is always a separation in the academic world between internal and external problems, between professionalism and the function of maintaining the social hierarchy. This also explains why student movements, in order to avoid this separation, which weakens their action, tend to resort to extreme methods and to close the university. At the same time, this extremism robs the student movement of its base and exposes its most convinced militants to face-to-face conflict with the police or the army under very unfavorable conditions.

It would therefore be artificial to present this academic protest movement as a multistage process in which organizational demands trigger the pressure for participation in the decision-making machinery, this pressure in turn providing material for a more general criticism of the political authority on which the university depends, while, at the same time, relying for support on the social demands that are most repressed by academic conformism. The elements of the problem are effectively those that I have just outlined, but their interrelationships are neither as direct nor as total. The scene of the action moves from one level to another. The student movement always plays a role that is simultaneously central and marginal. It is perfectly aware of this, since it constantly calls for the intervention of other protagonists and never defines its action in purely academic terms.

A university-based social movement can only exist insofar as the stage of going beyond the internal problems of the university is concomitant with an examination of the role of the university in society. Moreover, this debate must focus on the need to recover control over the university's scientific, technical, and professional productive forces from the present holders of political power.

4   Lastly, we must apprehend the ultimate level in the student protest movement, a level where the content is more cultural than social. Let us return here to ideas already outlined. The society directed toward its own technical and economic development is also the one in which uniformity is defended against change, and consumption against investment.

I am referring now to cultural orientations that cannot be defined at the level of class conflict and the struggle for power. American society, in its entirety, is one of consumption, and, at the same time, of investment, in the same way as rural society was formerly both a religious community and a society of small communities and transmitted social statuses.

Those who rebel today against the culture of the industrial or postindustrial society are not only the radicals, and they are not solely preoccupied with combatting the established powers. In place of a wild Promethean society, they appeal for a return to harmony, remembering the words of Jean-Jacques Rousseau, who in his day feared that Western Europe, in the wake of England, would be carried away by "progress." In place of the conquest of nature by man, they demand respect for the fundamental balances of the eco-system. They see man as part of nature, instead of opposed to it, like a worker faced with a sheet of metal.

The demographic explosion, the spread of pollution, the increasing threat to the natural production sources of oxygen, the exploitation of the world of the imagination by the mass media, or the destruction of personal relationships and sensory experience brought about by such techniques and forms of social organization as, for example, those resulting from the urban crisis—these and other sources of anxiety lead to movements that bring to mind Eastern Monachism or 13th-century Italian Joachism rather than political struggles. André Malraux has spoken of a crisis of civilization: when the gods are dead and, as a result, the image of man—of his soul or of his essence, which were mere reflections of the gods—has disappeared, when the belief in the hereafter is replaced by the cold shadow of death and the development of boundless forces, groups are formed that attempt to recover harmony, community, and self-expression.

This cultural demand may be associated to a greater or lesser degree with a defensive social action. Similarly, at the time of the utopian socialists, communities were formed in the industrial world but also on the fringe of it, nurtured by their opposition to industrial capitalism but also inspired by the idea of a utopia, the most elaborate of which, and also the closest to us, doubtless being that of Fourier. In total contrast to the world of movement, he proposed a world of equilibrium; instead of a society founded on investment, a society founded on communciation and the organization of "natural" needs.

The new fact is that these modern utopias are closely associated today with the topic of youth, because in the most industrially advanced countries, and in the United States far more than elsewhere, this period of life has assumed an increasing autonomy. The length of this period, which stretches from the time when the authority of the family and other socialization agencies begin to decline, and the time when the individual enters the labor force, is increasing. One might add that similar cultural phenomena must occur in old age, and here, once again, the United States sets the trend. But, in our societies, old age is still too marked by the wear and tear of work and by social isolation for it to be a time when new utopias are revealed with much impact. Youth, on the contrary, is at once isolated from the family, concentrated on the campus where academic authority is less and less exerted *in loco parentis*, and isolated from adult life by the prolongation of studies and the necessity, in a society of rapid technological change, for a training that is general rather than strictly professional. Claude Lévi-Strauss envisages our societies becoming more and more like regions in which cultures as different as those of the Hopi and Navaho would coexist. Marshall McLuhan's use of the theme of return to the tribe is well known. Others speak more traditionally of a generational conflict—an ambiguous term, for it is either a question of a separation, rather than a conflict, of generations, or else a conflict that does not set one generation against another but opposes to a system of power those who are subject to it and who cannot be sufficiently defined by their age. This ambiguity has its utility, however, for, at times, this cultural utopia is a complete withdrawal from social conflicts, and, at times, is laden with political demands. These two tendencies are constantly intertwined, especially in pop culture—that of the Beatles, the Rolling Stones, Woodstock, or protest songs and drugs.

In some countries, like France and Japan, the political tendency has the upper hand among the active youth; in others, like the United Kingdom, it is the cultural utopia that holds sway. The particularity of the United States, and especially California, is to have interwoven more closely than elsewhere these two linked and opposite tendencies.

Relation Between These Levels   Before we consider more fully the specific characteristics of the academic protest movement in the United States, it is essential to rapidly examine the reasons that underlie a particular type of articulation between these different levels of collective action.[2] It is, in fact, a question of knowing what reinforces the formation of a

[2] A first attempt at analysis has been presented in my book: *The Post-Industrial Society* (1971*b*).

social movement, or, on the contrary, what isolates the different levels from one another. What makes a social movement in embryo swing either toward an action of pure organizational demand or pressure on the institution, or toward a political or cultural action that is of general relevance but is in fact independent of a university basis?

1 In the first place, what factors raise the first levels of collective action to the level of a full-fledged social movement?

As far as the characteristics of academic organization are concerned, I advance the hypothesis that in its state of crisis it tends to separate internal problems from external problems—that is, the aims of restructuring the university from general social and political aims—whereas an organization that is relatively integrated and satisfactory for its participants enables a smooth shift to be made from organizational problems to general problems. The study of the labor movement has shown[3] that in the declining industries class consciousness is weak; the workers attempting to defend their particular situation come up against immediate difficulties that isolate them from the labor movement as a whole and from its desire to build a new society. If one takes the beginnings of the labor movement in the middle of the nineteenth century in France, for example, one sees in this world dominated by unemployment crises and formation of the proletariat two distinctly separate trends: one, inspired mainly by P. J. Proudhon, is centered on the autonomy of the workers, the defense of their skills, and the self-organization of the producers. The other, best expressed by the action of Louis Blanc and the Luxembourg Committee of 1848, is oriented toward state intervention and political action.

Similarly, in the French university of 1968 the problems of reorganization of the university and of general political struggle were relatively distinct. The organizational crisis of the university was obvious. (There was a very high proportion of failures and of dropouts, bad material conditions, a ranking system within the teaching body in which upward mobility was severely limited, underadministration, etc.) While the lecture halls on the ground floor of the Sorbonne resounded with revolutionary declarations, working groups on the upper floors prepared plans for the reorganization of the university. This separation is typical of the whole continent of

---

[3] See Touraine (1966) and Dofny et al. (1966).

Western Europe, for the organizational crisis of the universities was acute in West Germany as well as in Italy, in Spain as well as in France. The situation was quite different in the United States.

A parallel hypothesis can be applied in relation to the decision-making system of the universities. In the cases where it is incapable of dealing with the problems of adapting the university to social and economic changes (either because it is autocratic or bureaucratic), the desire expressed by the students or the teachers to take part in, and exert an influence upon, decisions leads either to an artificial integration without any real influence on the existing system, or is immediately transformed into a brutal confrontation with the entire political system. Institutional blockage diminishes the possibility of reform and therefore separates the internal from the external problems (see Crozier, 1970). Countries like France and Italy are examples of blocked systems, the simplest indicator to use being the degree of the institutions' autonomy within the academic system. From this point of view, West Germany and Japan had a more flexible system. Compared with Europe, the United States appeared to be endowed with flexible university institutions; however, the analyses that I have cited, particularly that of Lazarsfeld, show that factors of rigidity were also often present. There were, in fact, wide differences among the institutions. The University of California under Kerr or San Francisco State College under Summerskill, while situated within the Master Plan of California, which comprised important factors of rigidity, were evidence of an obvious effort to define the president as a mediator and negotiator. The problems concerning the internal government of these institutions and general political demands were therefore closely linked in both cases. On the other hand, observers are of the opinion that Columbia was in fact governed by Grayson Kirk and David Truman without the faculty or student government having an appreciable influence. Columbia was therefore, par excellence, the place where incidents in the university were most directly the expression of a movement of general significance and of a distinct separation between internal and external problems.

2 A second type of consideration must deal with the relation between the offensive and defensive facets of the social movement itself. Their synthesis does not depend upon the characteristics of the academic system but rather on confrontations within the academic institutions. Similarly, when problems of the labor market or a

general political crisis are given priority in the labor movement over those within the firm (particularly those concerning wage levels or working conditions), one observes a low degree of integration between the elite that protests and the mass that has been reduced to the ranks of the proletariat.

In recent academic history, a higher degree of integration is attained when the crisis is the result of a specific conflict within the university. The importance of both the black movement and the struggle against the war in Vietnam tended to produce in the United States, especially during the second part of the crisis (1969–70), a low degree of integration between, on the one hand, the action of the radical groups against the political power system and the university's connection with it, and, on the other hand, the movement of solidarity with the victims of the system. The American situation was close to that of the French student movement in its first period of important activity, that is, during the Algerian War and immediately afterward.

Inversely, in the French movement of 1968 or in Japan the distance between the two facets was small. In France there was the struggle against capitalist domination, a relative indifference to problems of state properly speaking (the demonstrators on the evening of May 24 shouted, while the President was broadcasting, "To hell with de Gaulle"), and an appeal to the proletariat, more especially fervent in France as the working class was mobilized in the biggest general strike of its history.

However, this first opposition between two types of national situations must be refined. In the first place, if it is true that in the United States the synthesis between the two facets of the social movement is superficial, and that they often tend to separate from each other, like the black movement and the movement against the war in Vietnam, it is also true that the synthesis of these two issues did occur on several occasions and, indeed, in an academic frame of reference. Although it is impossible to speak of a truly student and purely academic movement, the nature of the academic system has meant that in the United States, more than elsewhere, the fight against the war and the movement for black liberation have, through the autonomy and the open-mindedness of the academic world, managed to join—but not to forever combine—forces. Although elsewhere, in France or in Italy, the student movement is construed as something of a device for exploding more general social struggles, in the United States it appears to weld together different elements whose synthesis alone constitutes a social movement that the ruling class experiences as a direct threat.

The objection must then be raised that the unity of this social movement in other countries was artificial, that in the main the labor movement in Japan, West Germany, and even in France, did not respond to the expectations of the students whose supreme desire, as the students in the Sorbonne said, was for the workers to seize the flag of the revolution from the frail hands of the students. The synthesis was strongest during the eventful autumn of 1969 in Italy, an economically less-advanced country. But it is not so much the success or failure of the students that is at issue here as it is the conditions of formation of a social movement.

In the United States, the decisive importance of the war in Vietnam on the one hand, and of the black power movement on the other, at once assured the movement national significance that extended beyond the university and rendered its integration very difficult. The revolutionary groups that attempted to amalgamate the two met with such enormous difficulties that they themselves split.

3   Finally, on what does the union—to any extent—of the social movement with the cultural revolt depend? In the most highly planned societies, the state relies on traditional patterns of dependent or submissive behavior in order to restrict the desire to consume or to participate and therefore to reinforce the investment capacity managed by an authoritarian elite. Such societies are less likely to experience an autonomous cultural outburst than more liberal societies, where grass-roots movements are more important. (But in certain cases, like Italy, the archaic cultural frames of reference are so worn and the political authority so weak that cultural innovation is thereby reinforced.)

It may be thought that mass higher education, the cultural independence of the students on the campus, and the insistence on a consumer society (no longer attaching the same value to discipline and effort as was the case at the time of the economic takeoff) contribute to the autonomy of the cultural movement. The French, Japanese, or German student is still much more subject than the American to the control of school and family. He is less culturally "mobilized" and more dependent. This is why the cultural revolution in France went side by side with political action, as did the black flag with the red. The leadership of Daniel Cohn-Bendit, in fact, relied on their close association.

The slowness with which pop culture infiltrates into France, compared with its rapid spread in Great Britain, the United States, and English-speaking Canada, bears out the weakness of specifically cultural movements in France. The commune movement, or the teen-age culture, has more adherents in Germany than in France.

In reviewing these observations and hypotheses we are led to the conclusion that organizational crisis and institutional rigidity contribute to the formation of a movement of general significance that is directed toward the outside world and is distinctly separate from academic problems. But this movement, in which ideology plays an important part, has little likelihood of being able to organize an action of any permanence in the university. On the other hand, the American situation is such that the movement is closely connected with the university's internal problems, but splits when it goes beyond these limits. This split reinforces (and is reinforced by) the autonomy of the cultural revolt.

Although the desire to classify rigidly ever more complex local or national situations may be misleading, it is useful to present these conclusions in the form of a table. The aim of this table is simply to sum up the preceding remarks and to help in developing a more exact analysis, like the one that I intend to present of the United States.

TABLE 23 *Integration of the social movement*

Cultural movement	Organizational situation			
	Crisis decision-making system		*Normal decision-making system*	
	Rigid	*Flexible*	*Rigid*	*Flexible*
High				
Dependent	Sorbonne	Japan	Socialist countries	San Francisco State
Autonomous	Italy	Nanterre 1968	Columbia 1968	Berkeley FSM
Low				
Dependent	France 1962–65	W. Germany	Harvard 1969	U.S. Cambodian crisis 1970
Autonomous	Netherlands (provos)	W. Germany	Berkeley 1967–69	Great Britain

Table 23 requires a brief explanation. For France, it distinguishes between the Sorbonne and Nanterre. In effect, Nanterre, a new institution situated on an isolated campus, was a liberal university where negotiations between the administration, the students, and the teachers were without doubt much more developed than in the

Sorbonne, which was an amorphous mass and much more seriously underadministered. Nanterre, where a certain number of students were housed on the campus and were therefore more independent of their families, was constantly a scene of cultural revolution; one of the first incidents to take place there followed a lecture in 1967 on Wilhelm Reich, whose influence grew after 1968. It was then that Cohn-Bendit challenged the Minister for Youth in an incident provoked by cultural issues.

The Italian situation is varied and often fairly close to the French one. I have chosen, somewhat arbitrarily, to stress the existence of autonomous cultural issues in Italy, given the hold there of the traditional cultural order, represented by the Catholic church, and the reactions provoked by it; also, I have not found in France any occurrence similar to the one at Trento. I have put Germany in twice, for cultural issues have been both more current than in France and more associated with a specifically political analysis than in the United States. I have taken Great Britain as the example of an extreme situation where the formation of a social movement was especially difficult. I will come back later to the American examples.

To sum up, in the United States, forces that diverge at the summit tend to be reunited in a general movement due to the very weight of the academic world. The strength of the movement is in its base, the weakness at the top. This weakness is not necessarily unproductive, since it brings about the development of political, social, and cultural movements which infiltrate deep into American society. Inversely, in Japan or in France, a powerful social movement appears, particularly in Japan, as an impressive "event," but its reformist effects on the social body are limited. No event in the American university world, not even the revolt in the spring of 1970, shook American society in the way that the 1968 May movement shook France. But it is possible that the effects of the revolt, both on the academic system and on American society as a whole, are more diffuse and more enduring.

The opposition between France and the United States reduced here to highly simplified, all-inclusive images, is exactly that of the two opposing tendencies found in most social movements. The American movement is rich in cultural content and combats a modern adversary, both because the universities actively participate in the formation of the technocratic society and because the war in Vietnam is not a rearguard action of outdated colonialists but the action of dynamic imperialism. But where its ability to bring about changes and reforms is important, its revolutionary potentiality is low. The French movement on the other hand is confronted by a moribund university overtaken by its own growth; the central role it once played in the recruitment of an elite or of a technobureaucratic personnel is now filled by schools independent of the university. The student movement turns to the labor movement because the working-class culture, reinforced by the arrival of new industrial workers, difficult living conditions, and the authoritarianism of the employers and the state, still has a profound influence on French society. If the movement fathered at Nanterre is closer to the American situation, the most long-term trends of the student movement are more susceptible to a Leninist model of political action, a model based on the internal contradictions of the political system and the necessity of concentrating action on the destruction of the state's political power.

The force of the shock provoked by the movement of May was linked more to the archaisms of society and the state than with the response met by the much newer issues of the March 22 Movement. The rapid regression of the movement, starting in the fall of 1968, reinforced the movement's Old Left tendencies and increased the distance between these tendencies and certain forms of politico-cultural revolt; the latter remained uninstitutionalized and are severely repressed.

In all social movements, the desire to create a new world through the spontaneity of the people is combined with the necessity for an organized struggle against the ruling political power. The main revolutionary movements combine these two imperatives; the student movement, on account of its distinctive and limited social basis, has only combined them to a limited extent. On one side of the Atlantic it tended to follow one trend, on the other side, the opposing one. But in both cases we can speak of a social movement, because there was an attempt to combine these two aspects of its action in its awareness and its struggle.

THE PROTEST MOVEMENT IN THE UNITED STATES The American student movement has lasted for some six years (1964-1970) in its recent phase; it has been closely connected with the campaigns against the war in Vietnam and more indirectly with the black movement. Finally, it cannot be separated from the counterculture. Able to develop itself on the campus and supported by new cultural demands, it is at the same time involved in a direct and sometimes violent political action. It is certainly unable to act as an organized political form, but the various aspects of its action must be considered as part of one movement and not as autonomous reactions to unconnected social and political problems.

Crisis in Academic Organization

This heading, which corresponds to the first of the four levels of analysis outlined—organizational, institutional, sociopolitical, and cultural—can be studied by comparing the different campuses where incidents have occurred. Astin and Bayer (1970, p. 7) sum up their observations by concluding that the most closely affected institutions "tended to have environments which were incohesive; moreover, students and faculty had little involvement in the class, students were not on warm friendly terms with the instructor and they were not verbally aggressive in the class; finally, these institutions had relatively permissive policies concerning student drinking. Students in the protest-prone institutions tended to feel that there was little concern for their individual welfare . . ."

This is why incidents are unimportant in the private nonsectarian colleges, where there is a great deal of interest in the students as individuals. Inversely, the big research universities, where professors are little concerned with undergraduate education and teaching assistants are therefore more important, were very protest-prone. The students often divided into overcrowded classes with a high student to teacher ratio, were more dependent on their classmates and so the spread of protest was easier there (Byrne, 1965). More precisely, the academic situation favored the simultaneous development of three categories that Kenneth Keniston had distinguished very early on (Keniston, 1961, pp. 335–341): the activists, whom we shall come back to; the disaffiliated, who rejected a university where they felt themselves outsiders; and the underachievers, who were filled with resentment against the family and academic environment that forced them into studies for which they were not motivated.

This student discontent vents itself on the organization of their studies, especially the examinations. But, does this mean to say that the students would be in favor of a return to general education? Table 24 contains some results that throw light on student reaction. The students are mainly concerned with their personal liberty. It is particularly noticeable that the criticism of specialization that is usually attributed to students is much stronger among teachers, who respond to student agitation with something of a guilty conscience and tend to think that anything which

Undergraduate education would be improved if:	Faculty, %	Undergraduates, %
All courses were elective	20	53
Grades were abolished	32	59
Colleges and universities were governed completely by faculty and students	39	62
There was less emphasis on specialized training and more on broad liberal education	56	41
Teaching effectiveness, not publications, was the primary criterion for the promotion of faculty	75	95

TABLE 24 Attitudes of faculty members and undergraduate students

SOURCE: Martin Trow, (1970*b*)

would ensure greater cohesion in the teaching and the academic sphere is desirable. When questioned on the aims of education, these students almost unanimously approve of an aggregate of aims (88 to 97 percent of the replies are positive) including: "continue intellectual growth," "satisfy job requirements," "find myself," and "acquire detailed grasp of a special field." These answers do not give the impression that the teaching given in the university is thought to be contradictory.

S. M. Lipset's (1970) reaction can therefore be considered excessive. In his opinion, the reforms desired by the students would be a return to the past, if not to childhood, and signify their refusal to accept specialization and a purely professional student-teacher relationship. His opinion is worth quoting:

It may be argued that when the activists criticize the educational system today, they seek to retain the status of pupil and to have teachers rather than to be students of university professors. Although their demand is now couched in terms of the faculty taking an activist position in support of radical social change, it is a demand that their professors act like their schoolteachers, that they take part in "bull sessions" in which they discuss the totality of human experience, not simply their subject matter. When the students oppose grades, they are demanding the restoration of a particularistic relationship with their teachers, one in which they are not judged objectively according to highly specialized criteria, but rather continue to be treated as total human beings (ibid., p. 112).

One might agree with Lipset that student movements in general have effectively not given much serious thought to the grounds for judging specialization, but this fact demands a different interpretation. The stand taken by the student movement is one of struggle, and not one which proposes a management scheme for the university. They are concerned with demolishing the professionalist arguments of teachers, with demonstrating that effectively the university is not outside society, but within it—much more closely associated with the ruling classes than with any other class, or than with the cultural demands of the students. Their declarations are an integral part of a policy of agitation and confrontation. One can disagree politically with them, but to present their stand as infantile and as a rejection of specialized learning is not to do them justice. The figures I have quoted are evidence of this.

It is difficult to estimate the extent of academic discontent. Perhaps, in a situation of political calm in the universities one would be tempted to admit that it is widespread. However, since we are concerned here with evaluating the causes of a protest movement, it seems wise not to exaggerate it.

It is more exact to say that the working and living conditions in certain universities, especially in the larger and better ones (apart from the large private and traditional universities), have created a certain potential for action directed toward other ends. At Berkeley, for example, the student population is far more heterogeneous than at Stanford or Harvard; the proportion of dropouts among the undergraduates is much higher (40 percent as compared with less than 5 percent at Harvard and less than 10 percent at Stanford). The very size of the institutions weakens their integration as a community.

Above all, the development of the universities and the general social evolution have created a large category of students who aim at general, rather than professional, intellectual formation. Whereas, in the 1930s, in institutions like City College of New York, Wayne State, or Rutgers, there was forceful political activity among the upwardly socially mobile students, deprived by the Depression of professional openings, it is not in these institutions that the main political militancy of 1964–1970 is found. Now it is the middle-class social science and humanities students who are the most active, especially the freshmen and sophomores, who are even further removed from a directly professional training (Lipset & Altbach, 1966).[4]

But the student world was in no way one of agitation or strong radicalism. Louis Harris' survey and Philip Jacob's analysis (Jacob,

---

[4] We must, however, recall the important role of the TAs.

1958), among others, have clearly shown that the student world was fairly conformist, oriented toward "privatistic" goals, and by a great majority still supported the war in Vietnam.

The student movement did not originate with professional demands that extended first to the point of criticizing the government of the universities and then to the general policy of the American government and the ruling social class. On the contrary, an action developed within the university because, first the movement for civil rights, and then the struggle against the war, made increasingly direct criticism of its role in society and effectuated, at the same time, a much wider politicization of the student population. This clearly distinguishes the American student movement from others, which, particularly in Latin America, have called for innovation from the outset and have therefore been based on a vehement criticism of the functioning of the universities.

The student situation in certain institutions has created an environment favorable to protest, but the latter is not especially sustained by organizational demands. It is only, in my opinion, among the graduate students, and especially the teaching assistants, that demands of this type are more widespread. These students often feel exploited and irritated when faced with the demands of the Ph.D. But, it would really be an exaggeration to believe that the students of Berkeley or Columbia did not feel that they were in excellent universities where working conditions were good and where each individual had enough flexibility to organize his own program of studies. Finally, those who are the most discontented are precisely those who are not among the activists; all the surveys show the latter to be average, or above-average, students. Similarly, in industry, the militant workers are not the marginal ones but those who are more "central" than the average. It is not specifically in the student discontent that the principal root of protest should be sought.

Crisis in Academic Government The growth of the universities and the diversification of their activities entailed the development of their administrative bodies. But this administrative development was coupled with considerable confusion about the distribution of responsibilities. The regents gladly supported the imprecision of these functions. In fact, Byrne (1965, p. 17) said that if the faculty's sphere of decision had been precisely defined "more things might have been done which the public might have opposed and which the Regents themselves, as members of the public, would also have opposed. The Regents have, therefore, established a system of University government which gives the academic community comparatively little freedom to make potentially controversial or embarrassing decisions."

This disparity between the reinforcement of internal administration and the imprecision of political responsibilities is even further accentuated in California by the Master Plan. The state colleges feel themselves to be demoted to a lower level, since they are not permitted to set up doctoral programs. Moreover, each one of them is dependent on a general state college administration, directed by a chancellor who lives in Los Angeles. The rigidity created by this system is often referred to at San Francisco State College (Orrick, 1969). In fact, the statewide administration itself is somewhat displeased. It is difficult to fill executive positions when many executives in the system feel "underpaid, overworked and underappreciated." There are therefore numerous occasions for strain between the local and statewide administration or between the administration and the faculty senate. Moreover, the position of the student government, which in Berkeley had gone into decline after the tenure of President Wheeler, remains very ill-defined on the University of California campuses.

For the students, the administration is an unknown and distant world that gives credence to the idea that, in the last instance, everything is manipulated behind the scenes by the regents or the trustees and by a president or chancellor who is their accomplice through his many connections with the business world. The teachers, who are also further and further removed from the head of the system, suspect they participate in decisions only within the frame of reference of their department and are fairly hostile to the institution's government, from which they feel deliberately excluded.

But before considering the reactions of the students and the teachers, we must know whether this government — so ill-defined — usually acted in an authoritarian manner or not. The answer is that, on the whole, it did not. Today it is difficult to imagine the autocratic grip of a Butler governing a big American university. Of recent important presidents, Clark Kerr of the University of California is undoubtedly the best representative. He liberalized political activity on the Berkeley campus to the point of allowing communists to express themselves, which denotes a considerable change in comparison with the times of the loyalty oath at the beginning of the 1950s. His position was two-sided. On the one hand, he believed that if a student was punished for off-campus activities by the legal authorities, the university did not have to penalize him also, as the same crime cannot be punished twice. On the other hand, members of the university must not involve the name of the university in off-campus activities and must not use the facilities of the university for political ends.

Easy though it might be to portray the administration as overwhelmed by an entirely new course of events at the height of the Free Speech Movement, the author's experience in Europe leads him to feel that the administration actually had considerable room for maneuvering. To believe that the student movement could be pacified by more skillful tactics on the part of the president or chancellor would be, in my opinion, to underestimate its nature.

The case of San Francisco State College is an example of extreme liberalism, also outflanked by events. The college had organized an experimental college where the students themselves taught. It was also the first place where the Negro students organized themselves. At first, President Summerskill was attacked more by the conservatives than by the radicals, for he had supported a program aimed at increasing minority enrollment. This had subsequently been decreased by the application of the master plan, which introduced strict aptitude standards for admission into the state colleges.

In contrast to this cautious, but flexible, managerial attitude, other universities had governments that could only be termed weak. The problems of growth required such constant attention that the problems of functioning and of relations with the students receded into the background and were often left to the deans, who could ill take specifically political initiatives.

At times, weakness of government explained the development of the unrest. This was probably the case, for example, at Buffalo, where the campus found itself without a president in 1969. But difficult as it is to estimate what the situation might have been, here or there, if the president had been different, more decisive, or more flexible, the question seems to me of minor importance. For, although there continually were demands to participate in the government of the university, the radical students were obviously not mainly concerned with gaining seats on commissions. The weakness of the presidents was not occasioned by their personalities but by the fact that all their power was contained within a certain type of relationship between the university and the establishment and that it was this type of relationship that was attacked.

Crisis in government? If you will, but its extent can only be truly evaluated by examining the reactions of the students and the teachers.

1 On the student's side, the issue of freedom within the university, and therefore the clash with the administration on this issue, seems at first sight of prime importance. Both at Berkeley and at Columbia the outbreak was connected with measures taken by the administration. We must, however, take a closer look.

Students at Berkeley first aimed their attacks at the outside world. The civil rights campaign was the real starting point; some students left for the South in the summer of 1964. At the same time other demonstrations took place, like the sit-in at the Sheraton Palace Hotel in San Francisco. Meanwhile, at Berkeley, on the sidewalk at the corner of Telegraph and Bancroft, on land belonging to the university although situated outside the entrance gates, political activities of a general type were developing. The crisis broke out for good when the administration decided to resume control of this sidewalk. On September 30 the dean issued summonses to five students who had deliberately set up tables covered with political propaganda in the forbidden area. This provoked the sit-in on the steps of Sproul Hall, during which Mario Savio emerged as a leader. Eight students, including Savio, were suspended, and on October 1 a police car that had come to arrest a student member of the Congress of Racial Equality (CORE) was trapped for 32 hours. This crisis was not, however, directed toward institutional reform.

What was remarkable in the ensuing period was the impotence of the administration and the development of student action. The students, of course, were encouraged by Chancellor Edward Strong's decision on the ninth of November to dissolve the committee set up to study problems raised by the crisis, problems very rapidly overtaken by the larger problems of the university. Student action certainly had not been aimed at the recognition of student participation in decisions. The movement was, in fact, more expressive than instrumental. As we shall see at once, during this period it was the faculty that endeavored to play the main role.

At Columbia, where radical students opposed the construction of a gymnasium in Morningside Heights Park and thereby provoked a radical crisis, the role of problems internal to the university was even more limited. President Grayson Kirk was not accused of autocracy, but of attacking the Negro community; it was the arrogance of this rich university situated on the edge of Harlem that was exposed. Kirk had in fact negotiated with the leaders of the Negro community previously and had arranged that the gymnasium would serve both the inhabitants of Harlem and the students (although on separate floors). But it was not his method of approach that was in question; it was, much more fundamentally, the role of the university in society.

Meanwhile, the issue of student power materialized during the crisis—first in Berkeley in 1966, probably in imitation of black power. It was also raised in several other universities, particularly at Chicago, where the university refused to reappoint a radical faculty member, Marlene Dixon (Wallerstein & Starr, 1971, pp. 479–517). But it was mainly discussed within the SDS. At first considered favorably, student participation was subsequently opposed, especially by the most radical factions. Nevertheless, Mike Wallace, writing on behalf of the Columbia Strike Steering Committee in May 1968, was to demand the co-government of the university by the students and the teachers and the abolition of the trustees.

But the main tendency was expressed by Carl Davidson: "We are being trained to be oppressors and the underlings of oppressors" (ibid., p. 485). This attitude was shared by the March 22 Movement at Nanterre. The very existence of the student is already one of submission to social domination. The problem is how to get beyond this alienating existence and not how to live with it. The French leftists—in the autumn of 1968—opposed the extensive participation afforded within the framework of Faure's law.[5] Only the moderates and the communists accepted it and were elected to management committees. Although the issue of participation was unimportant at the height of the crisis and the topic of student power is of limited significance, in places where events were less dramatic or situated within a more cohesive context (for example, at Harvard in 1969 and particularly at Princeton at the time of the invasion of Cambodia), the theme of university government reform gathered momentum. But, as we shall see, the demands for this

[5] This "law of orientation of higher education," prepared by the Minister of Education, Edgar Faure, created councils at the university and the department level in which students received, at least in principle, almost half the seats.

reform were put forward just when the social movement was breaking up. The very nature of the antiwar movement—powerful but extremely heterogeneous—explains the fresh significance assumed by demands internal to the university. Their general context was more reformist than radical and was accompanied by a real decline of the New Left.

The radical groups, on the other hand, envisaged a revolutionary reform of the university, transforming it into a "People's University," as Jack McDermott demands in the radical periodical leaflet, *New University Conference Newsletter*. Students from the same university as McDermott, Southeastern Massachusetts University, published a brochure entitled "1984" (the cover of which showed a swastika superimposed over the American flag), attacking the role of the university in the service of the ruling class, both economically and ideologically; they also circulated an evaluation of the good qualities and the failings of each teacher. This can scarcely be taken as an attempt at participation, for it clearly represents both an attempt to judge from without and a break with previous criteria and procedure.

2   Though the issue of restructuring may not be entirely central to the student movement (with the exception of its most moderate fringes), it is of prime importance to the faculty, which on this issue displays both its hostility to the administration and its disagreement with the aims and means of the student movement.

The teachers, as we have seen, are an above-average liberal public-opinion group, and their political attitudes do not differ significantly from those of the students: 39.3 percent class themselves as liberals, 27.1 percent as middle of the road, and 25.5 percent as moderately conservative. The proportion of liberals is a little higher in the universities. A slight majority expresses unfavorable attitudes toward business; the majority condemns the action of the police at Chicago during the 1968 Democratic party convention (Bayer, 1970). Social science teachers are the most liberal, many having favorable attitudes toward students. Two-thirds think that "undergraduates are mature enough to be given more responsibility" for their own education. They admit that many good graduate students drop out because they do not want to "play the game" or "beat the system." Half of them agree that "most American colleges reward conformity and crush student creativity." They are hostile to student participation in the nomination of teachers, the admission policy, the curriculum, or the degree requirements, but they accept student participation in disciplinary procedures.

Here, for example, is the distribution of the teachers' opinions on the role to be given to the students, either in social matters or in academic matters.

	Social matters, %	Academic matters, %
No voice	0.5	4
Informal consultation	3.5	22
Committee membership, no vote	12.0	38
Committee membership, limited vote	15.0	27
Committee membership, equal vote	45.0	9
Entire responsibility	21.0	

SOURCE: Wilson & Gaff (1970).

These opinions do not imply a very clear-cut attitude toward a much more radical student movement. In fact, a survey revealed that at Columbia less than half the teachers acted in keeping with their generally liberal attitudes (Cole & Adamsons, 1969).

As we know, this professional liberalism is centered on the professional autonomy of the university. It is more widespread among teachers who have the highest reputation. But, since the student movement operates on another level, the teachers' behavior during a crisis depends mainly on their specifically political orientations. "When political identification (conservative, radical) is standardized, the effect of the other independent variables is considerably reduced" (Lipset, 1969, p. 102).

These political positions led only a very low proportion of teachers—mostly younger faculty members—to give full support to the student movement. The action of the vast majority varied from limited support to limited opposition. A small number took part in organizing the action of the administration (Boruch, 1969). A much greater number brought to the movement what the interviewed deans termed "sympathetic support" (49 percent). In only 9 percent of the cases, however, did the deans consider the teachers to be leaders, a figure that can still appear high. But it must be pointed out that the deans included all the incidents, many of which were absolutely peaceful—petitions, marches, and so forth.

Attitudes more favorable to the principles than to the means, with low active participation in a movement that is essentially the student's—these results probably apply to many other countries.

Yet, in the most dramatic cases, the faculty did actively participate, mainly to force upon the administration its right to govern. Laying claim to these rights is particularly prevalent in the best public universities, mainly because these institutions must compete harder to remain in the top ranks, whereas the large private universities have greater security of status. The public universities are also subject to more intense political pressure from the ruling political authorities. At Madison or Berkeley, the desire for faculty self-government is a response to these limitations, and also, more simply, to the problems of internal organization posed by the large number of campuses and departments (Lipset & Altbach, 1966). The teachers in these universities have to sit on many more committees than do those at Harvard, Yale, or Princeton. More basically, in these large and excellent public universities, the student body is more heterogeneous, and consequently the teachers are much less integrated into a prevailing ethos common to both the students and the governing body of the university (Meyerson, 1966).

The best-known case is that of Berkeley. After the first important incidents in October and November of 1964, the faculty senate, which was a source of incessant activity, passed on the eighth and tenth of December important resolutions that had far-reaching repercussions on the campus. On December 8, the faculty passed Resolution A, which accepted the principle of "advocacy" demanded by the students, and Resolution B, which created the Emergency Executive Committee. On the tenth, in Resolution C, they decided to create a committee to improve the functioning of the Berkeley Senate. Under this pressure, the regents accepted the right of advocacy, but refused to allow the faculty the right to discipline the students. We therefore see at the heart of this crisis the organization of a real political life among the faculty and the manifestation of a desire to act like a government. This, moreover, was the source of the violent clashes between teachers, the formation of parties, and the very tense atmosphere that reigned for a long time in departments like sociology, where participation in the movement was particularly widespread.

At Columbia, where the May 1968 crisis was much more violent, an ad hoc faculty group was formed that tried to negotiate with the students and the administration (Barton, 1968; Bell, 1968). It attempted to find a compromise whereby the students who had occupied the university buildings would be subject to a de jure punishment but a de facto pardon. Walter Metzger, who was a member of this committee, admitted that it failed because the faculty had so little organization and authority that its mediation was rejected by both sides (Metzger, 1970). After the intervention of the police, positions hardened and a group of teachers declared themselves in favor of deposing the president and setting up new regulations for government.

This general failure at the very height of the crisis proves that the matter at stake was not in the domain of the institution and that institutional change was both solicited and possible. The teachers took advantage of the crisis first of all to destroy the role of the university and college *in loco parentis.* The statements made by the American Association of University Professors, by the Association of American Colleges, and in very precise terms by the Crow Committee of Wisconsin University (February 1968) are all in this vein. But their main desire was to acquire a greater say in decisions. The growth of their role in this respect is perhaps one of the important consequences of the crisis.

The National Commission on the Causes and Prevention of Violence, presided over by Milton Eisenhower, concluded that there was a need to redefine the powers of the trustees, the president, and the faculty. The Cox Commission (a fact-finding commission appointed to investigate the disturbances at Columbia University in April and May 1968) published a very liberal report. It condemned the authoritarianism of the president and the insufficient role of the faculty. It was unfavorable to the ad hoc faculty committee, but concluded: "We are convinced that ways may be found, beginning now, by which students can meaningfully influence the education afforded them and other aspects of the University activities." In the mind of the commission, this opportunity for student participation was probably not separable from the determining role that the faculty was to have in the government of the university.

Finally, I must point to at least one case where part of the faculty played a different role and was an important protagonist in the movement. It is that of San Francisco State (Orrick, 1969). In the second phase of the crisis, after the nomination of President Hayakawa, the American Federation of Teachers started a long strike that ended in failure in February 1969. Hayakawa, having come to an agreement with the leaders of the Black Students Union (March

21, 1969), turned violently against the radical teachers. Liberal teachers like Marshall Windmiller took part in acts of repression against militant teachers like John Gerassi.[6]

This kind of repressive reaction is widespread. Because it wished to increase its control over the functioning of the university system, the faculty tried to act in a "responsible" fashion. A teacher must ensure the observation of the institutional regulations and under no circumstances give material or moral support to those who attack it. The Joint Committee to the Harvard Corporation on Charges Against Certain Officers of Instruction at Harvard University wrote, on September 8, 1968, with reference to the Stauder affair (an instructor of social anthropology who had participated in the movement against ROTC and the "racist" policy of the university and had stormed University Hall with the students): "In such circumstances the duty of an instructor is to dissuade students from persisting in such acts." It went on, "Those who display by their acts an unwillingness to accept the canons of free discussion and democratic choice as the guiding principles of university life show themselves to be so fundamentally at odds with the nature of a university committed to learning that they cannot, without the showing of important mitigating circumstances, have a place on its faculty" (Wallerstein and Starr, 1971, vol. 1, pp. 464, 465). This text certainly does not express the general opinion of the teachers. Many did not accept this identification of the demands of scientific research with its institutional and social frame of reference. Stauder was able to embarrass his judges by reminding them that Harvard teachers had been dismissed by the university for their antislavery campaigns.

But this text is good proof that the teachers, whose power had just been increased at the time of the crisis, do not attack the administration in the name of opinions held by the radical students. Their liberalism is in fact simply a corpus of opinions. To understand how this liberalism works, we cannot be satisfied with listening to its dictums but must examine its mode of behavior in a concrete situation of relationships and forces.

Liberalism is not so much a moderate position as an attempt to change the internal working of the institutions without either questioning their relationship to society or considering the influence exerted upon them by the ruling class and the political forces in power.

[6] See the exchange of texts between Windmiller and Gerassi in the *New York Review of Books,* quoted by Wallerstein and Starr (1971, vol. 2, pp. 341–369).

It is therefore necessary to distinguish between the actions of liberal teachers, who are increasingly isolated and who individually or in small groups have assumed the role of mediators or have become allies of the student movement, and that of the entire faculty, which defined—more and more conservatively as the crisis developed—a policy that opposed the procedures of the administration and the content of the radical students' action.

This interpretation of the faculty's role can be put into sharper focus by comparing it with the study done by Parsons and Platt (1970), who directly link their general analysis to an examination of the events that occurred at Harvard in the spring of 1969. The authors refer to the general idea that the central value of the university is cognitive rationality, which implies two corollaries: academic freedom and the obligation to contribute to the advance and the diffusion of knowledge. Thus, the higher the university's rank the less it can be managed bureaucratically (in the Weberian sense) and has to be managed collegiately. In these universities the value-commitment of the teachers exercises an influence that is independent of the power of the administration and is tending to surpass it in importance.

In the best universities the departments have greater autonomy and the administration intervenes less in the recruitment of teachers and in the organization of the teaching. The role of the chairman even tends to be weaker than in averagely differentiated establishments and to be replaced by members of the senior faculty. To quote Parsons and Platt (ibid., p. 154): "We conceive of high-differentiated academic systems as more likely to be influence systems, where influence is the emphasized medium of exchange and where power, while relatively diffused, is limited. The limitations of power and the preference for influence should thus lead to greater discrepancies between power and influence with increasing differentiation."

The authors see a proof of this argument in the fact that when Harvard was faced with serious incidents the faculty was practically a substitute for the administration. It was the faculty that, within the frame of reference of the department concerned, dealt with the affair of the social relations course 148–149, which had a radical political orientation. Also, in the Afro-American studies affair, the faculty approved both the creation of a department and the formation of a committee with equal student-teacher representation to organize the department. Finally, by means of the Committee of Fifteen, the faculty decided to examine the causes of the crisis that led to the occupation of University Hall on April 9, and to take sanctions against those involved. All this goes to prove that the foremost American university is also the one in which the faculty, in a serious crisis that threatened the values of the institution, most resolutely took the initiative, pushing the administration unceremoniously to one side. It is possible, however, to interpret otherwise facts whose reality is beyond question. At Harvard, Columbia, and Berkeley, to take only the particularly famous campuses, the faculty intervened in a clear-cut fashion, supplanting, or trying to supplant, the administration.

But, in my opinion, this faculty intervention has two distinct meanings. On the one hand, it is an attempt, at the height of a serious crisis of political authority, to release the university from the conflict and to affirm the priority of its intellectual vocation; on the other, it is the corporate action of the teachers to defend an academic freedom that then becomes the overlay of their own power. The first type of reaction cannot have a lasting effect. Everyone is ready to admit the prime importance of the university's scientific function, but that does not conceal the problems posed by the financing of research, by social recruitment, or by teaching conditions. As far as the second is concerned, it leads, I feel, to an extremely conservative position. On September 20, 1970 (see Carnegie Commission, 1971*b*), Harvard defined academic freedom in very restricted terms — as, in fact, the conditions for the effective professional functioning of the university — without any reference to problems of the relationship between the university and society. Thus the autonomy of the teachers can easily be seen as submission to this social order; moreover, it always appears to be more directly threatened by those who attack what they consider to be the dependence of the university. More simply, this professorial self-management either leads to the formation of a French-style bureaucracy or else reverts to an administrative authoritarianism that appears as a convenient and efficient guarantee against difficulties.

The power of the teaching body appears more as a parenthesis at the time of a crisis of power than as a solution resolving the fundamental problems of the university. The illusion that consists of reducing an institution to its technical activity of production has no more basis for foundation in academic life than in any other sort of activity. Problems of power are always posed. The academics support student demands in order to extend their influence; they oppose them when their power is attacked. At Berkeley, even the students on strike in 1966 no longer found the faculty support that the Free Speech Movement enjoyed in the autumn of 1964.

Nonetheless, despite their being branded as black sheep when they took part in radical actions, the teachers as a group scored a success as a result of the crisis. Sometimes, their responsibilities were lightened to make room for good specialists in the universities undermined by the crisis. More generally, they took advantage of the retreat of the administration. But their gains were limited. Lipset is even very apprehensive (1970, p. 117):

The increased "democratization" (more elected faculty committees) thereafter increases the importance of the role of the more conservative and scholarly less prestigious "committeemen" since they can now claim to be the elected "representatives" of the faculty rather than the appointed consultants of the administration. In effect, faculty elections often serve to give populist legitimacy to locally oriented, relatively conservative professional faculty politicians, who rise to the "top" because the "cosmopolitan," more research-involved, liberal faculty see campus politics as a waste of time in normal periods.

An interesting point of view, with which I would tend to agree except on one point. It is true that a new rank of teachers, administrators, and politicians is being formed and that it does not consist of the most notable intellectuals, who are engrossed in their work. But it would be erroneous to apply here the distinction between cosmopolitan and local so dear to Robert Merton. The teacher-politicians are not necessarily more conservative; on the contrary, they are as conscious of conflicts of interest as is a member of parliament. The political orientation of these negotiators depends upon the political forces at work in their particular institution; they can play a significant role in a university that is not uniquely a research center. Since Lipset proclaims himself hostile to the Soviet separation of teaching and research, he must accept the organization of a legislative level of the university. But it is obvious that it is not at this level that the decisive factors for the advance of scientific knowledge are situated, nor is it here that the social movements are formed. It is nothing more than a step toward the institutionalization of new labor conflicts.

We have considered at length the role of the teachers, in the first instance because they are one of the main protagonists on the university scene, but more especially because their intervention demonstrates both the importance and the limits of the institutional problems in the academic crisis. The American universities have been almost constantly the scene of a "political" process. This is true of Berkeley at the beginning of the crisis, and true also of the 1969–70 period, when incidents became widespread. Only at times of the greatest violence, during the strikes at Columbia and San Francisco State, has the role of the faculty been diminished, ending in complete failure at Columbia and Hayakawa's repression of the strike at San Francisco State with Reagan's approval.

The student movement was not principally aimed at participation in university government, but it was able to develop on the campuses over many years in the case of Berkeley, and the political impotence of the universities did not lead them to collapses of the type experienced by the French universities — especially the University of Paris — which were subject to control at once weak and repressive. While asserting the solidity of most American academic institutions, it is difficult to determine whether it is due to the nature of the student movement and its social context or to the working of the academic institution. It is, however, difficult not to accord the latter a certain importance.

The Negro "problem" and the black movement The students are dependents, treated as minors, defined by their situation as apprentices and not as workers, and subject to regulations imposed upon them. Certainly it is difficult for them all to feel themselves members of a "community of scholars." But they are also among the privileged, even in a country where higher education is widespread. This is particularly true when they are in universities that normally prepare them to be members of an elite group, or at least of the upper strata of society. Finally, most of them are in a temporary situation, since they are not going to spend their entire adult life in the university. All these aspects of student life explain how student culture and loyalty to an academic institution can be concomitant with what a leader of the SDS has termed a "sensitivity" to external problems and a desire to escape from a world that is too easy, too isolated, and too limited.

But remarks of this sort are very far from explaining the massive and militant student involvement in social struggles in which they are not the principal protagonists, whether in the United States or elsewhere. The campaign for Negro rights was the origin of the incidents in Berkeley; it also is one of the main issues for the SDS. What does it mean, and how did the relationship develop between the action of the white students for the Negroes and the efforts of the Negroes on their own behalf?

The error, which it is easy to avoid, is to think that there was a united front of the radical students and the black movement. There were more contacts between workers and students in France in 1968 than there were between students and black militants at Berkeley, Columbia, San Francisco State, or Cornell. Margaret Mead[7] has compared the student to a person living in a ghetto: both can only act as they like within the boundaries of a closed world, are outside political life, and are minors.

The comparison seems most artificial, and the unemployed youths in the ghettos are probably not very touched by it; Harlem certainly does not feel like Columbia, for which most ghetto youth is completely out of reach.

If one assumes, firstly, the point of view of the activist students, two completely different aspects of their relationship with the black community can be distinguished.

In the first place an awareness of the issue of equality can go from a kind of paternalism to extreme generosity — as for example, from the religious groups that launched tutorial programs for the black children of San Francisco's poor districts to the students from Columbia and elsewhere who joined the civil rights campaign in the South at the risk of their lives. This attitude of awareness does not differ in principle from that of the administrators at San Francisco State, who wanted to give the Negro a feeling of self-identity and to help him find his place in American society.

In the second place, the students' discovery of flagrant contradictions and injustices leads them to cast a critical eye on the values and social organization that the liberals use to denounce inequality and marginality. This is a bewildering revelation for the students, who discover they are both dominated and dominators, subject to the establishment and privileged themselves. They are intensely aware of the incoherence of their situation and their actions.

The march toward the exploited, toward the Negroes in the South or in the ghettos in the United States, or in the factories and the shantytowns in France or Italy, then tends to become a desire to break with the academic world — to get out of it in order to judge it from the outside and to change it both from within and from without. This second position is of necessity ambiguous, because

[7] In *Columbia University Forum,* Fall 1968; quoted in Wallerstein and Starr, (1971, vol. 1, pp. 423–429).

the student is neither the unemployed inhabitant of the ghetto nor the assembly-line worker.

If he becomes the ghetto dweller or factory worker, he ceases to be a student and no longer has any specific base for his action, his influence in his new surroundings being, by definition, minimal. If he remains a student, sooner or later he will come up against the distrust of the labor or Negro movement, which acts on the basis of a different social and cultural experience and which may consider the student a member of the dominant power group against which it is struggling. But this ambiguity does not prevent the student movement from having far-reaching consequences and, above all, from being an essential factor in the formation of a social movement, for it severs the double hold on the students that is maintained by the prevailing ideology and academic rhetoric.

In the United States, the march to the South by the students from the North is colored by this ambiguity. On the one hand, it indicates a desire for integration in which egalitarianism and modernization are naturally united. An end must be made to this unjust and archaic situation: in the name of moral values and of the Constitution, segregation and racism in the South must be suppressed.

At the same time, the students discover in the South, not only injustice and inequality, but also violence. Raised with the idea that a society is organized on the basis of values and institutions, they find that the law is impotent and that values are ideologies. They acquire a political conscience critical of society and learn to recognize relationships of opposition and not only of participation.

The nature of liberalism is even further transformed when its objectives are less distant. For example, in Europe, it is fairly easy to denounce apartheid in South Africa, but the Parisians thus moved are in general fairly indifferent to the situation of the Portuguese, Algerian, or Mali workers who live alongside them, apart from them, exploited and rejected. When Algerian children come to their children's schools, they complain that the academic level of these schools is being lowered and that, as a result, their children's chances for academic success will suffer. As we have seen, the American academic system had taken shelter behind an impervious barrier of professional criteria in order to rid itself of the Negro problem and problems posed by other ethnic groups. The California Master Plan had in fact isolated Negroes in the junior colleges on the grounds of their poor academic performance in high school. Moreover, many of the more traditional campuses are located far from the ghettos.

But as the Negro population in the large towns in the North increased, becoming more conspicuous as the white middle classes withdrew from the center of the towns and moved to the de facto segregated suburbs, the academic world became increasingly aware of a new problem. It was not that of a Southern racist society, for the big universities, nearly all in the North, did not feel themselves responsible for Southern racism and hoped to see it disappear, an attitude similar to that of their ancestors a century earlier. The new problem concerned the boundary of social segregation that passed through all levels of American society. The Negro problem is not one of a different society, but of a contradiction within a single society.

Universities often feel threatened when the population of the surrounding area becomes predominantly Negro. The value of certain of their properties could decrease. It might become harder to recruit the best teachers and students, etc. Columbia for example, felt itself besieged in its fortress of Morningside Heights, surrounded by Negroes and Puerto Ricans in an area of increasing social disorganization. The university, for very objective reasons, was worried about the consequences of the urban crises on its professional quality.

At the same time, the student discovered that even if he could go out of the university to support the civil rights movement, he was also taking part in an institution that produced inequality or segregation. He himself then turned against this institution and his own personal demands merged with those of the excluded. This leads us to consider two very different situations — two types of relationships between the student movement and the black movement.

In the first instance, we have the situation best represented by the Free Speech Movement. The students therein defined themselves in relation to the Negro *problem,* as they found it in the South, in Selma, and elsewhere. This problem was incorporated in a general protest, a political outburst, and a break with the academic rhetoric. The students demanded rights for themselves and for everyone. As dependents themselves, they appealed, almost symbolically I might add, to the dependent situation in which Negroes or other social groups live. The increasing proximity of the Negro problem in the North was probably a factor in sparking the revolt against dependence; the black movement was not yet sufficiently strong to prevent this liberal radicalism from speaking in its name, from appealing to a certain universality of values at the same time as to specifically political issues. This situation was ambiguous, as was that of the whole Free Speech Movement; it represented the extreme limit of a liberalism that was already pregnant with radical protest. This ambiguity corresponded to the Negro situation, which was at that time more than just a problem but not yet a movement.

Although it is true that many of those who took part in the action for the defense of civil rights in the South were not radicals, the Negro problem was the point of assembly for the militant groups: the Student Nonviolent Coordinating Committee (SNCC), more concerned with problems in the South, and the Congress of Racial Equality (CORE), which was already more aware of the problems in the North. The incident of the police car that was hemmed in by a crowd for more than a day on the Berkeley campus tells us something about the role of the civil rights movement in the student revolt. The student arrested by the police was a CORE militant, and many of the students arrested had taken part in numerous demonstrations for civil rights. The Negro problem forced the student out of the academic sphere, at once professionally respectable and ideologically integrated.

This role grew when a movement was organized, when, beyond the radicalism developed in the Negro petite bourgeoisie by the Black Muslims, members of the working class formed their own political groups. From these there emerged, due both to its leaders and to the distinctive repression used against it, the militant Black Panthers of Oakland, at the gates of Berkeley. Small in numbers, and strong in aggressiveness, leadership, and the use of symbols, the Panthers forced a break with the ruling form of society, suffered violence, and fought back. They had no more sympathy for the liberal universities than for white institutions in their entirety, or for the "pigs," as they labeled the police.

Soon, the Black Panthers began to be active in the universities. On the campuses it was the black students who became the extreme radicals, simultaneously rejecting the white radical students, who still belonged to a racist ruling society. This was the source of constant, often of violent, tensions. However, the autonomy of the academic world meant that by means of the clashes a certain convergence of struggles took place. For example, at San Francisco State, the role of the Black Student Union in the confrontation with the authorities was absolutely central. The Third World Liberation Movement was only a "front" organization, the Black Student Union being the driving force. But the movement was not purely and simply the penetration of the Black Panthers onto the campus. It is true that George Murray, an English teacher, was the Panther Minister for Education, but it is also true that the Panther leaders regarded the black students themselves with distrust; they were middle-class blacks, and it is a far cry from the urban culture of Fillmore Street in San Francisco to that of the most radical of campuses, even that of San Francisco State (Orrick, 1969; see also Bunzel, 1968).

On the other hand, as we have seen, the white radicals, students and teachers alike, while not playing a leading role, were constantly present in the struggle and in the picket lines. Finally, Hayakawa chose to negotiate with the black leaders, admitting the necessity of opening the college to minorities and of reforming the educational system.

The black leaders do not, then, totally reject the universities. Not only do they use the university's liberalism to express and organize themselves, but they try to obtain concrete results, to open the university to blacks and to force white racism to capitulate. Thus, at Northwestern in April 1968, the black students demanded that the university recognize its racism. Under their pressure, a text was signed on the fourth of May by the Afro-American Student Union and a committee representing the administration. The administration admitted its former racism and set up a committee of black leaders to organize the admission of blacks to the university and to set up courses in black studies. The trustees refused to sign the preamble in which the university's racism was denounced, but the important point is that the black movement aimed at changing the university admission policy for blacks and at gaining control of that policy for the black community.

Elsewhere, more extreme stands were taken. At Fisk University, for example, a statement was published in favor of a black university, defined in purely political fashion: "A Black University is open to all people who subscribe positively to Black liberation as defined by Pan-Africanism."[8] It was not by accident that this nationalist stand came from the South, for although the battle fought in the Northern universities led to many victories, in the end it could only weaken the Southern universities. This became clear when many white universities in the North competed to recruit black teachers for their faculties.

[8] Wallerstein and Starr (1971, vol. 1, p. 361). This source also contains information on the other examples I have mentioned here.

Nevertheless, the break between white liberals and black radicals in the North was maintained. The most extreme incident took place at Cornell, where blacks occupied Willard Straight Hall, the student union, and demanded amnesty for previous incidents. On a Monday, the faculty voted for maintaining the sanctions, and the blacks, fearing reprisals, armed themselves. The threat of a struggle with bloodshed loomed ahead. On Wednesday, the faculty capitulated, precipating a major crisis. The liberal administration of President James F. Perkins was violently denounced, and accused of giving in. Perkins had to resign.

The relationship between black and white radicals was also tense, as the strike at Columbia in May 1968 demonstrated. Hamilton Hall was occupied at the outset by blacks and whites together, but soon the blacks opposed the presence of the whites and refused to take part in the campaign against Kirk. They conducted their action alone, not even allowing the extremest element from the white collective to join them.

This example also shows — and this is the main point — the double nature, and consequently the relative autonomy, of the black radical students' movement. The creation of departments of black studies — or their equivalents — in a rapidly increasing number of institutions underlines this ambiguity. This is a radical type of action that goes against the traditional principles of the university, since blacks control these departments and speak in the name of black nationalism. Nonetheless, the action is also situated within the university, and not only formally so. When police repression and internal crises weaken a political movement involved in violent confrontation with the established order, these departments are forced to relate to the university in terms of the two words which form their title — black and studies.

To sum up, the black movement obviously outdistances the movement of the radical white students and is often opposed to it. But it also has objectives within the university itself, and on this common terrain the two movements reinforce each other, at least during the central phase of the academic crisis.

I would like to demonstrate, by means of a comparison, that this is more than a convergence or mutual reinforcement. At the beginning of the twentieth century in Western Europe, we see developing, alongside the growth of revolutionary syndicalism, the theme of proletarian culture that had already been strongly expressed during the Paris Commune of 1871. In France, this theme assumed significant proportions in the 1920s. A social class, living out its exploitation, tends to reject totally the dominant culture. In the same way, arabization in the former colonies sometimes assumed the form of a traditionalist "integration." But it can only be a first stage in the dialectic of social struggles, for a class is not defined by its existence, but by its role in class relations. The working class cannot confine itself to a proletarian culture without confining itself, in the name of independence, to an alienated culture. It cannot turn aside for any length of time from its central struggle for the collective control of the productive forces.

In the same way, while the black power movement is following a policy of separateness, the violence of which increases with the capacity of American society to integrate, it is important that communication between the black movement and other radical movements be maintained, even marginally. This contributes to the re-establishment of the dialectic of social struggle, and to the movement away from the aggressive defense of identity—an essential state for a dominated population—toward the search for a general social conflict. But, at the same time, this action in the university can easily become merely reformist if it is not initiated by a movement whose main objectives are to break off relations with, and to challenge, a social order that expresses power of the ruling groups. It is therefore not enough to speak of a black movement in the university. It is also necessary to speak of the part this movement plays in the formation of a wider social movement. The incomplete link between these two aspects of the same reality is one of the big weaknesses of the protest movement. Nonetheless, the action of the black movement has radicalized the rest of the student movement, especially at Columbia, and has therefore had a part in destroying the prevailing ideology of the university and in exposing the basic conflicts of the academic society, which likes to think of itself as being merely a community organized around values and techniques.

Radicalism and the Struggle Against the War

A social movement is formed only if a social group defines itself in opposition to another social group and defines the clash as one of opposing interests fighting for the control of social development; there are opponents and a stake. But this stake, which in the last analysis is the cultural model of the society, is not immediately definable as the objective. In a capitalist society, capitalists and the labor movement are involved in a clash of interests in which the stake is the control of "progress." But this stake has to take some material form. This explains the importance of the state, but the state is not the real stake in the contest; it is only the material social force around which the social movements organize themselves, both in their effort to participate in the social and cultural orientations of their society and in their antagonistic relationship. This explains the ambiguity of actions directed against the state. On the one hand, such actions are the most complete expression of a social movement whose aim is to "take power"; on the other, they do not correspond entirely to social movements, for the state is not purely and simply the ruling class. It is both less influential than the ruling class, to the extent that a representative political system or, more generally, a plurality of political influences do exist, and more influential, since it helps to transform a domination of class into a political and ideological domination.

At this point, let us refer to the example of the labor movement once again. In addition to its anticapitalist action, labor also engages in a specifically political activity, which may be reformist, in the French "republican" tradition, or violent and nihilistic, aiming at the destruction of the state. This political activity is constantly assuming a certain autonomy in relation to the rest of the labor movement. For example, in France at the beginning of the twentieth century, a mass socialist movement created by Jean Jaurès coexisted with an antimilitarist, antistate movement whose chief spokesman was Gustave Hervé. Neither movement identified itself completely with revolutionary syndicalism.

The same analysis can be applied to the American situation. The student movement became aware of its identity in the university; this identity found its purest expression in the Free Speech Movement. The Negro problem and the black movement superimposed the existence of contradictions and of conflicts in the larger society. The war in Vietnam and the campaign against it gave the movement its political dimension. But, concurrent with the development of this all-inclusive movement, the struggle against the state assumed a fairly large measure of autonomy, denoted, on the one hand, by the libertarians' rejection of the state, and, on the other, by the formation of a huge movement, somewhat more liberal than radical and very largely independent of a social movement in the sense we have defined.

Since the existence of state interests on the campus are plain to see, the links between the academic movement and the struggle against the state, and in particular its imperialistic activities, are many and obvious. Lipset, whom one can scarcely accuse of falling prey to radical slogans, wrote: "The university itself, in spite of its emphasis on being non-partisan and 'value-free,' is becoming increasingly involved in politics as professors take over roles as party activists, intellectual commentators on political events, advisors, consultants and researchers on relevant policy matters" (1969, p. 18).

Noam Chomsky (1969) attacked these new mandarins, who are not so much the servants of all society as servants of the society's ruling forces, in more violent terms. Institutes connected with the universities and engaged in research for political and military reasons have often been denounced or directly attacked by the radicals. The Institute of Defense Analysis at Columbia and the Stanford Research Institute have been vehemently indicted. But it is the inclusion of military preparation in academic life and in the curriculum that has been the most constant target of the attacks. Years ago the land-grant colleges introduced a premilitary training course onto the campus. The ROTC was created in 1916 and was long held high in student estimations, particularly as it enabled a fair number of them to finance their studies. But the situation of war, and therefore of mobilization, made ROTC a special target of movements directed against the war, especially during the spring of 1970, a time of total crisis.

A second aspect of the student campaign against the war derives from the situation of the students, who, being young, are themselves liable for the draft. But, truthfully speaking, their situation is ambiguous. They are more liable than others because of their age, but less so because they are students. Until the lottery system was introduced, the Selective Service Administration gave deferments to those whose work or program of studies was in the national interest—in the fields of science, technology, or education. This ambivalent situation provoked an extreme reaction in a country in which military conscription is exceptional. The antidraft movement —which involved refusal of the draft, the public destruction of selective service cards, the organization of a network of support for draft resistors, expatriation, and sometimes even desertion— was supported by some of the faculty. Although they did not wish to play a role in military selection, these teachers were, in fact, forced to so so, because good marks were necessary to get a deferment. The antidraft movement was closely linked to the action of the radical groups, for the support of a group is required by an individual who thus confronts the authority of the state and who has to endure prison, or go underground, or escape abroad. But it was also an autonomous movement, linked as much with a cultural movement as with political action, and supported as much for its defense of personal and collective identity and general pacifism as for its criticism of imperialism. The antidraft movement was an essential element in the spread of radical action and above all in the formation of an action that went beyond the narrow confines of the university. As the war developed and military victory seemed more improbable, the losses increased—as did the risk that the conflict would spread—and the movement against the war gained momentum. It was the moving force behind the biggest demonstrations, the marches on Washington, the moratoriums and the strikes in the universities in the fall of 1969, and finally the huge movement of spring 1970, in which all the issues merged—academic problems, the black movement, and campaigns against the war. It was then that the nationwide student movement was formed. In April 1969, 250 presidents of student governments and editors of student newspapers had already signed a statement circulated by the National Students Association that expressed opposition to the draft and support for draft resistors. The group "Resist" published "A New Call to Resist Illegitimate Authority." Both faculty and a rapidly increasing number of universities supported the action against the war. First Columbia, in September 1969, supported the October moratorium by 51 votes to 25 with 3 abstentions, then Harvard and many others; at the time of the invasion of Cambodia almost 500 institutions were on strike or had been closed by their administrations. The killings at Jackson State and Kent State lent considerable force and pressure to this movement.

Yet this very force indicated the increasing autonomy of this action in relation to the radical student movement. George Wald, who obtained the Nobel Prize for biology and teaches at Harvard, made a speech at MIT on March 4, 1969[9] that conveys very well the attitude of the liberals, preoccupied by the war and the reversal of the traditional American values that it implied.

Wald recalls that the United States was a land of refuge for many young people who had refused to serve in the army in Russia or in Central Europe. He wants a pacifist society and a land of liberty.

[9] Quoted by Wallerstein and Starr (ibid., vol. 2, pp. 4–12).

The main impetus for the moratoriums in October, November, and December of 1969 was provided by the liberals, who joined the radicals in a common cause. I cannot but recall here my own memory of the October moratorium on the campus of the University of California at Los Angeles—usually extremely quiet. There was a huge gathering in the evening, speeches by Hollywood stars, and an almost religious silence when, at the end of the evening, everyone lit a candle and sang "We Shall Overcome." I cast my mind back to an entertainment given by the Living Theater at Nanterre at the beginning of 1968; the members of the cast were singing "Peace in Vietnam" in an increasingly incantatory manner, when the revolutionary students rudely interrupted them with cries of "Victory in Vietnam," Daniel Cohn-Bendit heading the demonstration. How many of those who took part in the gatherings and marches in the United States were willing to undertake a critical analysis of the war and also of the causes for the victorious resistance of the Vietnamese? "Enough dead, enough stupidity, let's get out of this mire"—feelings in no way different from those of the increasingly large percentage of the French population that was opposed to the Algerian war. In the midst of this opposition, the radicals, to be sure, were a particularly active group, but powerless and relatively isolated.

Since 1965, opposition to the war has been the most obvious issue in student action, the one that enabled the mobilization not only of the campuses but also of the mass demonstrations in Washington and in other principal cities. The campaign against the war made possible the formation of a very wide front, which had in its first ranks intellectuals of high reputation. Their presence justified student action in the eyes of a number of moderate liberals.

Mass actions of this sort, more often tolerated than repressed, were elements of political pressure rather than of radicalization. From the point of view of the student movement, the action against the war was primarily important for having provided an organizational base, issues for action, and above all a means of getting out of the campus. But it was only rather vaguely connected with the other aspects of the movement. And those who, like Noam Chomsky, pushed the critical analysis of the action of the American government the furthest, did not give a great deal of importance specifically to the student movement.

The action against the war was mainly important for its break with the liberal illusion of the Kennedy period. Those who had spoken of "new frontiers" and the "great society" involved the United States in Vietnam, much as the social-democratic government of France, asserting the secular and progressive inheritance of the French Revolution involved that nation, most deeply in colonialism, specifically through the Suez Canal expedition and the kidnapping of Ben Bella. Carl Oglesby, one of the SDS leaders, was well aware of this when he declared that the fight against imperialism was directed not only against a small number of hidden capitalists, but also against liberals who expressed generous ideas but at the same time defended American colonial interests, especially in the Caribbean (Oglesby, 1966). If this fight did not contribute to any important extent to the definition of the nature of the powers that had to be fought, it did at least reveal the contradictions of a political system that took credit for being the defender of progress and freedom both at home and abroad.

The Revolutionary Groups

The component parts of the social movement—action within the universities and against their oganizational links to the government, action in support of the black movement, and action against the war—were sufficiently distinct for their merger in the spring of 1970 to be more spectacular than creatively organized. It was not in the mass movements, but in the action of the revolutionary groups, that the problems of how these parts related were posed most intensely and most consciously. It may seem excessive to grant so much importance to their brief and complex history, which rapidly takes on the appearance of nothing more than a confused tangle of debates and violent actions, but this would be a most superficial reaction. The history of all revolutionary movements appears confused at the outset, because by definition those who oppose the established social order cannot arrange their behavior and their ideas in the methodical fashion of those who dominate society and culture. The discussions within the socialist and communist movements are one of the best means of getting to know the problems of a society. Moreover, revolutionary groups, in America as elsewhere, are extremely interested in analyzing their actions, and the heat of their internal discussions leads each tendency to explain and justify itself at length. This literature is at times tiresome, because each protagonist who lives, by definition, in a contradictory situation, constantly invents a doctrine that gives an artificial unity to his behavior. Nonetheless, several of the texts collected by Wallerstein and Starr, who naturally enough grant special importance to the incidents and discussions at Columbia, are evidence of very shrewd analysis.

The existence of revolutionary student groups is not new in the United States; in the 1920s, the winds of rebellion against the official patriotism, religion, and provincialism blew through the universities (Handlin & Handlin, 1970, pp. 67–70). Colleges rebelled against their presidents, underground student newspapers were created, as, for example, *Critic* at Oberlin, *Gadfly* at Harvard, *Proletarian* at Wisconsin, and *Tempest* at Michigan. In 1925, the National Federation of American Students was created. But this movement quickly lost ground and was transformed into one of cultural protest. It was the era of the "lost generation," with its taste for alcohol, jazz, and cars. During the Great Depression and World War II, the movement became more intellectual and more political. Marxism penetrated the academic world by means of magazines and reviews. But, while certain Trotskyist groups engaged in original theoretical activity and enjoyed a limited influence, they relied more on groups of intellectuals in New York, many of whom were of European origin, than on the campuses.[10]

Completely different is the Free Speech Movement—a mass movement of great energy that had no organizational base—in which the personal role of the leading spokesman was considerable. Antiacademic issues, cultural issues (obscenity), the Negro problem, and then the issue of opposition to the war, reinforced by the proximity of the Oakland embarkation center, from which recruits and materials were sent to Vietnam—all these threads of the movement intertwined and mutually reinforced each other, forcing student action out of the university and into the city of Berkeley, where radical candidates almost won control of the municipal administration in 1971.

The history of Berkeley is also that of a microcosm where, more so than elsewhere, the components of the movement in its entirety were revealed.[11] The important period for Berkeley was the time when the movement was taking shape and giving expression to that process, rather than the time when a major effort was made to integrate the diverging components. This explains why the Berkeley

---

[10] Daniel Bell (1971) has recalled in particular the figure of D. Schachtman.

[11] The facts and various points of view regarding the Free Speech Movement have been presented in several books, among which is S. M. Lipset and Sheldon Wolin (eds.), *The Berkeley Student Revolt: Facts and Interpretations,* Doubleday, New York, 1965.

action lasted so long, why its ideological production was relatively limited, why its "expressive acts" were so important, and why its idealism was so significant for a whole generation of young Americans.

The important incidents at Berkeley, from the Free Speech Movement in the fall of 1964 to the strike of December 1966, marked the end of apathy. The students who had taken part in the civil rights campaign during the summer of 1964, and those who were involved in the struggle against the war in 1965, discovered an escape from the ambiguities of academic liberalism, and, more simply, from their feelings of impotence. Mario Savio, the leading figure of the FSM, clearly expressed these feelings immediately after the first incidents at Berkeley: "Society provides no challenge. American society in the standard conception it has of itself is simply no longer exciting. The most exciting things going on in America today are movements to change America" (Cohen & Hale, 1967, p. 252). The ruling elite wanted to put "an end to history," but the movement for civil rights and the student movement opened up new perspectives for the future. There was the discovery of action: "History has to be lived and felt and shaped" (Engler, 1968, p. 205). The Free Speech Movement was not a political organization but a movement whose action created militant followers and drew sympathetic support from the majority of students.

In its origins, the SDS was not far removed from this state of mind, as one can see from the Port Huron statement of 1962, adopted after SDS was formed by a group of dissidents, who, under the leadership of Tom Hayden and Al Haber broke away from the League for Industrial Democracy. But although the shared experience of the civil rights campaign often brought all student activities together, the SDS militants were always more directly concerned with the problems outside the campus. The FSM stood for student subjectivity, but the SDS wanted to expose itself directly to the problems of American society and launched the Economic Research and Action Project (ERAP) in several towns. Hayden, for example, devoted himself to it in Newark. Some leaders, like Carl Oglesby, were closer to the "romanticism" of SNCC; others, like Paul Booth, a student at Swarthmore, wanted the movement to have a more strictly political direction and organization. After the congress at Clear Lake in 1966, when, under the influence of Carl Davidson, the movement decided to carry its action over onto the campuses, it acted as an organized political group. It was favorably disposed to the ideology of the new working class imported from France and was interested in student unionism. But it was only starting in the spring of 1968 that the SDS took part in both the actions and discussions that were to place it at the center of events. Its main doctrinal text, the Columbia Statement, written by Paul Rockwell and adopted on September 12, 1968, clearly sets out the three main directions of the movement and affirms their interdependence:

- Columbia dominates Harlem, is appropriating its land, and is implementing a racist policy.

- The university is linked to the political and military leaders and is taking part in the war.

- Academic teaching is aimed at fragmenting the learning and intellectual life of the student by the separation of the departments and by the system of grades and examinations.

According to SDS the unity of the academic system, and therefore of the action against it, cannot be expressed in terms of values or of professional demands; it results from the integration of the university in the capitalist system and from the repressive role that it plays therein. It is therefore imperative to make a frontal attack on this system, to shatter its rhetoric of value-free professionalism and to attack, in particular, the liberal teachers, like James Shenton, whose courses were to be interrupted.

But from this time on, doctrinal unity covered divergences. At the time of the strike—of the occupation of Low, Avery (architecture), Fayerweather (social sciences), and the department of mathematics —a certain tension existed between the SDS labor committee, which played the main role at that time, but was to be expelled a few months later, and the most radical group, which was led by Mark Rudd. Action in the university was more important in the eyes of the labor committee, which was less in favor of the centralized party and more concerned with participation at the base. It also had not completely split from the liberal or radical groups that aimed at restructuring the university. Hayden himself attributed a positive role to these aims in an article in the June 15, 1968 issue of *Ramparts:* "They wanted to be included only if their inclusion is a step toward transforming the university."

But a few months later, Rudd's tendency, the Action Faction, militated against the Praxis Axis, which insisted on action at the base. This disagreement over the form that action should take concealed a more important difference of opinion. The members of the Strike Steering Committee, like Rusti Eisenberg, who criticized the behavior of SDS during the strike ("People did not believe they were electing a cadre. They thought they were choosing a representative leader.") gave priority to the student movement, with which they were in direct contact. Rudd, however, considered the black movement as the driving force of all revolutionary action. He adopted a Leninist stand—going as far as to write a text modestly entitled "What is to be done?" (September 1968)—and believed that the force of the movement was generated by the internal contradictions of society rather than by the subjective problems of the students.

The gap quickly widened. Some, like Lee Coleman, defended the issue proclaimed in the April slogan, "Shut down the Universities." On the other hand, Carl Davidson remained faithful to his own ideas, which were close to those of the critical German universities.

The first split distinguished between problems internal to the university and those involving the outside world, that is, those that were immediately concerned with the contradictions in society.

This was shortly followed by a second split, which confirmed the idea expressed above, namely that support for the black movement and participation in the anti–Vietnam war campaign suggested two different directions.

The Revolutionary Youth Movement (RYM), formed in order to corroborate the prime importance of general problems, split in its turn. RYM 1, which became the Weatherman led by Mark Rudd, accorded the main role to the black movement; RYM 2, which became the Mad Dogs, considered the struggle against the war to be more important. Mike Klonsky was the founder, and Davidson a member, of RYM 2.

The result was that the three components of the movement— academic action, the black movement, and the antiwar campaign— became the centers of three distinct and opposing tendencies, all of which were weakened by their internal struggles.

Thus, the ideological divisions, far from being confused (it is true that I have perhaps oversimplified them), reproduce exactly the problems facing a movement that is both in the university, where it has its militant base, and in the outside world, where it affirms that the university serves the ruling class and its policy of oppression and repression. Although these tendencies were closely associated with one another, and their interdependence was most seriously discussed within SDS, the split of that militant organization is convincing proof that there were limits to the integration of the movement's various components.

Whatever differences of opinion may pull it apart, the New Left is in no way prevented from having its own personality when compared with the Old Left and the moderate organizations. The Du Bois clubs, of Communist party origin, had a fairly wide influence, particulary at Berkeley, but their constant preoccupation with forming alliances with the liberals against the conservatives made them deaf to the newness of the student movement. The Young Socialist Alliance, which was linked to the Trotskyist Socialist Workers Party, was a more active group and was among the first to recognize the importance of the black movement, but it was paralyzed by its Leninist model of democratic centralism. The Progressive Labor Party and the Independent Socialist Club, the latter in California, were closer to the New Left. The Progressive Labor Party, however, maintained an extremely dogmatic, so-called Maoist line, to the point of making, at times, very strange political judgments. Moreover, much of the analysis made by the Independent Socialist Club was criticism of all previous socialist experiences. Both continued to attribute the greatest importance to the labor movement and were more sects than movements.

This multiplicity of tendencies is important. It indicates, at the least, that an organized political movement was not formed. This impotence was not the result of circumstances. The students do not constitute a class, are not a particularly exploited social category, and are not directly confronted by those in possession of social power. Even if we recognize that they are situated within the system of production of a social and economic order, they cannot speak in their own name alone; they must also speak in the name of others. Yet the revolutionary student movement is not the equivalent of the black movement, but only one of its supporters, and, as we saw at Hamilton Hall at Columbia, the black movement rejects this alliance. In addition, the revolutionary groups do not control the growth of the movement against the war. Finally, although the university may be allied to society and its ruling forces, it also has, on its own, enough power, autonomy, and political capacity to make impossible the limited academic action called for in the slogan "Shut it down."

Further, the emphasis on the tendencies to split should not be allowed to obscure the essential fact that these same tendencies were brought together and united by the radical students. This group therefore merits special attention.

The foreign observer is surprised at the extent to which the attention of social scientists in the United States has been naturally oriented more toward the study of the protagonists than to that of the situations and the movement itself. This choice was facilitated by the development of the behavioral sciences. At times it resembles an ideological choice, as if the movement were an answer to the personality, the conditions of education, and the particular experience of certain categories of students, rather than to the expression of social problems. If one believes that the university is primarily a community of scholars, linked to society by its universalist love for knowledge and instrumental action, it is, in fact natural to seek the cause of the movement, not in the university situation, but in the personality of certain students. I have also just explained that the unity of this "unorganized" movement depended primarily on the action of the student groups, which is another reason for justifying the importance of the protagonists. Their action could not have had such wide influence if their radical student members had been marginals. Their importance derives from the fact that they were both central to the academic culture and conscious of the society's general political problems. They differ from the dropouts who continue to live on the fringe of the campus, as well as from students who belong to what Martin Trow has termed the collegiate culture.

The very numerous studies published on this subject [12] reveal, in effect, three outstanding characteristics. In the first place, the radicals are good students, with particularly high scores in verbal aptitude and above-average theoretical orientation and social maturity. They come from an above-average social background. In short, they are not marginal to the university and have many characteristics with which "Academic Man" would like to credit himself. In the second place, they often come from liberal, even radical families, and, far from being in opposition to their parents' generation, they tackle the same issues as it did, while at the same time,

[12] There is a good recent résumé in Sanford (1968). Others include those of Keniston (1968) and Cavalli and Martinelli (1971). We shall return later to studies on the formation of the students' personalities.

criticizing its bourgeois attitude.[13] In consequence, while they belong firmly to the academic world, they are not imprisoned in it, for they have political perspectives. Finally, they have less racial prejudice and are more aware of community and international problems. They are, therefore, neither a young academic elite that would only be rebelling against the difference between the American ideals incarnated in academic teaching and the actual state of society, nor rebels who cannot tolerate the constraints of the academic world. Both their personalities and their acts are evidence that, within the protest movement, the problems of the university and the social and general political problems of American society have become synthesized.

The Cultural Revolt The movement's relative lack of integration gives considerable significance and even fairly wide autonomy to what one might call the cultural revolt. Beyond the political attack on the ruling class — on its political and ideological instruments — various elements of the movement have also rejected the cultural model of a society forced by science and technology to ceaseless change. The search for individual and collective identity — for an education that is a means of developing one's personality and not of participating in the system of production — are issues present in all the student movements and are to be found in very different cultural contexts. Alfred Willener (1971) was right to compare the French movement of May with dada and surrealism, on the one hand, and with movements like free jazz on the other. Our society of development and investment is also one of consumption, and although that consumption is denounced by the radical students as being an instrument used by commercial interests to manipulate consumer needs, it can also serve other functions: it can be a means of expression, or be associated with the world of the imagination, or with nature or happiness.

Keniston (1960) did well to remind us that Americans are particularly sensitive to this attitude toward consumption. In America, childhood is seen as a time of self-expression, nonspecialization, and affective relationships — a time when imagination can be expressed in action. The opposition between this world of childhood

---

[13] The interpretations of Lewis Feuer (1969) seem contradicted by the facts and do not give any precise analysis.

and that of the specialized and instrumental life of the adult is particularly evident in the intermediate world of school—a world that has greater autonomy and is more developed in the United States than elsewhere.

But in all countries it is impossible to identify the cultural themes of identity, equilibrium, and community with the ideology of a social class. These themes represent—as do those of technological and economic development—a general orientation of America's type of society, and each social class tinges them with its own hue. The most active students are from the upper middle class. Their militancy to a large extent rules out the commercialized forms of the theme of identity and harmony. Like the French and German students, the radical American students also attacked the bourgeois consumer society and the role of the mass media. The women's liberation movement, which was initially connected with the radical groups, was to spend most of its efforts on this criticism, and in particular on criticizing the image of the woman as a consumer object. This criticism was part of a more general attack on the inferior condition of women in American society, especially in the university. To this attitude of criticism was added a more positive desire for liberation and personal expression. Here, once again, in the Parisian context, one thinks of posters and graffiti. But there is a big difference between the two situations. In Paris, the cultural rebellion had little autonomy and was strongly integrated into political themes. Even when it was expressed autonomously, as for example by the "Situationists" in Strasbourg and Paris, it was more within the limited frame of reference of politico-cultural sects than as something belonging to the masses. Very recently, cultural themes have been taken up again by groups like "Vive la Revolution," which published the periodical *Tout.* But once again this is a limited group. Only the youngest college students and those at high school have given strong support to cultural themes, influenced to a large extent by the behavior of American youth. On the other hand, in the United States, cultural themes are a vital part of mass action. This is especially the case in California, as is illustrated by the Free Speech Movement and the struggle for People's Park. These movements were sustained both by political themes and by an almost mystical naturalism, reinforced by an obsession with purity, by nonviolence, and by the search for love and free expression in play and in imagination.

What part does this cultural revolt play in the student movement?

In the first place, it is independent of a specifically political movement. The development of higher education creates a new sphere for socialization, a new stage in the life-span, situated between adolescence and adult life (Parsons & Platt, 1970). A culture of the young is formed on the campus, dominated by the tensions inherent in the passage from the world of the family, which is personal and affective, to the adult world, which is one of hierarchies, rationality, and instrumentation.

Youth, in the words of Erik Erikson, is a "moratorium." Students are protected from certain constraints of adult life on condition that they remain in a dependent situation. In the United States, this youth culture does not conflict with the adult world as sharply as it does in underdeveloped societies, where the break between the "traditional" world and the "modern" world, according to the analysis of S. Eisenstadt (1956), is much more violent and partly explains why student movements in these countries have been active for so long. However, since the American family is more open to the outside world and more liberal, the formation of a youth culture there should not be accompanied by rebellion: "The general orientation appears to be, not a basic alienation, but an eagerness to learn, to accept higher orders of responsibility and to 'fit,' not in the sense of passive conformity, but in the sense of their readiness to work within the system, rather than in basic opposition to it" (Parsons, 1963, pp. 118–119).

But it is possible, in the same vein, to take a more disquieting view of the situation of youth: "In the West, we have to some extent shifted the children's burden on to youth. Youth now symbolizes the contradictions generated by our values and practices. Further, they live these contradictions" (Naegele, 1963, p. 59). Youth being the age, according to Erikson, of loyalty and diversity, that is, of both involvement and indetermination of the aims of action, the sensitivity of youth to social movements is great and is expressed more affectively than instrumentally, more culturally than in the form of an organized political movement.

Parson's analysis seems more in keeping with a previous situation than with the contemporary one. The role of the university as a socializing agent is what is usually termed its role *in loco parentis,* but revolts against this type of dependence are not new among American students. For example, early in the nineteenth century Princeton expelled half of its students (1806), Harvard half of its seniors (1823), and Yale some 40 students (1828). In addition, clashes over discipline became numerous at midcentury, decreasing in relative importance only with the beginning of the twentieth century. At that time, specifically political organizations began to appear on the campuses, the first being the Intercollegiate Socialist Society in 1905. During the 1920s and 1930s the main issues of the student movement were political, with pacifism in the forefront.

Cultural issues have appeared again in recent years but in a very different form. They are wholly linked to political issues, either directly or indirectly. When the role of the college *in loco parentis* is attacked, it is in the context of opposition to its role in the establishment and therefore to its political role. Young people rebel less against a discipline and regulations than against their dependent and isolated situation, which makes them passive agents of the establishment and thus prevents them from taking part in the reality of social conflict.

Before considering the cultural issues of militancy, we must consider cultural behavior that seems to have considerable autonomy and not to be linked to political attitudes. A great many writers have bracketed this behavior and militant political activity under the single term of alienation. Keniston, on the other hand, has emphasized the difference between the uncommitted and the militants. In his view, the cultural situation of the young is no longer the principal factor explaining the student movement. One must, on the contrary, make an absolute distinction — as one would for two types of personality — between the alienated and the committed, between those who ask the question "Who should be in the driver's seat?" and those who shout "Let's leave the car!" (Friedenberg, 1969). I would like to indicate what seems to me important, but also insufficient, in Keniston's analysis of the uncommitted (1965). The alienated outlook is withdrawal into oneself, a distrust of taking part in groups or in institutions, an attitude of the wary spectator who, as a fragmented self, is searching for experience, sensitivity, and a break in the social barriers, dreaming of synthesis rather than action. Keniston makes a good analysis of the childhood experiences linked with this alienation. But although the psychological characteristics of the uncommitted are effectively opposed to those of the militants, are they not both an answer to the same social situation? Is not the absence of commitment in the simple form of apathy, or in the more accentuated forms of alienation, already rejection and a break? In the second part of his book,

Keniston comes nearer to this theme while reflecting upon his analysis of American society and of the dictatorship of the ego. Noncommitment is an attitude of opposition to the prevailing norms of society that cannot take any form other than the "Heautontimoroumenos" of Baudelaire. Middle-class youths who no longer are impelled by the necessity for social ascension *refuse* to play the game, without being able to escape their condition or being urged into action by solidarity with the exploited. From the "beat generation" till the rise of the student movement, these youths testify to a situation of alienation that is both psychological and sociological. By this, I mean that they were subjected to roles, norms, and values that the ruling class imposes on society as a whole in the name of a "modernization" that is identified with its interests and its ideologies. These youth are not only marginals or in a state of anomie, but are virtual rebels who are reduced to living out psychologically conflicts that cannot yet be expressed socially.

Thomas Hayden also insists further on this impotence: "People are becoming more remote from the possibility of a civic life that maximizes personal influence over public affairs. There is a deep alienation of the student from the decision-making institutions of society" (Cohen & Hale, 1967, p. 277).

The difference between the era of the uncommitted and that of the young radicals is not only psychological, although this is of the greatest significance. It is also due to a change in the political situation that is well expressed by Paul Potter, writing in 1964:

For the first time, there are alternatives to the intellectual other than service to the Establishment or isolation from society, and these alternatives are being enunciated and proclaimed and implemented by social movements in the society. For the first time there is a base of power outside the university to which the intellectual can turn—which he can utilize in freeing himself from the structures of the university system. This, essentially, is another place to go. It is a home. It is not the home that any of us predicted. The home that we've been looking for is in the university, and the home the intellectual is finding is in social movements, political action and agitation (ibid., pp. 17–18).

The militants described in *Young Radicals* (Keniston, 1968) discovered themselves in extra-academic experiences and as "new veterans"[14] introduced the spirit of revolt onto the campus. It is

[14] The expression was coined by David Mallery (1966).

important to recognize that these militants are not rebels against their families, but, on the contrary, are young people who have strong links with their liberal-minded parents. Their political awareness does not coincide with an adolescent crisis, but happens after the latter has been resolved.[15] Here, it seems to me, Keniston distinguishes better than Richard Flacks (whose analyses are, however, extremely interesting) (1967, 1970) between the aspects related to an analysis of socialization and those relating to a political analysis. Flacks takes the thesis of Parsons and Eisenstadt and turns it around. In effect, he says that the conflict that the militants experience is not between a traditional family and a world of employment that is rapidly becoming rationalized (as is the case in the developing societies), but between a humanistic family background and a world that is still dominated by specialization and nineteenth-century values. "The discontinuities we refer to do not have to do with incongruence between a traditional family and a modernizing culture. If anything the reverse may be the case" (Flacks, 1970, pp. 348–349). This brilliant hypothesis is only partially satisfactory. It gives a good explanation of the role in cultural innovation played by these young people, for it is certainly true that many of the issues that they get involved in are best understood by upper-class professional people, who already live in a post-industrial society. But why should this cultural innovation take on a radical tone and associate itself with political and social opposition, rather than, say, producing another café society, somewhat more widespread than the previous ones? Evidence of humanism in the student movement is clearly in the Port Huron statement, adopted by SDS in 1962, but it is only one aspect and certainly not the most militant one. As I have pointed out, participation in the civil rights campaign and the struggle against the war in Vietnam complemented the movement's humanist views with a social negation and political criticism without which the movement would only have been a form—conservative by definition—of privileged participation in the consumer society.[16]

[15] Of the many studies on the relationship between education and political outlook, one of the best is that of Bloch, Haan, and Smith (1969). The authors contrast the dissenters, who gave a negative view of their relationship with their parents (who treated them severely and indulgently in turn), with the militants, who had an actively liberal upbringing.

[16] This humanistic liberalism is also found among the alumni—especially those from the best universities—who are liberals, but not radicals in any sense. See Spaeth and Greeley (1970).

It is this synthesis of cultural and political issues, this desire for a cultural revolution, that is important and that is expressed more forcefully in the United States than in any other country. It is always present in SDS and is also found, for example, in the newsletters of the New University Conference, where the Women's Caucus in particular voices its opinions frequently and with vehemence. With the Weathermen, the issue of violence is always accompanied by that of sexual liberation, particularly in the form of support for the gay liberation movement. The revolution cannot be concerned only with state institutions or economic organization. Because social domination has an increasingly total hold on the personality, any defiance of it must be total and challenge all forms of constraint, authority, and ideology, especially as regards sexual behavior.

This synthesis of morals and politics is best effected in relation to the most all-inclusive social problems, those that concern the organization of the world of everyday life. One of the most characteristic incidents in the history of the student movement was that of People's Park in Berkeley—characteristic precisely because it included radicals and "hippies," academic militants and nonstudents from Telegraph Avenue. [17] In the middle of April 1969 an organized group of radicals began to create a community park on an unused block of south-campus land that was owned by the University of California. After several weeks of work, during which hundreds of people turned a muddy parking lot into a park, the university, on May 16, erected a fence around the land. This act provoked a demonstration in which police, using shotguns, killed one person, blinded another, and wounded several more. For several weeks Berkeley lived in a state of siege, occupied by the national guard and subject to constant surveillance by helicopters. On May 22, a pacifist march—participants were carrying the flowers they wanted to plant—brought in its wake fresh police violence.

The fervor of these few days was unmitigated; appeals to love, to nature, and to free expression were met pathetically by the brutality of the police and the obstinacy of the academic administration. Some spoke of infantilism. Why not? In fact, it was a cultural and political clash between the world of play and imagination,

---

[17] Whittaker and Watts (1969). This study shows that this category—roughly 3,000 people—had results higher than the student average on the majority of items of the Omnibus Personality Inventory.

which is also that of participant democracy, and the apparatus of social repression.

Actually, a certain tension always exists between political and moral issues; newspapers like the *Free Press,* the *Berkeley Barb,* the *Berkeley Tribe,* and the *Village Voice* are not far from falling into the lowest commercialization of all forms of sexual life, but their alliance in a revolutionary stand is more important. Some may object that there is nothing new in this and that Western Europe—especially Germany at the beginning of the twentieth century—had already witnessed this type of alliance between social and moral issues. It seems to me, however, that this alliance is of much greater significance today, and that it is, in fact, what gives youth its central role in the new social movements. Defense of personal identity only becomes militant when it is supported by the forces of sexuality and of imagination against the demands of the ego, which are constituted by the constraints of the ruling society.

In the meantime, this cultural revolt—which is a sign of the times—cannot find an institutionalized political expression. Once played out, it tends to return to cultural forms of expression in which political commitment is replaced by a simple desire for schism, for remoteness, and for withdrawal. After the uncommitted came the young radicals; then new uncommitteds appeared who retained some of the vague and rather demobilizing issues of the movement—like pacifism, the search for an equilibrium with the environment, the return to primitive communities, or the setting aside of the technological society. Now, once again, the attitudes are more indicative of a crisis than of a preparation for, and a living out of, the conflicts. But, whatever the future may be, even if a separation occurred today among the various components whose synthesis has given the student movement its personality, it seems to me that the indissoluble link between social and moral issues will not continue to be the most important characteristic of the forces of political opposition in the United States.

General Characteristics of the American Movement We must, in concluding, recall certain characteristics of the American movement. I have attempted to analyze its components and their relationship. We must now consider its form.

What strikes me first is its duration, its capacity for development in a university, especially at the University of California at Berkeley. It seems to me that this duration has two main causes. First, the academic institutions are sufficiently organized and flexible for unrest to develop there without breaking them. The Sorbonne crumbled under much less important events than those that marked the beginning of the Free Speech Movement. It is true that later on more violent crises led to more rapid and violent repression and to the closing of the university. But the capacity of many universities to reply was rather remarkable. The action of Kingman Brewster at Yale is an excellent example. Secondly, this duration is linked to the significance of cultural issues. The duration of the movement is therefore directly proportional to the strength of the first and last components I described in this type of movement. On the one hand, there is academic action, and, on the other, cultural protest. In cases where the central elements of the movement (those that support the black movement or a radical movement against the war) are most important, the movement is more intense, as in the case at Columbia or even at San Francisco State.

The second characteristic is violence. Its importance is inversely proportionate to the length of the movement and is particularly linked with the direct intervention of the black movement and, as an adjunct, with the intervention of the police. Violence was limited, because in general it denotes the hidden presence of a social movement behind a social crisis. The absence of a "manifest" movement, ideologically organized and socially integrated, is in most cases linked with repression. This is the case in countries dominated by a colonial power; terrorism, encouraged by the cultural and social disorganization of the dominated country, is the first reaction. The obstacles may also be due to the entry of a group into a new class situation; this is the case when workers of rural origin enter the urban laboring class. This occurred in Western Europe in the middle of the nineteenth century and again at the beginning of the twentieth century. It happened again very recently in France, and especially in Italy, where the transfer of rural manpower to the town and to industry is still sizable. In all these cases, agricultural workers who were uprooted and turned into urban proletarians attacked the social order through violence rather than through an organized movement, for they lacked both the integration into a type of production and the social relationships necessary to form such a movement. Finally, the obstacles may also be due to difficulty in integrating the elements of the social movement itself. In this context, violence is a dramatic effort to unify the movement, analogous to the political suicide by means of which militants attempt to revive the cohesive forces of a movement that has split.

The American movement has therefore constantly oscillated between this long-duration type, which is both academic and cultural, and a more political type, which is characterized by shorter and more violent thrusts forward.

The relative separation of these two aspects explains the third one—the feeble ideological production of the movement. Since this production is much stronger when the general sociopolitical elements are more powerful, it is not surprising that the only really noteworthy production has been by SDS, even though its significant period of activity was brief. This meager output is particularly striking when it is contrasted with the production in West Germany, where, sustained by the tradition of the school of Frankfurt, the movement was able to maintain a critical university at Berlin for a long time. Out of that institution came a number of important doctrinarians, by whom the French, who were also somewhat unproductive, were significantly influenced.

Just before the outbreak of the crisis, Egon Bittner (1963), taking a Weberian stand, attempted to redefine the general characteristics of a radical movement. Among these were charisma, the control of doctrine, the strength of integration, the importance of sacrifice, and the capacity to use external hostility for its own reinforcement. A description of this type is ill-applied to the American movement, even to SDS, its most radical group. Although certain radical movements, as, for example, Messianism, are effectively "closed" movements, the American movement was "open." It was neither a sect, nor a church, but more of a loosely integrated body of social criticism, of attempts to get a hold on the social order in order to transform it or demystify it. Its utopian nature is almost always associated with an idea of reform. It is less concerned with re-creating a community world than with exploding the ideological cohesion of a system whose injustice, violence, and repression it wishes to expose. Because it is so open, it is not burdened with a characteristic common to many movements, that is, a duality between the community of protesters and an intelligentsia that controls the relations between the inside and outside world. This intelligentsia is the basis of the movement and in consequence unites criticism and political action so closely that the formation of a doctrinal code is weakened by it.

The third characteristic contrasts with the last one, the movement's deep penetration into American society and culture. The foreigner who occasionally lives in the United States is amazed at the extent of the changes that take place between one trip and another. Academic unrest, of course, does not cause these changes, but is both a part and a sign of change.

At the same time, the university is the place where the problems of American society have transformed themselves most unmistakably into an awareness of crisis. America was proud of her colleges and universities, in which she saw her preferred reflection — liberal and organized, idealistic and pragmatic. Because of this, the crisis in the university led her to doubt her values and, further still, to doubt whether it was in terms of values that she was to understand herself.

After 20 years of ever-increasing power, of development in many fields, of leadership of a large part of the world, American society has been "hoist with its own petard." The spirit of liberty and nationalism that is still keen in this erstwhile British colony protested against American arms and capital in various parts of the world. Young people rejected established values. The black population, or its most active elements, followed by other ethnic groups, such as the Mexican-Americans and the Indians, did not consent to integration, or else denounced its lies and limits in the North, where de facto segregation was still maintained or reinforced.

A society accustomed to seeing its reflection in the shape of monuments and principles now had nothing but a shattered image of itself. It had to learn to define itself in relation to the nature of its power and its conflicts, and by what it excluded or repressed as much as by what it affirmed and rewarded.

The institutionalization of labor conflicts and the waning of union militancy practically eliminated general social conflicts for 20 years. Large-scale confrontations were replaced by strategies and transactions. The capacity of political institutions seemed sufficiently large to ensure controlled social change in all domains.

In the 1960s, however, the age of affluence, which for a time seemed to mark the end of ideologies, came to a close. Violence erupted in the ghettos and then on the campuses, bringing the violence of Vietnam closer to home. Once the Negro problem had become a black movement, legal institutions could not control it alone. The trial of the Chicago Eight did not give an attractive image of justice. The Democratic party was incapable of responding to the social upsurge, which extended from extreme liberalism to radicalism. The social sciences, which had developed tremendously, were in most cases surprised by the new social movements; many young teachers and graduate students began to rebel intellectually and politically against the ideological-professional establishment. The women's liberation movement criticized certain of the most central aspects of American culture.

But I am struck as much by the extent of the crisis, by the manner in which it was experienced by the academic world, as I am by its substance. There was a multiplicity of initiatives, far-ranging discussions, and attempts at reform. In an instant, we shall examine the meaning and the limits of this critical attitude. It is sufficient here to recognize that the academic world retains extreme vitality. In cases where the university is above all a tool to reproduce the social order, a social crisis and a new policy can only overthrow it. The French Revolution simply abolished the universities, along with all the corporations, and the Chinese cultural revolution closed the universities, which were accused of reproducing an old-fashioned type of culture.

Because the American academic system was more a tool of production than of reproduction of the social order, it was within it that forces of social and cultural opposition manifested themselves, and it was also within it that forces of integration and of protest confronted each other and were able to reconstruct a political dynamic. But this does not mean that the movement that broke out in 1964 can, in the short run, continue to develop. Both in the United States and in France, the movement of the past few years can only split and be dispersed. In the spring of 1970, at the time of the invasion of Cambodia and of the killings at Kent State and Jackson State, people in the United States were led to believe that the synthesis of all the components of the movement was taking place. At no other moment was the unrest so widespread or so violent (Astin, 1971). A Carnegie Commission study of university presidents showed that 57 percent of academic establishments had experienced a "significant impact" from the crisis.[18] Among the best universities (those receiving substantial federal grants), one-third experienced strikes and almost as many had "destruc-

[18] Peterson and Bilorusky (1971). The first part of this report examines the response to the incidents of May 1970 on campuses across the nation; the second part is a case study of the reconstitution movement on the Berkeley campus of the University of California.

tive demonstrations." Above all, the demonstrations reunited the most diverse issues, not only opposition to the war and the black movement, but also the ecological movement and academic demands.

This extreme crisis, however, disclosed the split in the movement rather than its integration. The academic world was impressed by the Princeton Plan, and by the decision of this important university to delay its reopening in the fall so that its students could participate in the 1970 electoral campaigns. Yet, extraordinary as this decision may appear to be, it seems to me to indicate more of a turning point in the move toward the institutionalization of the clash, in the same way, moreover, as do the internal administrative measures taken by the university to associate the students with its management.

The reconstitution movement at Berkeley, initiated on May 6 by the Wolin proposal,[19] was nonviolent and moderate. It tried to get extended support outside the campus. Radicals felt isolated, and the campus administration did not try to oppose such a quiet activism. By October, the May fever had completely disappeared.

The struggle against the war itself could only unite the movement if public opinion were convinced that America, far from disengaging itself from the conflict, was plunging deeper into it by a fresh offensive and was running the risk of a clash with China that could lead to a world war. Few people seem to have adopted an interpretation of this type. I have already pointed out that the movement against the war did not develop significantly; it was relatively vague and sustained by pacifism, even "realism," rather than by a desire to criticize American imperialism.

Finally, the cultural issues gradually separated out from the specifically political issues, and the fall of 1970 witnessed more symptoms of withdrawal — into the communes or pop culture — than offensive actions. The move from the exhilaration of spring to the bitter and resigned apathy of fall was harsh. A movement activated by radicals and revolutionaries — situated in a society in a state of crisis but not in a revolutionary situation — can only split up. In the States, the universities in particular retained considerable efficiency, along with an increased capacity for negotiations and initiative. Moreover, the black movement remained nationalist instead

---

[19] "This campus is on strike to reconstitute the University as a center for organizing against the war in Southeast Asia" (Peterson & Bilorusky, 1971, p. 103).

of contributing to the formation of a class movement, and, subject to violent repression, was weakened by internal dissensions. On the one hand the movement generated cultural and institutional changes, and on the other its vital forces evaporated in the by-ways of sectarianism.

It would be a mistake to believe that a crisis that is coming to an end can be gradually absorbed by institutional mechanisms. Even if the break is complete between the academic reformers and the visionaries of the communes, even if participants in the new class struggles are unable to organize themselves and find for themselves direct political expression, the movement marked a change in American society in two ways. Firstly, it taught American society to recognize itself as the stake in a conflict and not as a community united by values. Secondly, the idealistic illusions of the ruling forces were destroyed and the way opened for fresh conflicts, institutionalized or not.

Perhaps, in concluding, we should return to our point of departure and, instead of describing the characteristics peculiar to the student movement, ask ourselves, "Is this a social movement?" If not, what is it? We can no longer say that the students were rebelling against their parents' generation and against all authority symbolic of paternal authority. I have cited the results of a sufficient number of surveys that present evidence totally opposed to this interpretation. Nor can we say that what has happened in and around the academic system in the course of the past few years is the expression of a crisis of this system. Easy though it may be to enumerate the difficulties experienced, the system is nevertheless expanding, its resources are plentiful, and teachers and students are aware of its qualities. Nor is the crisis one of government, though discontent in this respect is considerable.

But we can say that there is a student crisis, even if there is not an academic crisis—a gap, as Flacks says, between the culture of a new bourgeoisie and the more traditional apparatus of the establishment. But why have the personal problems of a certain category of students become a social problem? Why did they become activists, and why did their works and actions gain such an audience among the other students, the teachers, and the general public? (It matters little whether their opinions were favorable or hostile.)

We must therefore go further. At the least, this student elite was aware of the contradictions in American society—the injustice done to the blacks, and the scandal of the war in Vietnam. They reacted to them with the sensitivity of reasoning youths, with the violence of those who are themselves sheltered from misery and exploitation, and with the freedom of expression of those who are assured that they cannot so easily be dismissed from the factory or the office and who do not have to worry about the family budget. Is this type of answer sufficient? These students were directly affected by the war. They opposed the university, which was within immediate reach, not only distant and indistinct opponents. They felt that by remaining silent they were, if not victims, at least prisoners and accomplices of a social system that they opposed. Once these objections have been removed, the simplest one still remains—namely, that it was not a social movement because it was a rebellion of a limited number of people and lasted a limited time. The year 1970–71 was astonishingly calm in all the universities. This surprised many of those who had lived through the incidents of spring 1970. In a few years time, we may consider these years of crisis to be a historical event—an event which had its importance, but which did not reveal or forecast any permanent problems and attitudes. In Europe and in the United States, public attention had already been diverted from these problems and is now preoccupied with the international monetary crisis, inflation, unemployment, or various problems of domestic policy.

This is a valid objection. A nationalist, or a labor, movement has its ups and downs, periods with greater or lesser activity, but the nationalist will and the working-class consciousness are only considered the sources of social movements because they are persistent expressions of opinion.

If it is a social movement, then what should we call it? Is it the student movement? But the students, numerous as they may be, are only a limited group. They are not central to a society. It is not even very obvious to whom they are specifically opposed.

The struggle against the war played an important role in academic unrest, but this war was not waged against the students. Its main victims were not the students, but, primarily the Vietnamese, and, to a lesser extent, young Americans among whom the students were underrepresented.

I admit these objections for the United States, and for France or Japan, on condition that we define their relevance. The students did not collectively oppose those who dominated them simply in the name of their own interests or with a view to educational reform. They also spoke and acted on behalf of other groups and waged a campaign that was not especially oriented toward their own demands. But, because the university is no longer uniquely the memory or the mind of the social body, it is wholly insufficient to say that the students were merely the conscience of a society with problems. The university is now an essential element in the functioning of society, which has never been true in the past. The students' actions were not only inspired by the prickings of their consciences, but were also a result of their experiences and of their lives.

This dual role defines the content of their social movement and its relevance. They fought in the name of their education, of their personality, and of their identity against the academic, economic, and political machine that would employ them, and against a state whose imperialism is inseparable from the power that the ruling class — that of the managers of the large production, information, and consumption plants — excercises within its frontiers. But, at the same time, they were the vanguard of all the masses, and also the vanguard of a mass to which they belong; in this, their movement differed from the populist intellectual movement and even from the early stages of their own movement when SNCC and CORE were hatching grounds. This role of vanguard has been possible because students are concentrated on the campus, have a low degree of subjection to the daily constraints of employment, salary, and authority, and possess higher quality information and a greater ability to communicate.

What their movement does reveal is that the problems of education have become central social problems that challenge not only the society's ideology, but also its political system and mode of production. Our type of society gives increasing importance to organizational forms and to the management of relationships between people; previous societies were mainly concerned with the organization of man's relationship to nature. Our development depends more on systems of communication than on sources of energy. Given the above, there is no longer any fundamental difference between the domain of economic life and that of education or information. All are part of the process of production.

The students are those who have lived through new problems and at the same time were the first to feel themselves now part of a much larger and more integrated whole. The university, we repeat, is no longer only the locus of ideology; it is also that of production, and therefore of political choice.

What differentiates the student movement in the United States from that in Japan or France is that it is located in a solid and modernized academic system. The "affirmative" issues—cultural innovation, the image of a new type of man, and new concepts of human relationships—receive more attention there than in other countries, whereas, the "negative" or critical issues are not as clearly defined. This is also why the link between the radical students and their liberal modern families has seemed so important to American observers. It is noteworthy that the militants questioned by Keniston were very willing to speak about their childhood, whereas in France, for example, questions about the family in similar conditions have met with keen resistance. French students seemed to fear a psychological interpretation of their action and preferred to speak more of the situation that they were opposing than of their personal reason for involvement. But why think that a social movement only exists when the image of the almost natural contradictions of the existing society asserts itself, as if the role of collective action were only to force these objective contradictions to explode? The American radical movement is very far from this Leninist point of view but close to many other social movements, including a large part of the labor movement. Utopia is affirmation, definition of the objective, and consequently also commitment of the personality to its hopes and dreams as much as to its rejections and wrath. Keniston and others have very aptly noted the sense of continuity among the young radicals. This is the movement's source of its psychological and cultural richness, but also of its specifically political weakness. In France, we find similar aspects in the 22nd March Movement and the outburst of the first days of May 1968. The French utopia was more brilliant, but also less enduring, because the university was in crisis and because the labor conflicts were still very weakly institutionalized. The organization of the state, like that of the methods of education, was archaic. The movement tended increasingly to fall back on outmoded schemes of thought and organization, drawing from these archaisms, which were part of a society full of archaisms, a greater capacity for action and political organization.

All social movements are incomplete. They tend either toward the defensive—criticism and involvement in a struggle against a social crisis—or toward the offensive—associating the social struggle with the defense of new forms of social and cultural activity. In the first case, the movement may be merely the expression and the tool of the move from one ruling class to another. In the second, it may be reduced to a movement for institutionalized reform that does not threaten the ruling class and only contributes to its modernization.

A social movement also never has the complete, integrated, and balanced personality of a doctrine or of an analysis. It oscillates ceaselessly between the twin poles of criticism and utopia. For example, the unity of the American radical movement is not that of a party or of a theory. It resides in the complementarity and the tensions of SDS and the FSM, of pacifism and of black power. It is a social movement because there is a high degree of interdependence between these different, and often opposed, elements. This diversity and these tensions only cease to exist (at least openly) when the social movement is replaced by a new political power and state. The assumption of power in one sense denotes the success of an opposition movement. But, at the same time, it subjects the movement to the demands of a new ruling class and to the power that the latter manages to accumulate. Finally, it is the new ruling class that becomes the possessor of the tools of the opposition movement and of what that movement created.

The very fragility of the radical student movement, with its low degree of integration and its internal conflicts, along with its dynamic potential and the extent of the irreversible changes that it produced, proves that it is effectively a social movement.

6. *Integration or Disintegration of the Academic System*

The life and development of the academic system in recent years do not precisely parallel those of the protest movement, just as the protest movement is not confined to the academic world. Despite the criticisms of technological civilization, and the efforts to withdraw from it, there is no general rejection of scientific and technical knowledge, nor even of the professional activity of teachers and research workers. Those who want to replace the promethean model of industrialization by the search for a new balance between man and his environment look to the development of new knowledge and new techniques as well as to social and cultural change.

It is the right time to examine general problems, because the growth of the student population is slowing down. The enrollments doubled in the 1960s; they will increase by only one-half during the seventies, level off during the eighties, and then grow again, but at a slower rate (The Carnegie Commission . . . , 1971). No immediate material or political problem is hiding the necessity of long-term choices. In its functioning, moreover, the university mechanism encounters problems that are not directly related to the student revolt. In the year 1971, many an administrator was more worried about the financial crisis in his university or college than about the few political demonstrations on the campus. The student movement shook the society—its ideology even more than its political system or its economic bases. But as the movement's action became more radical, it became increasingly removed from specifically academic problems, or rather a growing discrepancy developed between the various levels of its action. As I have already pointed out, we should not be misled by the explosion of spring 1970. In the United States, after 1968, the cultural revolt leads either to withdrawal or to innovation marginal to the university world; political action proper strives for ways of thinking and forms

253

of organization that lead to the isolation of small groups; academic problems appear to be autonomous, especially as the teaching and research apparatus shows no sign of crumbling. In the rear of a movement challenging the orientation and the power of American society, academic institutions have therefore retained or recovered their initiative, which may find expression either in a backlash, in an attempt to impose reforms from above, or in the establishment of new decision-making procedures.

The idea of academic reform did not arise from the independent thinking of administrators and teachers; it was a reaction to the student revolt, although not specifically to the confrontation between radicals and the establishment. The general topic of reform covers three types of problems:

In the first place, the scope of the protest movement awakens us to changes that were already underway long before 1964. We should ask ourselves whether or not the student movement is already part of a new type of university and contributes to the acceleration of changes quite independent of its own objectives. The image of the multiversity has been attacked by the radicals, but it clearly has at least one thing in common with the student revolt: both destroy the old image of the university acting *in loco parentis* and professing to be a repository of values.

In the second place, the university authorities attempt to respond to the student movement either by trying to redefine once again the university's role as an educator or by rethinking the relations between gown and town, between the campus and the community.

Thirdly, there is a much more essential question concerning the very existence of the university. We see in the People's Republic of China the systematic destruction of the intelligentsia as a social category, and therefore of the university as an autonomous sphere, and even of the students as a professional and social group.

Despite the distance and opposition between China and the United States and other industrialized countries, it is normal that the existence of the academic system as an autonomous entity, and of the "studentry" as an age group and a professional category, should be questioned in the United States as well.

When dealing with the first type of problem, the student movement can be seen as one aspect of a more general trend; when dealing with the second, we observe the effect of this movement on the internal decision-making system in the colleges and universities. The third type of problem discloses the impact of this movement on the nature and functions of the academic system.

I will discuss each in turn.

THE MULTIVERSITY AND THE NATIONAL ACADEMIC SYSTEM

The academic system has been challenged. Its functioning has provoked the criticism of numerous teachers and students; its administrative methods have been attacked by the faculty; its links with the ruling elite have been contested by the radical students, who have succeeded in launching and sustaining mass movements; its "racism" has been denounced by the black movement. All these attacks have exploded the myth and the rhetoric of the academic community. But these assaults on the university can also be seen as coinciding with changes that had already been initiated within the academic system by some of its more alert leaders.

The academic crisis destroys the role of the university acting *in loco parentis;* on this point the agreement between S. M. Lipset, for example, and the radical students is complete. Not only does the university cease to be defined as an educational agency, but the very idea of a university based on a unifying principle is brought into question. If the general education theme was the most characteristic feature of academic ideology in the aftermath of the First World War, Kerr's idea of the multiversity has been the most original one produced by the university world during the last two decades (1963).

Kerr proceeds from the idea that the universities are naturally conservative because of their important role as transmitters and codifiers of the cultural heritage. They have, in fact, changed only in response to outside pressures.

According to him, the most dangerous and ossifying concept of the university is that of Newman, who wanted to organize the entire activity of the university around a humanist model, thereby saving the spirit of Oxbridge at a time when the great English universities were already engaged in an important process of opening up and diversifying. But Flexner's illusion is hardly less dangerous.[1] He believed in the possibility of replacing the traditional unifying principle by a more modern one—the concept of profes-

---

[1] See Kerr's preface to the new edition of Flexner's *Universities.*

sionalized scientific research—without any real analysis of how appropriate this German model would be for another country.

Between the two wars, Lowell and Hutchins tried to return to a global conception of education and to re-create what Metzger (1970) calls the similarity between the teaching profession and the clergy. Their efforts, however, were doomed to failure.

Kerr also suggests a complete reversal of the traditional approach: the unity of the university derives not from its function but from its administration. It can develop only to the extent that it can respond to varying demands, accept the coexistence of basic and applied research, train scientists and high-level professionals (as well as middle-level technicians), and combine teaching and research.

There is a temptation, at first glance, to see these ideas as a return to the generation of the great founders, White and Eliot. But such a comparison would be artificial. These presidents did indeed want to open the university to outside demands and encourage the internal diversification of its institutions, but they were inspired by a certain "idea" of the university expressed through its participation in the cultural model of nineteenth-century society. A belief in progress, combined with confidence in the progressivism of American society, was their basic principle, going beyond the opposition between the British college and the German graduate school to confer a social mission on the university. Kerr developed his ideas at a time when such a synthesis was no longer possible, particularly because of the increased professionalism of the academic world, and because direct communication and harmony could no longer exist between the external and internal demands to which the university had to answer. That is why he did not propose an "idea" of the university. Rather he searched for a way of coordinating distinct and often conflicting functions. This is an administrative, not an ideological problem. It is similar to the problem confronting any large organization, which, becoming increasingly diversified, can function only by coordinating sharply differentiated subunits, each with its own different or competitive operational norms and strategies. Here we reach the extreme limits of secularization.

But the meaning of this is ambiguous. By destroying the inner life—the "spirit" of the university—this concept, on the one hand, makes of it a political arena in which various social interests conflict, where the tumult of the outside world penetrates more freely.

And Kerr did in fact follow a policy of liberalization after Sproul's bureaucratic and paternalistic management. On the other hand, this concept leads to direct reproduction within the university of the power relationships between forces at work in the outside world, and therefore beyond expressions of protest and conflict to the university's integration into the prevailing order.

It is because of the coexistence of these two tendencies in Kerr's analysis that he came to confer an extremely important role upon the university president. It is he, and he alone, who can combine these two tendencies, act as mediator between them, and convert their contradictions into the dynamics of the university institution. But the other side of the coin is that the president may be torn between these two tendencies. Once the social forces in motion come seriously into conflict he will find himself under attack from the radicals as well as the conservatives. At first attacked on his left, Kerr was finally to become a victim of Governor Ronald Reagan's hostility — these two kinds of attack are easy to understand. Under pressure from the most conservative elements of the state, the Governor of California wanted to express his opposition to the endemic agitation at Berkeley. Thus a new majority on the Board of Regents, whom the governor appoints, dismissed the president in order to counter what was seen as a threat to the principles of law and order.

To the university apparatus, the radical students oppose the image of an academic community in which all are free to participate and express themselves. This highly mobilizing utopian conception does not, however, constitute a program of government. Since every university belongs to the society that finances it and makes use of its graduates or the results of its research, it is not easy to visualize how it could function as an independent community. Kerr's idea of the university could certainly imply the penetration of the university by the ruling forces of the society, but it could also make possible the participation and autonomy of the student community. I would even go so far as to say that the resort to an integrating image of the university seen as a community necessarily implies a close dependence on the ruling social forces, since the ruling ideology of such a community would necessarily be the ideology of the ruling classes. Indeed it is in the name of liberal and communitarian ideas that the university has placed itself in the service of the established order. How is it possible to allow the existence of opposition forces and cultural demands independent of the needs and restrictions of the social order, without destroying the ambition of the university to organize around any values whatsoever, and without turning it into a political arena where negotiations and transactions find their place as well as conflicts and confrontations? The creation of black studies departments was perhaps a significant example of this new political role, and for this reason it shocked those teachers who wanted to defend the purity of professional values.

It is to be expected that when a basic conflict breaks out that cannot be directly institutionalized, each of the adversaries will propose an overall, integrated, communitarian image of the university: employers speak of integration, while the revolutionary workers speak of cooperation or self-management. But there is no other system of self-management than the recognition of normal conflicts between the productive apparatus—whether controlled by the market, the oligopolies, or a planning agency—and the interests of the workers. The rejection of the multiversity during the struggle does not prevent it from being a framework in which the recognition of student opposition is more easily conceivable than in the university, defined as the seat of values.

This conception of the multiversity does more than confer a central role upon the president. It must also be accompanied by a serious attempt to organize the entire academic system. When a college or a university was defined by its spirit, and as a community, each one was an independent unit, linked to a local community, to a national trend of ideas, or to an educational outlook. The multiversity idea, on the contrary, gives far more importance to the academic system. Varying functions cannot be combined unless they are organized; a complex system must be differentiated at the same time as its unity is maintained. This was the idea behind the California Master Plan, which organized the relationships of the multicampus University of California with the whole system of state colleges and public junior colleges. The latter were completely open, whereas entrance to the state colleges was restricted to the upper third of high school graduates, and entrance to the university was limited to the upper eighth. The University of California had the responsibility of preparing students for the doctorate. It was possible, however, for a certain number of students to pass from one level of the academic system to a higher one, from a junior college to a college to the university. This was the most ambitious structure ever created at the state level. As we have seen, some of its effects—the development of a central bureaucracy and the reduction of minority enrollment in the state colleges—contributed to unrest on several state college and university campuses, for example, at Berkeley and San Francisco State.

But this structure clearly emphasizes the direction in which a large part of the academic system is going. The era when the organizational unit was the campus belongs increasingly to the past; we can discern the trends toward a broader organization at several different levels.

First of all, there is the development of the multicampus systems. Here are some examples:

Multicampus system	Number of campuses	Number of students
State University of New York	65	314,000
City University of New York	11	123,000
University of California	10	147,000
California state colleges system	19	288,000
University of Texas	10	74,000
State University of Florida	7	80,000
University of North Carolina	7	46,000

SOURCE: *Report on Higher Education* (1971, pp. 23–27).

In the state of New York, there exists an even more general system. The State University of New York is a legal entity that gives charters and accreditation to all the public and private institutions, schools and colleges.

Above the state level, regional groups are formed, such as the Southern Regional Education Board, the New England Board of Higher Education, or the Western Interstate Compact for Higher Education. In all, 39 states are covered by such regional organizations.

Finally, at the national level, a large number of organizations have gradually introduced a measure of unity into the system[2]: for example, the American Council on Education, the College Entrance Examination Board, the Educational Testing Service, the Woodrow Wilson Fellowship Program, and the National Merit Scholarship Corporation. The importance of federal intervention was underscored by the conversion of the U.S. Commissioner of Education into an Assistant Secretary for Education.

[2] For all these forms of organization, see Perkins (1966, pp. 66–77).

Lastly, I have already mentioned the role of the foundations, which was particularly important before the extensive development of the federal research funds, although the Ford Foundation, created in 1951 with considerable resources, gave a new impetus to their effort. We cannot speak of the progress either of research or of coordinated, long-term programs without mentioning the Rockefeller, Carnegie, Ford, and Russell Sage foundations, as well as many others.

The proliferation of these organizations might seem a threat to the autonomy of the academic system itself, but James Perkins, an outstanding champion of the organization of a specifically academic system, believes that only a rapid move from autonomy to systems of higher education can assure that ultimate decision making will be in academic rather than political hands.

So there develops at all levels an administrative organization that appears independent of any orientation the university might have and tends to interpose itself between the specifically academic activities of teaching and research and the centers of decision and influence. The president and the administrators must serve both as mediators and as managers capable of predicting and dealing with the tensions, the obstacles, and the attacks.

The importance of this trend is that it tends to satisfy — though not without conflict — the faculty's desire to gain a larger role in the administration. The ambiguity of the faculty demands, which has already been noted, was reinforced by the academic crisis. Resentful of the increasing role of the administration, the faculty would indeed prefer a collective type of government. When faced with pressure from the students, however, it quickly takes refuge behind the administration, which it nevertheless disavows from time to time. More basically, it has been shown that the professors' attitude has two components: attachment to the institution and attachment to the profession. Since it is hard to believe that these two reference groups always coincide, a system of government that combines the role of the executive with that of the legislature, in line with the ideas of Parsons, is probably the one most apt to satisfy both the teachers and many administrators. The probable victims of such an arrangement would be the trustees and especially the political authorities of the states. Already governors and administrators are beginning to show irritation with, and even hostility toward, the increasing political autonomy of the universities, which seems to them to open the door to the very ideas and behavior they condemn. As far as the students are concerned, we could, from this general perspective, adopt Irving Horowitz's (1970, pp. 70–71) hypothesis that they play an increasing role in the decision-making system, but as organized workers. The progress of trade-union organization among the teaching assistants is a sign of this trend. This unionization tendency is also probably strengthened by the broader social base of university recruiting.

There exist, therefore, tremendous forces operating at all levels in favor of the increasing organization and integration of the academic system, forces whose development seems a normal consequence of the weakening of the conception of the university as an educational agent.

EDUCATION AND COMMUNITY SERVICE But the same phenomenon could be interpreted in a different way. It could be said that in rejecting education as its main function, the academic system becomes a system of production — production of diplomas and knowledge. Universities would then become mere business enterprises, a trend that would inevitably arouse strong opposition. Can the universities — preoccupied by their own power and isolated from the society by an increasingly massive bureaucratic apparatus — respond to those very demands to which such bureaucratic machines are the least sensitive, those of the students and those of the nonruling forces of the society?

Among these reactions, two profoundly different tendencies should be distinguished.

One answer to the student protest is to revive the tradition of the liberal arts colleges, since they have been least affected by the movement. Numerous measures have been taken with a view to making the curriculum more flexible, giving more freedom of individual choice, and re-creating a more integrated human environment. The federations of colleges — the cluster colleges — make possible both this greater flexibility and the high degree of concentration of resources that higher education demands. In its 1969 catalog, for example, Old Westbury College, which belongs to the State University of New York, pleaded warmly for this recognition of the Oxbridge tradition as opposed to the depersonalization of the multiversity. John Harris (1970) goes further. According to him, the university has been oriented almost exclusively toward competitive achievement and has therefore sacrificed education. It should become "a secular church," where all the activities are geared to the personality of the students and are therefore determined with their participation. One of the coauthors of this book, Thomas E. McCallough, calls for a humanist university, a place of communication and participation, of discovery and identity. Borrowing the expression of Paul Goodman, he wants the university to teach "what is common, integral and humane." In more professional terms, Metzger (1970, pp. 604–607) would like to see the university assume some of the roles of a church—such as the preparation of neophytes—which implies a wide differentiation of teaching and research and a redefinition of the authority of the teacher and his relationship to the students.

As usual, emphasis on education can have very different meanings. For some it means restoring community cohesiveness, for others it means restoring the relevance of education, and therefore giving more initiative to the students in the choice and organization of their studies.

The most elaborate expression of this conception, turned inward toward education and communication, is found in the *Report of the Assembly on University Goals and Governance* (American Academy of Arts and Sciences, 1971). In writing this report, Martin Meyerson and Stephen Graubard synthesized the efforts of various work teams whose members came from many universities. This text calls for a basic change in the academic system. "An academic system that was forged in the latter decades of the 19th century, came to maturity in the 1920s and 1930s and was remarkably uncritical of itself in the 1950s and early 1960s when it grew to unprecedented dimensions, is now required to rethink its fundamental orientations."

The university, the report states, must first of all recover real control over its activities. "There is no reason for universities to serve as holding companies for large laboratories or research projects that are not linked to their educational program. The attraction of large expansions of staff and facilities should be resisted" (thesis no. 42).

The report goes on to say that the university should not act as a public service. It lacks the means of dealing directly with social problems such as the urban crisis, poverty, and the environment. It should be devoted to teaching and to the research that is linked to it. Still this teaching has to be modernized and made more flexible in its forms and duration. This implies a reform of the university administration, giving the faculty and students the right to "nominate" outside trustees, although not necessarily to elect them. The role of the students should be increased, but more at the level of the departments than at that of the university. The spirit of these reforms should spread throughout the academic system, but experiments with the suggested measures will be easiest in the private colleges and universities, for these institutions are less subject to political pressures. Finally, we should defend the existence of high-standard institutions, for which "selective support, public and private, is essential and ought to be fought for."

These examples of the main theses presented in the report illustrate its enlightened conservatism. No radical measures are called for, only a reinforcement of the inner life of the college or university —a reduction in the ambitions of a system that is overcommitted and whose spirit of innovation finds expression nowhere better than in the private, elitist colleges and universities. Since the attacks against the university derive from its too numerous bonds with the economic, social, and military leaders, these bonds should be cut when they are not specifically linked to the needs of academic research and teaching.

While the multiversity strives to be wide open to the outside world and expects to derive its unity from the managerial ability of its president, the assembly report, published in Cambridge (which of course is no accident) insists on the necessity of restoring the university's unity of content and spirit. This same report, however, contains a certain number of suggestions that seem to indicate a different orientation. "Whether the instruction be formal or informal, in a ghetto or in a foreign university, evidence of accomplishment should be quickly recognized" (thesis no. 38). The idea here is to open up the university, to encourage off-campus work. But this does not contradict the previously mentioned thesis. Although it is good for the student to acquire practical experience in the world, to go through his *Wanderjahre,* the college or university should keep its distance, remaining outside the world of power and social problems. The latter have no place in the university except as professional experience.

The direction taken by those who want to bring the university closer to the community in which it is located is a different, and even an opposite, one. Their central theme is that of the urban civilization. Although many campuses have been built in the very heart of the cities, the prevailing spirit in the American academic sphere has been to maintain the separation of the university and the city. The university has its own space, isolating it from the city.

"Within the concept of the modern city, the idea of 'campus' is archaic. The wide open spaces, the monumental and inflexible architecture, and the insulation combine into an anti-urban phenomenon. The campus is more than a place: it is a system. It assumes turning the flow of human relations inside. Its success depends upon imposing an isolated contrived community upon the lives of its inhabitants" (Birenbaum, 1968, p. 58). John W. Ryan, (1967), Chancellor of the University of Massachusetts in Boston, has become a passionate advocate of an Urban Grant University Act, which would make possible a "creative partnership" between the various public authorities and academic institutions. The university located in the heart of the city would give more scope to continuing education (Liveright, 1968) and create institutes to serve the cultural development of the entire population—e.g., Institute for Occupational and Professional Development, Institute for Personal and Family Development, Institute for Civic and Social Development, and Institute for Humanistic and Liberal Development. To these institutes could be added agencies for study counseling, adult education, or urban problems.

In a more limited way, some universities have created programs in which the education stems from problems of the outside world. The University of Cincinnati, for example, has established a community service program enabling field teams of undergraduates to help ghetto children and to participate in various community endeavors (Ritterbush, 1970). The College for Human Services in New York tries to answer a complementary need: opening higher education to students who have no preparation for it. These students are from low-income families and are definitely older than the average. Half of them have no high school diplomas, and selection is based primarily on motivation. Theoretical courses are designed to answer the needs of the students, and the teachers are both college graduates and professionals (U.S. Department of Health, Education and Welfare, 1971). In the same way, Northeastern University has a "work-study approach for technical training," and there is a similar program at Staten Island Community College. Special programs for the educationally "handicapped" proliferate, such as the one at the College of DuPage, near Chicago, or the SEEK program (Search for Education and Elevation of Knowledge) in New York. Studies show that the results obtained by "risk students" are no lower than those of others (Nicholson, 1970), and that in many jobs where employers require advanced degrees, the professional achievement of those without them is just as high. Even at a high level, according to Ivor Berg (1969, p. 46), there is no salary differential after 15 years between graduates of Harvard Business School and others. Higher education's monopoly on the access to high-level jobs should therefore be questioned.

The Open University theme, launched in Great Britain, where so many new ideas and initiatives in the field of higher education originate, has now been taken up in the United States. R. Masters (1971) thinks that the frequent defacement of university buildings by the students reflects their rejection of the university space, and De Carlo (1969, p. 27) states that the idea of specifically academic buildings may soon be considered outdated. The most thorough criticism is that of Ivan Illich,[3] who demands the complete separation of education from the teaching system, which he believes should be destroyed so that education would no longer set up new social barriers or strengthen existing ones. Instead, education would provide the means whereby the community could fulfill certain of its needs, but would keep those means from becoming an instrument of social domination in the guise of an autonomous professional organization.

The more immediate question can be raised as to whether the colleges and universities, as presently constituted, really fulfill their professed normal function of vocational training. The reasons for the continual extension of schooling are not always positive ones. A recent report by André Lichnerowicz (Lichnerowicz & de L'Ain, 1970) in Paris expressed a more critical judgment:

The university tends increasingly to play a new role for society, that of keeping the youth out of the production circuit as long as possible. The labor market might be upset by the sudden influx of too many graduates. Too many established positions and privileges might be threatened, and in some countries adults would no longer be able to hold two jobs, still a rather frequent practice in certain occupations. The employers hope, moreover, that by postponing the average hiring age they will be able to recruit youths who will have released all their aggressiveness toward society during their academic career.

The university, then, plays the role of a "parking lot." In many countries, including the Democratic Republic of Germany, the Fed-

---

[3] See, for example, Illich's "Descolariser la société," *Temps modernes,* Paris, 1970, pp. 475–495, and *Une société sans école,* Editions du Seuil, Paris, 1971.

eral Republic of Germany, Sweden, etc., measures have already been taken or proposed to reduce the length of higher education. Similar steps have been taken in the United States, particularly by MIT and Cornell. The Carnegie Commission (1970*b*, pp. 16–23) has suggested more generalized measures, such as reducing to three years the time needed for the B.A., and introducing two new intermediate degrees between the B.A. and the Ph.D.: a Master of Philosophy, to be obtained two years after the B.A., and a Doctor of Arts, to be obtained four years after the B.A. The M. Phil. will be for those who intend to teach in the high schools and the lower level of the colleges, while the D.A. will be for those who intend to go into university teaching.

These proposals raise the general problem of whether education should be limited to a particular period of life and should put all its resources at the service of those youths who, because of their social background, received the best cultural preparation, or whether it should give an opportunity to those who have to go more directly into the work world and want to raise their level of knowledge. For a long time, adult education was a mere appendage to real academic work, and its prestige was low. In view of the immense resources today devoted to education, if adult education is taken seriously, it will involve a real political option, requiring a significant shift of resources. At the very least this might mean that the increase of educational funds devoted to youth would have to be limited in order to give a more significant social role to continuing education and therefore to the establishment of closer links between the university and those who have already entered the work world.

All these efforts and ideas add up to the image of an academic system wide open to the life of the community, able to adapt to different levels of cultural preparation rather than being hemmed in by the selectivity of a Scholastic Aptitude Test.

This involves a real dismembering of the university, for it would have to forsake its walls and its norms and put its instruments at the service of various social categories for whom diversified approaches are needed.

The academic system has been connected to society from the top, through the social elite and through federal subsidies. All those whose efforts we have been discussing want rather to connect it with the base of society.

These initiatives would take on significant meaning only if the good intentions were reinforced by the pressure of necessity. Can such an orientation of academic activities be considered so long as the idea of science as the motor of development, of national power, and of social balance remains alive? While the role of scientific and technological development in the cultural model of our society cannot be contested, a more precise question can be raised as to the nature of the relationship between science and development and the continuity and closeness of the links between them. It is because this continuity and this closeness are said to exist that some claim that the university serves society more directly by becoming more professionalized.

Carl Kaysen's ideas are particularly relevant in this connection (1969). He questions the direct usefulness of science, and the image of science as input and technology as output. It would be more accurate to say that science is a flow of knowledge added to an existing stock from which emerges a flow of technology. It is therefore not obvious that the acceleration of scientific progress directly results in an acceleration of technological progress. The latter can derive from a more rapid use of scientific knowledge. A Department of Defense study shows that only 10 percent of the innovations in the field of new weaponry are due to pure science. The logical conclusion to be drawn from these facts is that, while scientific research should be developed, it is not necessarily through this channel alone that social development in general, or even technological development, can best be helped. Another argument in favor of the central role of science in the educational system is that science corresponds directly to the values of an achievement-oriented society. This is, however, a spurious argument, since it could be claimed with equal force that science conflicts with the values of a democratic society, since it is always elitist, and that it is not entirely justifiable to expect the general public to make a large sacrifice for a category of people who are so different from the majority, so incomprehensible and shut off by their elitism.

Kaysen thinks that the financial crisis of the universities, and particularly the curtailment of some research funds, is not a temporary but a lasting problem. In recent years the proportion of financial assistance to the universities earmarked not for research but for buildings, scholarships, and loans has increased; it rose from 5 percent of federal aid in 1963 and 1964 to more than 20 percent in 1965 and nearly 30 percent in 1966. In the future it seems likely that more attention will be given to the training of experts, the solution of political problems, or the search for a better way of utilizing talents. The scientific world—although its importance will remain high—will tend to live in greater isolation; it will even see its growth slow down and its central role in the academic system diminish.

There is indeed then an academic crisis. But this is not to say that the university's scientific professionalism has been successfully attacked by student pressures. What is coming to an end is the period in which the identification of science and power was politically so strong and ideologically so solid that it was impossible to raise separately the problems of education on the one hand and of power on the other. The great word—science—covered everything, especially in the mouths of those whose activity could be described as scientific only to the extent that everyone in the academic world calls himself a scientist.

The crisis of American power, together with the strength of the social movements originating in the ghettos and the campuses, led to a new analysis of society and to the distinction Kaysen makes between scientific progress and technological progress and also, therefore, between scientific progress and academic organization. Science need not be the loser because of being deprived of its role as a quasi-religious guardian of the social order; certainly critique of the institutions and of the functioning of society has much to gain by such a development.

It is not, in my opinion, an adequate answer to the problems of the university to try to plunge it back into the community, to dismember it—that is, to separate a type of education that has become a form of social work from research concentrated in a few institutes inside and outside the universities, leaving between these two extremes the existing middle level of professional training, halfway between scientific knowledge and social practice. The link between education and the community could lead to the generalization of the system of community colleges—which frequently serve a "cooling out" function rather than being an adjustment to the demand for education—and to the elimination of the distance between technical and general education. What is rather vaguely called the community may be simply the local elite. Leaving in their hands the lower levels of education can only have the effect of strengthening conservatism and hierarchy. To avoid this, much depends, of course, on the general political and social conditions, but the university has a responsibility to concern itself actively with these issues and to intervene in order to prevent the segregation of its various activities. In this sense, the concept of the multiversity, as a recognition of the breakdown of any substantive principle of unity, is today more relevant than ever. But it has to be deepened and modified in the light of the current crisis.

Every academic system is faced with the real problem of deciding between two alternatives. On the one hand a system can maintain the distinction between the different levels of knowledge—basic research, applied research, and the practical application of research —that correspond to a social hierarchy of institutions depending on their wealth and prestige, and a social hierarchy of students and teachers, with an aristocracy of creators, a middle-class of appliers, and a working-class of utilizers. On the other hand, the system could develop enough unity to be dehierarchized and desegregated in such a way that the cultural backgrounds of the different social categories do not prevent the free circulation of all among these various types of activity.

This seems to me to imply the combination of two main conditions. In the first place, the university will have to diversify its approach to the various types of activity in which it is engaged. A mathematics department and a social work department cannot be organized in the same way. In the former case, internal criteria of coherent knowledge would prevail; in the latter, the main consideration would be the social demand, provided its true nature is known. In the second place, unity should be guaranteed by the opportunity for the students to combine different types of activity that would be judged by different criteria, and, above all, by the participation of all the social agents concerned in the management of the system. Such participation would be illusory unless the necessarily predominant influence of the ruling forces were balanced, not by the action of dignitaries from various strata of the population, but by the action of the students and the educators, convinced that their main social role is to be a power against the power structure, an institution against institutions, knowledge against ideology. The separation of knowledge from the ruling apparatus is almost inconceivable without a political commitment on the part of the universities to throw all their weight into the scales against the control of knowledge by the powers-that-be. This is not the place to examine the considerable difficulties inherent in such a conception of the university, and especially the danger of a sort of coalition of conflicting ideologies tending to weaken or reduce the role of scientific or even merely professional knowledge. My intention is not to propose a conception of the university, but to point out the problems that seem to arise following the shaking of the academic ideology, and merely to examine the conditions of survival for the universities. It might, of course, be claimed that their survival is not desirable and that the last remaining links should be destroyed between the high-standard academic centers and the professional universities and proliferating service institutions. But if, rightly or wrongly, this solution is discarded, it seems to me that the only choice is between the reconstruction of the old system — but this time with a greatly strengthened capacity to create a social hierarchy from the ruling elite to the lowest ranks of the service class — and the combination I have outlined of a differentiation of functions with a determined attempt at the democratic control of the whole system.

The debate now underway revolves around these three conceptions of the university. The political history of the university is only beginning to replace ideological discourse; it is a great step forward to speak of the "uses of a university" rather than the "idea of a university." Is knowledge to be simply an instrument of social domination masked by a liberal ideology, or is it to regain its true role through social protest, criticizing ideology, and combatting the private appropriation of knowledge and its identification with the power structure, making possible a genuine debate on the social uses of knowledge?

The birth of entirely new student and academic movements indicates, if nothing else, the social significance of these problems. Once scientific knowledge becomes a means of production, the struggle for the social control over the knowledge apparatus becomes an essential aspect of political struggles. The debates just mentioned between different conceptions of change in the academic system are truly significant only if we recognize that the unity of any society's structural conflicts, i.e., the unity of class and power relationships, underlies the diversity of ideas. The greatest danger in the present situation, in the United States and elsewhere, is that after a new, prolonged, and violent crisis, disappointment, repression, and the understandable desire to return to one's usual concerns combine to weaken the capacity for discussion and initiative, clearing the field not for a political vacuum but rather for involuntary choices, which are based simply on the most immediate interests of the prevailing social order.

From this point of view, the situation in the United States appears more favorable than in many European countries, for through their force and autonomy, American academic institutions express greater imagination and a greater ability to define problems and invent solutions. During the entire first part of its history, outlined here, the American academic system, while growing and diversifying, tried to find its intellectual and moral unity, and eventually thought it had found it in general education. The second period, on the contrary, witnessed the dissolution of this unity. Such a development could lead to the breakup of the system. But it could also lead to the recognition that the unity of the university, like that of society itself, is but a unity of conflicts, conflicts generated by its efforts to determine what kinds of social control will be exercised over its ability to act upon itself.

CONCLUSION The American academic system's preferred image of itself is one that projects an increasing independence, from the time of its secularization up to the successful achievement of professionalization. At the beginning of the nineteenth century, colleges and seminaries transmitted the values of a community. Teachers were mere employees, badly paid and held in low esteem; their role was not even essential in the socialization of youth. By the middle of the twentieth century, the universities have become powerful institutions. Moreover, the teachers have gradually gained control of features essential to their management, to the recruitment and promotion of their colleagues, and to the organization of research—for which individuals rather than institutions receive the financial allocations. Their rights are recognized and their security of employment guaranteed, at least for those who have tenure. Knowledge is respected and the teachers are paid at higher rates. Society recognizes that scientific research and higher education are factors essential to its own development.

Independence has replaced dependence, and the bonds of tradition have been shattered by freedom in research.

An outline sketch of this type, all the details of which could easily be penned in, is a correct description of certain aspects of the evolution of the academic system. It is, however, dangerously misleading. First, it arbitrarily isolates certain features of a situation that can only be understood in its totality. Second, it reduces the meaning of a situation to the understanding of one of its protagonists, namely academic man; the latter is thus judge and plaintiff and tends to identify his intentions with the social meaning of his actions.

To define the academic system solely in terms of the professionalization of the teachers, or in terms of the objectivity of science (which comes to the same thing), would be to forget that between the scholar and scientific knowledge there is a stratum of interventions and limitations.

- Not all academics are scholars; not all the knowledge created and transmitted in the universities consists of propositions that can be scientifically proven.

- The majority of those employed by the academic system are engaged in teaching tasks, and teaching is not the simple extension of research, just as not all students are future research workers.

- The characteristics of the student population—be it their social origin, their personal relationships, or their professional opportunities—depend very little on the intervention of the teachers.

- The development of scientific or intellectual work depends upon decisions and choices that are not taken uniquely on the basis of scientific considerations. Their financing does not directly respond to the scholars' requirements.

The list of these elementary conclusions can be extended ad infinitum. I have only referred to them as a reminder of the extent to which it is arbitrary to take for granted a direct and abstract liaison between the teacher and "values," and to reduce the academic system to the organization of this privileged relationship.

While those who are not academics may find these remarks obvious and of no great interest, we must nevertheless bear in mind that as a general rule it is academics who study universities and that they have a most understandable tendency to analyze it from their point of view. (It is always difficult for a priest not to start a study of his religion by examining the relationship with his god and to make a critical analysis of the social—not the religious— determinants of the language, organization, and practices of the religious life.) It is all the more difficult because in many cases the appeal to "sociology" only reinforces the fault in vision that it is supposed to correct. In effect, the more one insists on the social hindrances that stand in the way of creative activity, the more it appears that one is putting all that is secondary to one side in order to reach the essential—that is, faith, art, and knowledge.

As a reaction to this idealism it is tempting to adopt a diametrically opposed approach. Given society as it is—its class relationships, its political system, and its organizational structures—teaching can be considered as a mechanism for the transmission from one generation to the next of norms and values, of vested interests, and of inequalities. Teaching is only a form of ideology; if you change society, you must change both the organization of the university and the content of both teaching and research. There is no doubt that this reproductive function is one of the essential roles of the university. But can we content ourselves with a statement of this sort?

It has in any event to be completed. A society is not static—and an industrialized society is even less so than others. We are therefore led at least to say that universities assure a continuity within this change and that they maintain a fundamental social structure while adapting to change. For example, they maintain class relationships, while at the same time effecting a certain amount of individual social mobility and modifying the professional and cultural characteristics of one part of the population.

This statement is similar to the one that we first criticized, which assumed a fixed point of comparison, namely, the values represented by scientific learning. The second assumed another, namely, class relationships. In both cases academic activity serves a social postulate to which it is subject and on the nature of which it has no influence whatsoever.

This statement neglects an essential fact: knowledge is a force of production. At the outset of this study, I added that it was linked to the cultural model. It is as impossible to say that this production is institutionalized and organized independently of class relationships and the political situation as it is to declare that it is only an ideological tool for the reproduction of class relationships.

It is misleading to discuss the relationship between the university and society if this small word *and* leads us to define the position of the university in relation to a society defined as not including the university, or exclusive of the production of knowledge. This would be tantamount to studying how the soul of the university is incarnated in the social body.

We must first, therefore, destroy these fictitious persons—the university and society—and consider the various social roles of knowledge. I refer here to my opening remarks (in the general introduction), where I distinguished between the three main roles, which I termed theory, adaptation, and ideology.

Knowledge is theory insofar as it constructs an image of man, nature, and their relationships, and as it is considered as a normative orientation in a given society. In this respect, it is a basic element of social organization and defines the field of social relations. At the same time, it is directly involved in these relations and more precisely in the most fundamental of all—the class conflict. Knowledge of adaptation because it is linked to social organization and primarily to vocational training. In this respect, it is a social resource utilized by a political system to achieve a certain production and therefore a certain transformation of social activity. The interplay of political forces determines the social uses of knowledge.

Finally, knowledge is ideology to the extent that any ruling class is capable not only of pursuing its own interests but of using its ideology to enforce an order on society as a whole and to maintain the same both by repressive measures and by methods of socialization. In this respect, the universities have the double task of repression and of embedding the prevailing norms in the mental structures of the citizens.

But it is not sufficient to distinguish these "functions" of the academic system. Do they in practice overlap?

It may be maintained that the ruling class is sole possessor of the model of learning and the cultural model, that the political system is merely a means of reinforcing its domination, and that the language of a society is nothing but the ideology that the ruling class imposes on it; if this is so, the university is merely the instrument of the ruling class. The context is that of a closed society, which can, moreover, be technically dynamic right up to the time of its disintegration. The latter is caused both by the pressures of an uncontrolled environment and by the upsurge of demands repressed in the very collective consciousness itself by the dominant ideology.

The same reasoning applies if we replace the ruling class as the principle of order by the power elite, or, better still, by an institutional expression of the collective consciousness and of the social and cultural consensus.

If, on the contrary, it is maintained that society is entirely open, that social classes are competitors capable of exerting a certain influence on each other, that the political system is a network of variable strategies, and that the language of society has no unity other than the totality of opinions expressed, the university appears as directly linked to values. These values may be hidden from sight in the disorder or disorganization of society, but they are the only justification for its existence.

One can imagine such situations existing. But the first (that of the closed society) is more likely to be found in low-differentiated societies that evolve slowly, where there therefore generally does not exist any specifically academic organization but other more comprehensive forms for educating the young.

As to the second (the open society), which represents a society with no power, it seems to presage a generalized crisis in which the university would probably be dissolved, like all the other institutions. To say that the university serves values, or, on the other hand, that it serves the ruling class, is the equivalent of saying that our society belongs to one of the two types that I have just rapidly outlined above. But it probably would be more useful to examine less schematically the situations that lie between these two extreme types, situations that have the advantage of corresponding to an observable reality.

The extent to which a ruling class has a hold on the cultural model, the extent to which the political system is open or closed, the degree of stability or change in the form of work of a society— these combine with one another to bring the academic system closer to one type or another, and to give varying importance to each of its functions.

The general characteristics of American society are such that these three functions exist simultaneously, that is to say, they mutually limit one another, which allows us to conclude that the academic system is open and consequently that it is purely a locus of tensions.

This is apparent at first sight when we consider the crisis of the 1960s, which was at once class conflict, crisis in government, and a cultural revolt. During this period the production role of the university was challenged as was its place in the ruling apparatus of society; a critique was made of its decision-making system and of its adaptation to requirements; and its ideological role of integration into the social order was rejected. The inventiveness and the significance of this movement would not be so great if society and the academic system were not also "open," if the radical students had been forced to say "their" university. The openness of society by no means signifies that class conflicts are reabsorbed into a pure complex of influences and strategies, and the dominant ideology into an open discussion. It means that the development of conflicts within a society is permitted through a differentiation of the problems, by the presence and the capacity for action of opposing social forces; and by the existence of a model of learning and of a cultural model that are endowed with autonomous forms of social existence and which are not in the sole possession of the ruling class.

The opposition forces in this context are neither fundamentalist movements, attempting to recover the purity of their values, nor forces of total rupture that have no other perspective than to contribute to the disintegration of a society undermined by contradictions and by the accumulation of repressed needs.

In other social situations, profoundly different social movements have more reasons for constituting themselves. In a dependent society, maintained in a situation of underdevelopment by foreign domination, the opposition can only aim at breaking up the society; there is no internal dynamic other than the pattern of uprising followed by repression. It is still more useful to compare the American academic situation with the French one, which is very different and situated in a society that, despite archaic aspects, cannot be termed underdeveloped. The crisis in government and the crisis in organization are in the French case much more acute. In particular, higher education is compartmentalized so as to maintain at the top levels of formation a highly selective social recruitment. On the other hand, in large parts of the university, and especially at the level of the young teachers, the academic rhetoric has been overtaken by an ideology of opposition, or at least of distrust, with regard to the powers-that-be. In this type of situation, the student movement is much more a rejection than a counter-project. All the problems come one on top of another; there is a general crisis in the academic system that gives the movement a large revolutionary potential but also little influence. It goes much further in its attack on social order and threatens the regime, but its main "contestation" disintegrates after this outburst as a result of the organizational and institutional crisis of the university. The liveliest tendencies of the student movement always understood this and attempted to move outside the university. What remains of the May '68 movement in the university is expressed much more by a confused ideological production than by a capacity for political action or a true intellectual criticism. This situation does not result from the tendencies and the nature of the student movement, but from the state of decomposition of the academic system. The weakness of the American movement is the reverse; while it has extensive influence on national culture and academic organization, it has only low political capacity. Since it has insinuated itself deep into society, it is difficult for it to retain its aspect of ferment for social opposition. It therefore becomes reformist more quickly.

To conclude, we must return to the idealistic interpretation that I criticized at the outset.

The facts that this interpretation invokes lead to the introduction of an idea that contradicts it, and that completes and corrects the theme of relative autonomy of the social problems of the university.

The more professionalized the academic system, the greater the importance of its role in social production; and the more predominant its theoretical role, the deeper is its consequent involvement in class conflict. These three attributes are inseparable from one another.

I have distinguished three stages in the history of American universities over the past one hundred years. The integration of the academic system increases from one stage to the next because its production role becomes increasingly fundamental and its role in social reproduction becomes less important. The more the teachers become professionals, the less they are educators and the closer they are to being producers.

The role of education in a society whose cultural model is "abstract" is primarily ideological. By "abstract," I mean a society whose ability to act on itself is slight enough for this creativity not to be perceived as a social practice but as a principle transcending practices, a society, for example, whose cultural model is not science and technology but a suprahuman order, state absolutism, or even the "laws" of the market. On the other hand, the more a society defines itself in relation to its capacity for change and no longer in relation to the rules of its functioning and its perpetuation, the more teaching is closely associated with the production of knowledge. In the first situation the integration of the educational system can be extreme. But the history that we have outlined begins later, at the point when the organization of movement prevailed over the maintenance of order. This is why the integration of the academic system was slight at the end of the nineteenth century. Education of the bourgeoisie, adaptation to social and economic changes, and production of a new cultural model and of new class relationships coexist within the same system. The attempts in the period between the world wars to restore to education a fundamental importance — the attempts of Lowell, of Hutchins, and the whole of the general education movement — are only attempts, and reactionary at that, which clash with both the increasing diversification in educational demands and the increasing professionalization of the teachers; the failure of these efforts is obvious. On the other hand, we have seen how, in the most recent period, there has been an increasing tendency towards the formation of a hierarchical academic system of which the Ph.D. represents the main unifying element. Between the research universities and the young colleges a continuity exists that is based on the stratification of a society of production.

The role of the university in the social change controlled by the technobureaucratic class is, then, the most important, rather than its role as the transmitter of a heritage. The proof of this is the appearance of the student movement. If the ideological role of the university were predominant, the students would only be the "heirs," by turn conformist, apathetic, or bohemian. In this case, what explanation is there for their rebellion? It was not only the expression of a sensitivity to the internal strains of a society, or an awareness of a desire for modernization — that is to say, to the spread of the reign of innovating technocrats. The weakening of the ideological role of the university is well demonstrated by the progress of what is called, somewhat vaguely, a subculture of youth; yet the very existence of that subculture is evidence of the limited influence exerted by the academic system. Similarly, the old forms of working-class culture dominated by overall dependence, both in work and outside work (an extreme form of which was the company towns), gradually dissolved as society became more mobile and more differentiated. This does not mean that the social conflicts disappear, but that their nature changes because the dominated classes are now more subject to the management of change than to the maintenance of stability.

As the ideological role of the university recedes, a corresponding aftereffect emerges — the progression of academic rhetoric, the main themes of which (professionalization and academic freedom) have been referred to on several occasions. These themes become significant only because academic activity is directly involved in the production of the cultural model of the society, which leads the scholars to claim that they are directly situated, in all aspects of their activity, at the level of "values." This claim leads them at times, but always to a limited extent, to defend themselves against the ascendancy of social power, but in fact much more frequently helps them to conceal the existence of this power and to feel themselves threatened by protest movements that openly challenge it. But let me once again insist that this rhetoric cannot be assimilated into the ideology of the system. It is not a force of integration of society, but an attempt at integration at the level of the university itself, of the "citadel of learning," or of the academic "sanctuary." It must be pointed out, firstly, that this rhetoric is used within the class relationships and ideological action of the ruling class and, secondly, that it is an ambiguous "defensive" action. The behavior of the teachers during the crises of the 1960s is a good demonstration of this.

This book, in its entirety, is an attempt to argue the following proposition:

The progress of scientific knowledge and of its role in social development has replaced crises of socialization by social conflicts of general relevance, through which the class relations and struggles specific to technocratic society begin to take form. The university, because it is a center of production and diffusion of scientific knowledge, is increasingly becoming the main locus of the social conflicts of our times. Conflicts of this type are reinforced by the crisis in academic government and by challenges to the dominant ideology, but it is the conflicts themselves that give their true significance to these crises and controversies.

The university is not tending to become the locus of professionalization — it is increasingly a place of production and of social conflicts.

It is natural that the managers of the system (by reforming the government of the university and by changing or weakening its ideological role) should attempt to eradicate or institutionalize the fundamental conflicts that have appeared. Everything I have said here leads to the conclusion that these conflicts will not disappear, because they are at the heart of American society, of its production, and of its class relationships, and because they reveal the struggle for the possession of its model of learning, its forms of accumulation, and its capacity for development.

References

American Academy of Arts and Sciences: *Report of the Assembly on University Goals and Governance,* Cambridge, Mass., March 1970.

American Council on Education: *National Norms for Entering College Freshmen, Fall 1970,* Washington, D.C., 1970.

Ashby, Eric: *Any Person, Any Study: An Essay on American Higher Education,* McGraw-Hill Book Company, New York, 1971.

Astin, Alexander W.: *Who Goes Where to College?* Science Research Associates, Chicago, 1965.

Astin, Alexander W.: "Undergraduate Achievement and Institutional Excellence," *Science,* vol. 161, pp. 661–668, Aug. 16, 1968.

Astin, Alexander W.: *The College Environment,* American Council on Education, Washington, D.C., 1969.

Astin, Alexander W.: *Campus Unrest, 1969–1970,* American Council on Education, Washington, D.C., 1970a. (Mimeographed.)

Astin, Alexander W.: "Measuring Student Outputs in Higher Education," *The Outputs of Higher Education,* pp. 75–83, Western Interstate Commission for Higher Education, Boulder, Colo., July 1970b.

Astin, Alexander W.: "New Evidence on Campus Unrest 1969–1970," *Educational Record,* vol. 52, pp. 41–46, Winter 1971.

Astin, Alexander W., and Alan E. Bayer: *Antecedents and Consequents of Disruptive Campus Protests,* American Council on Education, Washington, D.C., 1970. (Mimeographed.)

Astin, Alexander W., and Calvin B. T. Lee: *The Invisible Colleges: A Profile of Small, Private Colleges with Limited Resources,* McGraw-Hill Book Company, New York, 1972.

Astin, Helen S.: *The Woman Doctorate in America,* Russell Sage Foundation, New York, 1969.

Barton, Allan H.: "The Columbia Crisis: Campus, Vietnam and the

Ghetto," Bureau of Applied Social Research, Columbia University, New York, July 1968. (Mimeographed.)

Baudelot, Christian, and Roger Establet: *L'Ecole capitaliste en France,* Maspero, Paris, 1971.

Bayer, Alan E.: *College and University Faculty: A Statistical Description,* American Council on Education, Washington, D.C., 1970.

Bayer, Alan E., and Alexander W. Astin: "Violence and Disruption on the U.S. Campus, 1968–1969," *Educational Record,* vol. 50, pp. 337–350, Fall 1969.

Bell, Daniel: *The Reforming of General Education,* Columbia University Press, New York, 1966.

Bell, Daniel: "Columbia and the New Left," in D. Bell and Irving Kristol (eds.), *Confrontation,* Basic Books, Inc., Publishers, New York, pp. 67–107, 1968.

Bell, Daniel: "The Post-Industrial Society: The Evolution of an Idea," *Survey,* vol. 17, pp. 102–168, Spring 1971.

Bell, Daniel, and Irving Kristol (eds.): *Confrontation: The Student Rebellion and the University,* Basic Books, Inc., Publishers, New York, 1968.

Ben-David, Joseph: *Fundamental Research and the Universities,* OECD, Paris, 1968.

Ben-David, Joseph: *American Higher Education: Directions Old and New,* McGraw-Hill Book Company, New York, 1971.

Ben-David, Joseph, and Abraham Zloczower: "Universities and Academic Systems in Modern Societies," *European Journal of Sociology,* vol. 3, pp. 45–84, 1962.

Berelson, Bernard: *Graduate Education in the United States,* McGraw-Hill Book Company, New York, 1960.

Berg, Ivor: "Rich Man's Qualification for Poor Man's Job," *Trans-action,* March 1969, p. 46.

Birenbaum, William: "Cities and Universities: Collision of Crisis," in Alvin C. Eurich (ed.), *Campus 1980,* Delacorte Press, New York, 1968.

Bittner, Egon: "Radicalism and the Organization of Radical Movements," *American Sociological Review,* vol. 28, no. 6, pp. 928–940, December 1963.

Block, Jeanne H., Norma Haan, and M. Brewster Smith: "Socialization Correlates of Student Activism," *Journal of Social Issues,* vol. 25, no. 4, pp. 143–177, Fall 1969.

Blocker, Clyde E., Robert H. Plummer, and Richard C. Richardson, Jr.: *The Two-Year College: A Social Synthesis,* Prentice-Hall, Inc., Englewood Cliffs, N.J., 1965.

Boruch, Robert F.: *The Faculty Role in Campus Unrest,* American Council on Education, Research Reports, vol. 4, no. 5, Washington, D.C., 1969.

Bourdieu, P., and J. C. Passeron: *Les héritiers,* Editions de Minuit, Paris, 1964.

Bourdieu, P., and J. C. Passeron: *La réproduction,* Editions de Minuit, Paris, 1970.

Bowen, William G.: *The Economics of the Major Private Universities,* McGraw-Hill Book Company, New York, 1968.

Brown, David G.: *The Mobile Professors,* American Council on Education, Washington, D.C., 1967.

Bundy, McGeorge: "Were Those the Days?" *Daedalus,* vol. 99, no. 3, pp. 531–567, Summer 1970.

Bunzel, John A.: "Black Studies at San Francisco State," in Daniel Bell and Irving Kristol (eds.), *Confrontation,* Basic Books, Inc., Publishers, New York, pp. 22–44, 1968.

Bushnell, J. H.: "Student Culture at Vassar," in Nevitt Sanford (ed.), *The American College,* John Wiley & Sons, Inc., New York, 1962.

Byrne, Jerome C.: *Report on the University of California,* Los Angeles, 1965. (Mimeographed.)

Caplow, Theodore, and Reece J. McGee: *The Academic Marketplace,* Doubleday & Company, Inc., Garden City, N.Y., 1965.

Carnegie Commission on Higher Education: *Less Time. More Options: Education Beyond the High School,* McGraw-Hill Book Company, New York, 1970*a.*

Carnegie Commission on Higher Education: *The Open-Door Colleges: Policies for Community Colleges,* McGraw-Hill Book Company, New York, 1970*b.*

Carnegie Commission on Higher Education: *The Capitol and the Campus: State Responsibility for Postsecondary Education,* McGraw-Hill Book Company, New York, 1971*a.*

Carnegie Commission on Higher Education: *Dissent and Disruption: Proposals for Consideration by the Campus,* McGraw-Hill Book Company, New York, 1971*b.*

Carnegie Commission on Higher Education: *New Students and New Places: Policies for the Future Growth and Development of American Higher Education,* McGraw-Hill Book Company, New York, 1971*c.*

Cartter, Allan M.: *American Universities and Colleges,* 9th ed., American Council on Education, Washington, D.C., 1964.

Cavalli, Alessandro, and Alberto Martinelli: *Il Campus Diviso,* Marsilio, Padova, 1971.

Chomsky, Noam: *American Power and the New Mandarins,* Random House, Inc., New York, 1969.

Clark, Burton R.: "The 'Cooling Out' Function in Higher Education," *American Journal of Sociology,* vol. 65, pp. 569–576, May 1960*a.*

Clark, Burton R.: *The Open-Door College: A Case Study,* McGraw-Hill Book Company, New York, 1960*b.*

Clark, Burton R.: *Educating the Expert Society,* Chandler Publishing Company, San Francisco, 1962.

Clark, Burton R., and Martin Trow: "The Organizational Context," in Theodore M. Newcomb and Everett K. Wilson (eds.), *College Peer Groups,* Aldine Publishing Company, Chicago, 1966.

Cohen, Mitchell, and Dennis Hale (eds.): *The New Student Left,* Beacon Press, Boston, 1966.

Cole, Stephen, and Henri Adamsons: "Determinants of Faculty Support for Student Demonstration," *Sociology of Education,* vol. 42, no. 4, pp. 315–329, Fall 1969.

College and University Bulletin, American Association for Higher Education, Washington, D.C., May 15, 1969.

Connery, Robert H. (ed.): *The Corporation and the Campus,* The Academy of Political Science, Columbia University, New York, 1970.

Corson, John J.: *Governance of Colleges and Universities,* McGraw-Hill Book Company, New York, 1960.

Crane, Diana: "Social Class Origin and Academic Success," *Sociology of Education,* vol. 42, pp. 1–17, Winter 1969.

Crozier, Michel: *La société bloquée,* Editions du Seuil, Paris, 1970.

De Carlo, Giancarlo: "Why/How to Build School Buildings," *Harvard Educational Review: Architecture and Education,* vol. 39, 1969.

Demerath, Nicolas J., Richard W. Stephens, and R. Robb Taylor: *Power, Presidents and Professors,* Basic Books, Inc., Publishers, New York, 1967.

Dennis, Lawrence E., and Joseph F. Kauffman (eds.): *The College and the Student,* American Council on Education, Washington, D.C., 1966.

De Vane, William Clyde: *Higher Education in Twentieth Century America,* Harvard University Press, Cambridge, Mass., 1965.

Dofny, Jacques, Claude Durand, Jean-Daniel Reynaud, and Alain Touraine: *Les ouvriers et le progrès technique,* Colin, Paris, 1966.

Donovan, Elizabeth, and Carol Kaye: "Motivational Factors in College Entrance," in Nevitt Sanford (ed.), *The American College,* John Wiley & Sons, Inc., New York, 1962.

Dykes, Archie R.: *Faculty Participation in Academic Decision Making,* American Council on Education, Washington, D.C., 1968.

Eisenstadt, Samuel N.: *From Generation to Generation,* The Free Press, Glencoe, Ill., 1956.

Engler, Robert: "Social Science and Social Consciousness," in Theodore Roszak (ed.), *The Dissenting Academy,* Random House, Inc., New York, 1968.

Erikson, Erik H. (ed.): *Youth: Change and Challenge,* Basic Books, Inc., Publishers, New York, 1963.

Eurich, Alvin C. (ed.): *Campus 1980,* Delacorte Press, New York, 1968.

Fein, Rashi, and Gerald I. Weber: *Financing Medical Education: An Analysis of Alternative Policies and Mechanisms,* McGraw-Hill Book Company, New York, 1971.

Feldman, Kenneth A., and Theodore M. Newcomb: *The Impact of College on Students,* Jossey-Bass, San Francisco, 1970.

Feuer, Lewis S.: *The Conflict of Generations,* Delacorte Press, New York, 1968.

Fichter, Joseph H.: *Graduates of Predominantly Negro Colleges: Class of 1964,* U.S. Department of Health, Education and Welfare, Washington, D.C., 1967.

Flacks, Richard: "The Liberated Generation: An Exploration of the Roots of Student Protest," *Journal of Social Issues,* vol. 23, no. 3, pp. 52–75, July 1967.

Flacks, Richard: "Social and Cultural Meanings of Student Revolt: Some Informal Comparative Observations," *Social Problems,* vol. 17, no. 3, pp. 340–357, Winter 1970.

Flexner, Abraham: *Universities,* Oxford University Press, New York, 1930.

Flexner, Abraham: *Medical Education in the United States and Canada,* reproduction of 1910 edition, Arno Press, New York, 1972.

Folger, John K., Helen S. Astin, and Alan E. Bayer: *Human Resources and Higher Education,* Russell Sage Foundation, New York, 1970.

Foucault, Michel: *Les mots et les choses,* NRF, Paris, 1966.

Friedenberg, Edgar Z.: "Current Patterns of Generational Conflict," *Journal of Social Issues,* vol. 25, pp. 21–38, April 1969.

Gross, Edward, and Paul V. Grambsch: *University Goals and Academic Power,* American Council on Education, Washington, D.C., 1968.

Gruson, Pascale: "Du monopole napoléonien à la république des professeurs," unpublished thesis, Paris, 1970.

Gurin, Patricia, and Daniel Katz: *Motivation and Aspiration in the Negro*

College, a report for the Office of Education, Bureau of Research; Survey Research Center, University of Michigan, Ann Arbor, 1966.

Handlin, Oscar, and Mary F. Handlin: *The American College and American Culture: Socialization as a Function of Higher Education,* McGraw-Hill Book Company, New York, 1970.

Harris, John (ed.): *The American University: Some Dilemmas and Alternatives,* Institutions of Higher Education of Georgia, Athens, 1970.

Harris, Seymour E.: *A Statistical Portrait of Higher Education,* McGraw-Hill Book Company, New York, 1972.

Harvard University: *General Education in a Free Society,* 1945, in Richard Hofstadter and Wilson Smith (eds.), *American Higher Education: A Documentary History,* 2 vols., University of Chicago Press, 1962.

Hayden, Thomas: "Student Social Action: From Liberation to Community," Spring 1962, in Mitchell Cohen and Dennis Hale (eds.), *The New Student Left,* Beacon Press, Boston, 1966.

Heiss, Ann M.: *Challenges to Graduate Schools,* Jossey-Bass, San Francisco, 1970.

Hofstadter, Richard, and C. DeWitt Hardy: *The Development and Scope of Higher Education in the United States,* Columbia University Press, New York, 1952.

Hofstadter, Richard, and Walter P. Metzger: *The Development of Academic Freedom in the United States,* Columbia University Press, New York, 1955.

Hofstadter, Richard, and Wilson Smith (eds.): *American Higher Education: A Documentary History,* 2 vols., University of Chicago Press, 1962.

Hook, Sidney: *Academic Freedom and Academic Anarchy,* Cowley, New York, 1969.

Horowitz, Irving L.: "The Trade-Unionization of the Student Seventies," *New Society,* vol. 16, no. 406, pp. 70–71, July 9, 1970.

Huntington, Samuel P.: "The Changing Culture at Harvard," *Harvard Alumni Bulletin,* Sept. 15, 1969; quoted in McGeorge Bundy, "Were Those the Days?" *Daedalus,* vol. 99, no. 3, pp. 531–567, Summer 1970.

Hutchins, Robert M.: *The Higher Learning in America,* Yale University Press, New Haven, Conn., 1936.

Hutchins, Robert M.: *Freedom, Education and the Fund,* Meridian Books, Cleveland, 1956; in Theodore Caplow and Reece J. McGee, *The Academic Marketplace,* Doubleday & Company, Inc, Garden City, N.Y., 1965.

Illich, Ivan: *Deschooling Society,* Harper & Row, Publishers, Incorporated, New York, 1971.

Illich, Ivan: *Une société sans ecole,* Editions du Seuil, Paris, 1971.

Jacob, Philip: *Changing Values in College,* Harper & Brothers, New York, 1958.

Jaffe, A. J., Walter Adams, and Sandra G. Meyers: *Negro Higher Education in the 1960's,* Frederick A. Praeger, Inc., New York, 1968.

Jencks, Christopher, and David Riesman: "Patterns of Residential Education: A Case Study of Harvard," in Nevitt Sanford (ed.), *The American College,* John Wiley & Sons, Inc., New York, 1962.

Jencks, Christopher, and David Riesman: *The Academic Revolution,* Doubleday & Company, Inc., Garden City, N.Y., 1968.

Kaplan, N.: "Sociology of Science," in Robert Faris (ed.), *Handbook of Modern Sociology,* Rand McNally & Company, Chicago, 1964.

Kaysen, Carl: *The Higher Learning, the Universities and the Public,* Princeton University Press, Princeton, N.J., 1969.

Keniston, Kenneth: "Alienation and the Decline of Utopia," *American Scholar,* vol. 29, no. 2, pp. 161–200, Spring 1960.

Keniston, Kenneth: "The Faces in the Lecture Room," in Robert S. Morison (ed.), *The Contemporary University, U.S.A.,* The Daedalus Library, Houghton Mifflin Company, Boston, 1961.

Keniston, Kenneth: *The Uncommitted: Alienated Youth in American Society,* Harcourt, Brace and Company, Inc., New York, 1965.

Keniston, Kenneth: *Young Radicals: Notes on Committed Youth,* Harcourt, Brace and Company, Inc., New York, 1968.

Kerr, Clark: *The Uses of the University,* Harvard University Press, Cambridge, Mass., 1963.

Kerr, Clark: "Remembering Flexner," in Abraham Flexner, *Universities,* rev. ed., Oxford University Press, New York, 1968.

Kidd, Charles V.: *American Universities and Federal Research,* Harvard University Press, Cambridge, Mass., 1959.

Knoell, D. M., and L. L. Medsker: *From Junior to Senior College: A National Study of Transfer Students,* American Council on Education, Washington, D.C., 1965.

Kruytbosch, Carlos E., and Sheldon L. Messinger (eds.): *The State of the University: Authority and Change,* Sage Publications, Beverly Hills, Calif., 1970.

Lazarsfeld, Paul F.: "The Sociology of Empirical Social Research," *American Sociological Review,* vol. 27, no. 6, pp. 757–767, December 1962.

Lazarsfeld, Paul F.: "An Episode in the History of Social Research: A Memoir," *Perspectives of American History,* vol. 2, pp. 270–337, 1968.

Lazarsfeld, Paul F., and Wagner Thielens, Jr.: *The Academic Mind,* The Free Press, Glencoe, Ill., 1958.

Lee, Eugene C., and Frank M. Bowen: *The Multicampus University: A Study of Academic Governance,* McGraw-Hill Book Company, New York, 1971.

Lichnerowicz, Andre, and Bertrand Giorod de l'Ain: *Vie active et formation universitaire,* report of l'Association d'Etudes pour l'Expansion de la Recherche scientifique, Paris, November 1970.

Lipset, Seymour M.: "American Student Activism in Comparative Perspectives," *Seminar on Manpower Policy and Programs,* U.S. Department of Labor, Washington, D.C., 1969.

Lipset, Seymour M.: "The Politics of Academia," in David C. Nichols (ed.), *Perspectives on Campus Tensions,* American Council on Education, Washington, D.C., 1970.

Lipset, Seymour M., and Philip G. Altbach: "Student Politics and Higher Education in the United States," *Comparative Education Review,* vol. 10, no. 2, pp. 320–349, June 1966.

Lipset, Seymour M., and Sheldon S. Wolin (eds.): *The Berkeley Student Revolt: Facts and Interpretations,* Doubleday & Company, Inc., New York, 1965.

Liveright, A. A.: "Learning Never Ends: A Plan for Consulting Education," pp. 149–175 in Alvin C. Eurich (ed.), *Campus 1980,* Delacorte Press, New York, 1968.

Maccoby, Herbert: "Controversy, Neutrality, and Higher Education," *American Sociological Review,* vol. 25, no. 6, pp. 884–893, December 1960.

McDill, Edward L., and James Coleman: "High School Social Status, College Plans and Interest in Academic Achievement," *American Sociological Review,* vol. 28, no. 6, pp. 905–918, December 1963.

Machlup, Fritz: *The Production and Distribution of Knowledge in the United States,* Princeton University Press, Princeton, N.J., 1962.

Mallery, David: "Society and the Campus," pp. 131–136 in L. Dennis and J. Kauffman (eds.), *The College and the Student,* American Council on Education, Washington, D.C., 1966.

Massachusetts Institute of Technology: *Creative Renewal in a Time of Crisis,* Cambridge, 1970.

Masters, R.: "L'Université sans murs," *Le Monde,* Feb. 23, 1971.

Mayhew, Lewis B.: *Graduate and Professional Education, 1980: A Survey of Institutional Plans,* McGraw-Hill Book Company, New York, 1970.

Mead, Margaret: "The Wider Significance of the Columbia University Upheaval," pp. 423–429 in I. Wallerstein and P. Starr (eds.), *The University Crisis Reader,* vol. 1, Vintage Books, Random House, Inc., New York, 1971.

Medsker, Leland L.: *The Junior College: Progress and Prospects,* McGraw-Hill Book Company, New York, 1960.

Merton, Robert K.: *Social Theory and Social Structure,* rev. ed., The Free Press, Glencoe, Ill., 1957.

Metzger, Walter P.: "The Crisis of Academic Authority," *Daedalus,* vol. 99, pp. 568–608, Summer 1970.

Meyerson, Martin: "The Ethic of the American College Student: Beyond the Protests," in Robert S. Morison (ed.), *The Contemporary University, U.S.A.,* The Daedalus Library, Houghton Mifflin Company, Boston, 1966.

Millett, John D.: *Financing Higher Education in the United States,* Columbia University Press, New York, 1952.

Morin, Edgar: *Journal de Californie,* Editions du Seuil, Paris, 1971.

Morison, Robert S. (ed.): *The Contemporary University, U.S.A.,* The Daedalus Library, Houghton Mifflin Company, Boston, 1966.

Morse, Bradford: "The Veteran and his Education," in Alice Rivlin, *The Role of the Federal Government in Financing Higher Education,* Brookings Institution, Washington, D.C., p. 67, 1961.

Moscovici, Serge: *Essai sur l'histoire humaine de la nature,* Flammarion, Paris, 1968.

Naegele, Kaspar: "Youth and Society: Some Observations," in Erik H. Erikson (ed.): *Youth: Change and Challenge,* Basic Books, Inc., Publishers, New York, pp. 43–63, 1963.

Nichols, David C., and Olive Mills (eds.): *The Campus and the Racial Crisis,* American Council on Education, Washington, D.C., 1970.

Nicholson, E.: *Success and Admission Criteria for Potentially Successful Risks,* Brown University, Providence, R.I., 1970.

Oglesby, Carl: "Let Us Shape the Future," speech delivered during the Nov. 27, 1965, march on Washington, in Mitchell Cohen and Dennis Hale (eds.), *The New Student Left,* Beacon Press, Boston, 1966.

O'Neill, June: *Resource Use in Higher Education: Trends in Output and Inputs of American Colleges and Universities, 1930–1967,* Carnegie Commission on Higher Education, Berkeley, Calif., 1971.

Orrick, William H., Jr.: *Shut It Down! A College in Crisis,* The National

Commission on the Causes and Prevention of Violence, Washington, D.C., 1969.

Otten, C. Michael: *University Authority and the Student: The Berkeley Experience,* University of California Press, Berkeley, 1970.

Panos, Robert J., and Alexander W. Astin: *Attrition among College Students,* American Council on Education, Washington, D.C., 1967.

Parsons, Talcott: "Youth in the Context of American Society," pp. 93–119 in E. Erikson (ed.), *Youth: Change and Challenge,* Basic Books, Inc., Publishers, New York, 1963.

Parsons, Talcott: "The Academic System: A Sociologist's View," *Public Interest,* vol. 13, pp. 173–197, Fall 1968.

Parsons, Talcott, and Gerald M. Platt: "Considerations on the American Academic System," *Minerva,* vol. 6, pp. 497–523, Summer 1968.

Parsons, Talcott, and Gerald M. Platt: "Age, Social Structure and Socialization in Higher Education," *Sociology of Education,* vol. 43, pp. 1–37, Winter 1970.

Perkins, James A.: *The University in Transition,* Princeton University Press, Princeton, N.J., 1966.

Peterson, Richard E.: "The Student Left in American Higher Education," in Seymour M. Lipset and Philip G. Altbach (eds.), *Students in Revolt,* Houghton Mifflin Company, Boston, 1967.

Peterson, Richard E., and John A. Bilorusky: *May 1970: The Campus Aftermath of Cambodia and Kent State,* Carnegie Commission on Higher Education, Berkeley, Calif., 1971.

The Philosophy of Education of the Joliet Township High School and Junior College, Joliet Board of Education, Joliet, Ill., 1950; in Clyde E. Blocker et al., *The Two-Year College,* Prentice-Hall, Inc., Englewood Cliffs, N.J., 1965.

Pierson, George W.: *The Education of American Leaders,* Frederick A. Praeger, Inc., New York, 1969.

Pinner, Frank: "The Crisis of the State University," in Nevitt Sanford (ed.), *The American College,* John Wiley & Sons, Inc., New York, 1962.

Platt, Gerald M., and Talcott Parsons: "Decision-Making in the Academic System: Influence and Power Exchange," pp. 133–180 in E. E. Kruytbosch and S. L. Messinger (eds.), *The State of the University,* Sage Publications, Beverly Hills, Calif., 1970.

Potter, Paul: "The Intellectual and Social Change," in Mitchell Cohen and Dennis Hale (eds.), *The New Student Left,* Beacon Press, Boston, 1966.

"Record Number of Black Students Accepted by Ivy League and Seven

Sisters Colleges," *College and University Bulletin,* American Association for Higher Education, Washington, D.C., May 15, 1969, p. 2.

Rémond, René: *Les Etats-Unis devant l'opinion française,* 2 vols., Colin, Paris, 1962.

Report on Higher Education, U.S. Department of Health, Education and Welfare, Washington, D.C., 1971.

Riesman, David: *Constraint and Variety in American Education,* University of Nebraska Press, Omaha, 1956, and Doubleday & Company, Inc., Garden City, N.Y., 1958.

Riesman, David: "The Meandering Procession of American Academia," *Harvard Educational Review,* vol. 26, no. 3, pp. 241–262, Summer 1956.

Riesman, David: "The Academic Career: Notes on Recruitment and Colleagueship," *Daedalus,* vol. 88, no. 1, pp. 147–169, 1959.

Riesman, David: "Universities and the Growth of Science in Germany and the United States," *Minerva,* vol. 7, pp. 751–755, Autumn–Winter 1968–1969.

Riesman, David, Joseph R. Gusfield, and Zelda Gamson: *Academic Values and Mass Education,* Doubleday & Company, Inc., Garden City, N.Y., 1970.

Ritterbush, Philip: "Adaptive Response in Higher Education and Research," *Daedalus,* vol. 99, pp. 64–67, Summer 1970.

Rivlin, Alice M.: *The Role of the Federal Government in Financing Higher Education,* Brookings Institution, Washington, D.C., 1961.

Rivlin, Alice M., and June O'Neill: "Growth and Change in Higher Education," in *The Corporation and the Campus,* The Academy of Political Science, Columbia University Press, New York, 1970.

Rossi, Alice S.: "Equality Between the Sexes: An Immodest Proposal," in Robert J. Lifton (ed.), *The Woman in America,* Houghton Mifflin Company, Boston, 1965.

Roszak, Theodore (ed.): *The Dissenting Academy,* Doubleday & Company, Inc., Garden City, N.Y., 1968.

Roszak, Theodore: *The Making of a Counter-Culture,* Doubleday & Company, Inc., Garden City, N.Y., 1969.

Ruml, Beardsley, and Donald H. Morrison: *Memo to a College Trustee,* McGraw-Hill Book Company, New York, 1959.

Ryan, John W.: "The University of Massachusetts in Boston," *Massachusetts Review,* pp. 499–504, Summer 1967.

Sampson, Edward E. (ed.): "Stirrings out of Apathy: Student Activism and the Decade of Protest," *Journal of Social Issues,* vol. 23, July 1967.

Sanford, Nevitt (ed.): *The American College,* John Wiley & Sons, Inc., New York, 1962.

Sanford, Nevitt: "The College Student of 1980," pp. 176–199 in Alvin C. Eurich (ed.), *Campus 1980,* Delacorte Press, New York, 1968.

Savio, Mario: "An End to History," in Mitchell Cohen and Dennis Hale (eds.), *The New Student Left,* Beacon Press, Boston, 1966.

Schmidt, George P.: *The Liberal Arts College,* Rutgers University Press, Newark, N.J., 1957.

Seeman, Melvin: "On the Meaning of Alienation," *American Sociological Review,* vol. 24, no. 6, pp. 783–791, December 1959.

Sewell, William H., and Vimal P. Shah: "Socio-Economic Status, Intelligence and the Attainment of Higher Education," *Sociology of Education,* vol. 4, pp. 1–23, Winter 1967.

Sewell, William H., and Vimal P. Shah: "Parent's Education and Children's Educational Aspirations and Achievements," *American Sociological Review,* vol. 33, no. 2, pp. 191–209, April 1968.

Shils, Edward: "The Hole in the Centre: University Government in the United States," *Minerva,* vol. 8, pp. 1–7, January 1970.

Skolnick, Jerome: *The Politics of Protest,* Ballantine Books, Inc., New York, 1969.

de Sola Pool, Ithiel: "The Necessity for Social Scientists Doing Research for Government," *Background,* August 1966, quoted in M. Windmiller, "The New American Mandarins," in T. Roszak (ed.), *The Dissenting Academy,* Doubleday & Company, Inc., Garden City, New York, 1968.

Spaeth, Joe L., and Andrew M. Greeley: *Recent Alumni and Higher Education: A Survey of College Graduates,* McGraw-Hill Book Company, New York, 1970.

Stadtman, Verne A.: *The University of California, 1868–1968,* McGraw-Hill Book Company, New York, 1970.

Summerskill, John: "Dropouts from College," in Nevitt Sanford (ed.), *The American College,* John Wiley & Sons, Inc., New York, 1962.

Tannenbaum, Abraham J.: "Alienated Youth," *The Journal of Social Issues,* vol. 25, no. 2, April 1969.

Touraine, Alain: *La conscience ouvrière,* Editions du Seuil, Paris, 1966.

Touraine, Alain: "Crise et Conflit," *Cahiers internationaux de sociologie,* pp. 5–24, January–June 1970.

Touraine, Alain: *The May Movement, Protest and Reform,* Random House, Inc., New York, 1971a.

Touraine, Alain: *The Post-Industrial Society,* Random House, Inc., New York, 1971*b.*

Trow, Martin: "The Democratization of Higher Education in America," *European Journal of Sociology,* vol. 3, pp. 231–262, 1962.

Trow, Martin: "Bell, Book and Berkeley," in C. E. Kruytbosch and S. I. Messinger (eds.), *The State of the University,* Sage Publications, Beverly Hills, Calif., 1970*a.*

Trow, Martin: *National Survey of Higher Education and the American Council on Education, Washington, D.C.,* Carnegie Commission on Higher Education, Berkeley, Calif., 1970*b.* (Unpublished.)

Turner, Ralph H.: "Sponsored and Contest Mobility and the School System," *American Sociological Review,* vol. 25, no. 6, pp. 855–867, December 1960.

Veblen, Thorstein: *The Higher Learning in America,* Augustus M. Kelley, Publishers, New York, 1918.

Veysey, Laurence R.: *The Emergence of the American University,* University of Chicago Press, 1965.

Wallerstein, Immanuel: *University in Turmoil,* Atheneum Publishers, New York, 1969.

Wallerstein, Immanuel, and Paul Starr (eds.): *The University Crisis Reader,* 2 vols., Random House, Inc., New York, 1971.

Whittaker, David, and William A. Watts: "Personality Characteristics of a Non-Conformist Youth Subculture," *Journal of Social Issues,* vol. 25, pp. 65–89, April 1969.

Willener, Alfred: *The Action Image of Society,* Random House, Inc., New York, 1971.

Wilson, Robert C., and Jerry G. Gaff: "Student Voice, Faculty Response," pp. 181–188, in C. E. Kruytbosch and S. L. Messinger (eds.), *The State of the University,* Sage Publications, Beverly Hills, Calif., 1970.

Wolfle, Dael L.: *America's Resources of Specialized Talent,* Harper & Brothers, New York, 1954.

Wolfle, Dael L.: *The Home of Science,* McGraw-Hill Book Company, New York, 1972.

Index

*This book was set in Vladimir by University Graphics, Inc.
It was printed on acid-free, long-life paper and bound by
The Maple Press Company. The designers were Elliot Epstein
and Edward Butler. The editors were Nancy Tressel and
Janine Parson for McGraw-Hill Book Company and Verne A.
Stadtman and Sidney J. P. Hollister for the Carnegie Commission
on Higher Education. Bill Greenwood supervised the production.*